THE ROMANCES OF JOHN FOWLES

THE ROMANCES OF JOHN FOWLES

Simon Loveday

St. Martin's Press   New York

Printed in Hong Kong
Published in the United Kingdom by The Macmillan Press Ltd.
First published in the United States of America in 1985

ISBN 0–312–69107–6

Library of Congress Cataloging in Publication Data
Loveday, Simon, 1949–
    The romances of John Fowles.

    Bibliography: p.
    Includes index.
    1. Fowles, John, 1926–   —Criticism and inter-
pretation. I. Title.
PR6056.085Z74 1984   823'.914   84–13396
ISBN 0–312–69107–6

To the author of
The Anatomy of Criticism

Contents

Acknowledgements

I should like to thank the following for permission to use copyright material: Jonathan Cape and Little, Brown for permission to quote from *Shipwreck*, *Islands*, and *The Enigma of Stonehenge*; Anthony Sheil Associates for permission to quote from the English editions of *The Collector*, *The Magus* (both versions), *The French Lieutenant's Woman*, *The Ebony Tower*, *Daniel Martin*, *The Tree*, and *Mantissa* (copyright © J. R. Fowles Ltd), and Little, Brown for permission to quote from the American editions; the BBC for permission to quote from unpublished interviews with John Fowles; and the University of East Anglia for permission to quote from an interview recorded on videotape there. In all these cases, acknowledgement is also due to John Fowles. Finally I should like to thank the editor(s) of the *Journal of Narrative Technique* for permission to use material which first appeared in that journal.

I am particularly grateful to John Fowles himself, who volunteered to read through the typescript of this work, did so with minute care, and made a number of factual corrections and helpful comments.

As may be clear from the text that follows, my principal intellectual debt is to the work of Northrop Frye. But there is a less obvious debt to be acknowledged, namely to the work of Edmund (now Sir Edmund) Leach, formerly Reader in Anthropology at Cambridge University. I would like to express my gratitude to both for the stimulus (and pleasure) which I have derived from their work.

Throughout the writing of this book I have been enormously helped by advice, encouragement, and detailed critical comments from Ann Jefferson, of St John's College, Oxford, and Ritchie Robertson, of Downing College, Cambridge.

My greatest personal debt is to my wife Jill, without whom many things, including this book, would never have been possible.

Oxford, 1983

List of Abbreviations

Page references for quotations from the fiction of John Fowles are to the English paperback editions. The following abbreviations have been used. Full details are given in the bibliography.

Works by John Fowles:

C   *The Collector*
A   *The Aristos* (references are to the revised edition, 1968)
M1   *The Magus*
FLW   *The French Lieutenant's Woman*
ET   *The Ebony Tower*
DM   *Daniel Martin*
M   *The Magus: A Revised Version*

Chronology

1926 31 March: John Robert Fowles born in Leigh-on-Sea, a small town near the marshes of the Thames estuary. His father owns a tobacco business with several small shops in London.

1939 Goes as a boarder to Bedford School.

1940 His family move to a Devon village. Fowles immediately falls in love with the intricate and intimate West Country landscape.
Has a minor nervous breakdown at school and spends a term at home in Devon with his parents.

1944–47 Completes his school career in fine style as Head Boy and Captain of Cricket, and enters the Royal Marines.
Spends most of his military service giving pre-commando training on Dartmoor.

1947–50 At New College, Oxford, reading French.

1950–51 *Lecteur* in English at the University of Poitiers.

1951–52 Teacher of English at Anargyrios College, on the Greek island of Spetsai.
Meets his future wife on the island.
Starts work soon after leaving on what will eventually be *The Magus*.

1954–63 Teaching English as a Foreign Language in London.
Working on a number of fictional and non-fictional projects.

1954 2 April: John Fowles and Elizabeth Whitton are married.

1963   Publication of *The Collector* (by Cape, the first publishers who were offered it. Total sales, excluding the United States, over 550,000 by 1984; film version appears in 1965).

1964   Publication of *The Aristos: A Self-Portrait in Ideas* ('against the advice of almost everyone who read it').
Fowles gives up teaching.

1966   Publication of *The Magus* (American edition had appeared in 1965. Total sales, excluding the United States, over 500,000 by 1984; film version appears in 1968).
John and Elizabeth Fowles move to Underhill Farm, near Lyme Regis (the Dairy of *The French Lieutenant's Woman*).

1968   Move from Underhill Farm (which is gradually sliding into the sea) into Lyme Regis itself.

1969   Publication of *The French Lieutenant's Woman* (total sales, excluding the United States, over one million by 1984; film version appears in 1981).

1973   Publication of *Poems* (collected verse from 1951–1972).

1974   Publication of:
The Ebony Tower, a collection of five short stories (total sales, excluding the United States, óver 240,000 by 1984);
Cinderella, a translation of Perrault's fairy tale;
Shipwreck, a collection of photographs by the Gibson family for which Fowles has written an introduction and commentary.

1977   Publication of:
Daniel Martin (total sales, excluding the United States, over 240,000 by 1984);
Ourika, a translation of a little-known French novel of 1824.

1978   Publication of *Islands*, a collection of photographs of the Scilly Isles by Fay Godwin with an extended essay by Fowles on the metaphorical significance of islands.

1979   Fowles becomes Honorary Curator of the Lyme Regis Museum, the result of an increasing interest in local history 'which I see as an aspect of natural history' (personal letter).
Publication of *The Tree*, a collection of photographs by Frank Horvat with an extended autobiographical meditation by Fowles.

1980   Publication of:
The Enigma of Stonehenge, a collection of photographs by Barry Brukoff with an introduction and historical background by Fowles;
Monumenta Britannica, Parts One and Two, an edition by Fowles (annotated by Rodney Legg) of the works of the seventeenth-century antiquarian John Aubrey.

1982   Publication of:
Mantissa, a playful account, cast in fictional form, of the sources of literary inspiration;
A Short History of Lyme Regis, an expanded version of a booklet originally produced for the Lyme Regis Museum.

1983   Publication of *Lyme Regis, Three Town Walks*.

1 John Fowles: the Life and the Work

John Fowles is not only a prolific writer. He is also an extraordinarily successful one. Three of his five works of fiction have been made into films; two (*The Collector* and *The Magus*) have sold more than 500,000 copies; and sales of *The French Lieutenant's Woman* are already well over a million. In addition he has published poetry and photographic essays; he has written numerous reviews and introductions; and he has translated from the French both for reading (*Eliduc*, *Cendrillon*, *Ourika*) and for the stage (*Don Juan*, *Lorenzaccio*).

Fowles came to writing relatively late. His first published work, *The Collector* (1963), did not appear until he was 37. His childhood was suburban[1] and (as with the heroes of all his fictions) fairly solitary:[2] but in 1940 his parents decided to move away from the danger of air attack and to take a cottage in a Devon village. For the thirteen-year-old Fowles the experience – described factually in *The Tree* (1980), and re-created fictionally in *Daniel Martin* (1977) – was a revelation. The village life, and above all the natural beauty of the secluded Devon valleys, caught his imagination and appealed to him profoundly. Indeed he has consistently maintained that nature is not only his primary interest, but also 'the key to [his] fiction' (*The Tree*, p. 46).

In 1939 Fowles had started as a boarder at Bedford School. A year later the shock of public-school life, together with a certain resentment at being excluded from the Devon idyll throughout the school term, combined to produce a kind of minor breakdown. Fowles spent the next term with his parents in Devon. On his return to Bedford he found himself able to adapt to it very successfully; when he left he was Captain of Cricket and Head Boy (see Boston, 1969, and Amory, 1974, for further details). He then went into the Royal Marines for his compulsory military service (see the Foreword to *The Hound of the Baskervilles*, 1974, for an account of this period) before going up to New College, Oxford, to read French. After leaving Oxford he went to teach abroad, his experience including two years in Greece on the

1

island of Spetsai: the latter is the original for the Phraxos of *The Magus*, though Fowles emphasises (*M*, p. 9) that the events of the book have no direct connection with his stay on the island. He then returned to England to continue teaching.

For much of the 1950s, in addition to his teaching, Fowles was working on what was eventually to become *The Magus*, as well as on other (to date unpublished) novels and on a travel book. When Fowles submitted the latter to the novelist Paul Scott, then working as a literary agent, Scott suggested that his talents lay in fiction. Encouraged by this, Fowles tried his hand at a short novel in the crime genre, and the outcome – *The Collector* – was an instant success. As a result Fowles was able to devote all his time to writing. Sales of *The Magus* (1965) were even greater. Shortly afterwards Fowles and his wife left London (though they still have a flat there) and moved to Lyme Regis. In 1969 he published *The French Lieutenant's Woman*, considered by many critics to be his finest work; in 1974, *The Ebony Tower*, a volume of short stories; in 1977, the massive *Daniel Martin*, and in 1982 the slim volume *Mantissa*.

In one sense Fowles's writing career, though slow to start, has been a fairly straightforward success story. He is widely known as a writer of fiction, and it is as such that I shall seek to analyse his work for most of the course of this book. But this does not necessarily correspond to his own view of his own work. He remarked in an early interview that for him writing was always 'a form of teaching', and that he would rather be 'a sound philosopher' than 'a good novelist' (Newquist, 1964, pp. 220 and 222). The importance he attaches to philosophy is emphasised by the publication of *The Aristos*, a collection of thoughts, as his second book (1964); despite its deservedly cool reception from critics, Fowles issued a revised edition in 1968 and wrote a preface for its re-issue in 1980. In recent years Fowles seems to have reverted to this earlier fondness for genres other than fiction: since 1975 he has published only one full-length work of fiction, but three 'essays' (*Islands, The Tree,* and *The Enigma of Stonehenge*), several translations, and numerous introductions and reviews. We might add that his fiction, too – if *Daniel Martin* and *Mantissa* are anything to go by – is tending to renounce the narrative exuberance and descriptive colour of the early work in favour of a more reflective content. To some extent this is bound up with the way Fowles has always written: from the very first his fiction has been heavily intercut with didactic passages. In this sense the trend away from fiction is the realisation of an urge always present in his work to move from entertaining to instructing. But it springs also

from other factors, and is ultimately related – as I shall seek to show –
to his ambivalent attitude towards his chosen fictional form, and
perhaps also towards the whole enterprise of fiction. This area of
discussion, however, I shall defer until the final chapter.

As we come to look at Fowles's work in greater detail we shall find a
limited number of themes recurring in it very consistently. These
themes – which are prominent in both fiction and non-fiction – can be
grouped under four headings: the Few and the Many; the domaine;[3]
the contrast between the masculine and the feminine character; and
the importance of freedom. The next few pages will be devoted to
analysing these themes; in the chapters that follow I shall seek to bring
out the part they play in Fowles's five principal fictions.

'Heraclitus saw mankind divided into a moral and intellectual *elite*
(the *aristoi*, the good ones . . .) and an unthinking, conforming mass –
hoi polloi, the many', writes Fowles, appropriately enough in *The
Aristos*. 'One cannot deny', he goes on, 'that Heraclitus has . . . been
used by reactionaries: but it seems to me that his basic contention is
biologically irrefutable' (*A*, p. 9, emphasis in original). This statement
is essential to an understanding of Fowles's work because it is the key
to a three-fold structure (old man, hero, and heroine) which in one
transformation or another recurs in every one of his full-length
fictions. In this pattern the wise old man (respectively G. P., Conchis,
Dr Grogan, Breasley, and to a certain extent Professor Kirnberger)
represents the Few. Round about are ranged a number of characters
intermediate between *aristoi* and *polloi*, Few and Many, one of whom
(Clegg, Nicholas, Charles, David, or Dan) will undergo an ordeal to
decide whether or not he is eligible for full membership of the elite.
And in every case the agent of change, the physical object of the hero's
symbolic quest for 'election', is a woman – Miranda, Alison, Sarah,
Diana, or Jane.

Though Fowles describes this pursuit of excellence as the 'principal
theme' of *The Aristos* (*A*, p. 9), its workings in that book are mostly
submerged. Much more of the iceberg shows in *The Magus*, but its
treatment is not entirely typical either there (as we shall see in Chapter
3) or in *Daniel Martin*, where the issue is complicated by the fact that
Dan, the seeker, is himself acting as mentor for the much younger
Jenny. For a full exposition of the theory we must look to *The French
Lieutenant's Woman*. Here Fowles writes that 'every culture . . . needs
a kind of *self-questioning, ethical elite* . . . that is bound by certain rules
of conduct, some of which may be very unethical . . . though their
hidden purpose is good: to brace or act as structure for the better

effects of their function in history' (*FLW*, pp. 256–7, emphasis added).

This account of the Few can be taken as definitive, but we may pause briefly to bring out one or two of its implications. In the first place, words such as 'self-questioning' and 'unethical' point to the essentially detached nature of such an elite: that is, it stands sufficiently far back from immediate social concerns to see things in a larger framework and a longer perspective than those of mere political expediency. Secondly, its allegiance (as we see from the phrase 'function in history') is to *evolution* – a concept borrowed from biology which Fowles throughout his work applies to the social sphere. Finally, this elite is closely linked to two other concerns of Fowles's work whose importance will emerge below: collecting (its members 'all . . . reject the notion of *possession* as the purpose of life', *FLW*, p. 257) and freedom (since for Fowles freedom is the measure of social evolution).

In the case of the second theme, the domaine, we find ourselves dealing once again with a structural principle of the fiction. The action of Fowles's narratives typically withdraws from the opening setting to some kind of natural refuge or retreat: in the closing stages the move is reversed. The clearest form of this is seen in *The Magus*, which is divided into three parts corresponding to Nick's moves from London to Phraxos and back to London. But the pattern recurs throughout Fowles's fiction, and where any of it is missing (Clegg's failure to return to normal life in *The Collector*) or obscured (as in the complex patterns of *Daniel Martin*), that fact is itself significant.

The importance of the domaine is well brought out elsewhere in Fowles's writing. *The Aristos* aside, he has written four full-length works of non-fiction. All four of these (*Shipwreck, Islands, The Tree, The Enigma of Stonehenge*) are concerned in varying ways with privileged and almost sacred places where 'the top-hamper we call civilization' (*Shipwreck*, p. 10) is stripped away and the imagination can roam freely. The metaphor (or myth) which best brings out the significance of such places for the author is that of Robin Hood, a myth Fowles has been using since at least as far back as 1964 (see 'On Being English But Not British'). The two key images for Fowles are the outlaw – personified as Robin Hood – and the island; the forest seclusion of the former is of course only a version of the sea-girt 'isolation' of the latter. Nor is it accidental that both images are characterised, not only by the absence of society, but also by the presence of nature. As we shall see, there is for Fowles a profound affinity between nature and human nature. He writes that 'The two natures, . . . human and non-human, cannot be divorced' (*The Tree*,

p. 106); and at the deepest level, when Fowles's heroes enter their domaine they penetrate not only into nature but also into their own natures.

'Men see objects, women see the relationship between objects' (*M*, p. 413). The third theme, the contrast between the masculine and the feminine character, is particularly prominent in Fowles's writing. Like the first two themes, it functions above all as a fact of the fiction: men develop towards women, not vice versa. Fowles's female characters reign over the private sphere, the world of intuitive knowledge, sensibility, the emotions, and what Dan calls 'right feeling' (*DM*, *passim*). By extension they are associated with creativity, both in their own right (see for example *A*, p. 157) and as muses (see *ET*, pp. 81–2, and *Mantissa*, *passim*). Conversely men exercise dominance in the public sphere, the world of science and systematic classification, of action, violence, and war (*M*, p. 413). It follows from this that Fowles associates men with orthodoxy, conformity, and repression; he remarks in *The Aristos* that in the Genesis myth 'Adam is stasis, or conservatism; Eve is kinesis, or progress', and he is harshly critical of 'the selfish tyranny of the male' (*A*, p. 157). The epitome of repressive maleness for Fowles is the patriarchal Old Testament God he associates with conventional Christianity, 'the venomous tyrant of *Genesis 3:16–17*' (*A*, p. 16, emphasis in original), and his opposition to this aspect of religion burns fiercely through his writing.

Contained within Fowles's treatment of the masculine mentality is a topic which almost merits discussion on its own, namely the question of categorising, classifying, and above all *collecting*. Dreadful warnings about the dangers of collecting run through Fowles's work (Conchis remarks in *The Magus* that 'collecting ... extinguishes the moral instinct. The object finally possesses the possessor', *M*, p. 178); in each case we find the vice exclusively associated with men. De Deukans, a melancholic and finally suicidal figure despite his enormous wealth, will have no women about him except the vengeful Mirabelle (*M*, pp. 177–8); Charles, until he falls in love with the unclassifiable Sarah, enjoys collecting and classifying fossils; in *Daniel Martin* Anthony, ultimately like de Deukans a suicide, hunts orchids as botanical specimens, not as things of beauty. Science, for Fowles, is an extension of the same vice: by classifying things under headings we possess them, yet we miss what is most valuable in them, their individual essence (see especially *The Tree*, pp. 44, 48). This feeds back into the fiction in the form of a recurrent masculine tendency to 'reduce women to the status of objects' (*M*, p. 413). The classic treatment of this is to be found in

Fowles's first published novel, appropriately titled *The Collector*, in which a man captures and holds prisoner the girl he loves. The story makes the point more eloquently than any analysis could: the male captor Clegg stands for having, Miranda for the opposing principle of being.

In this connection it is interesting to consider Fowles's latest work, *Mantissa* (published in 1982). This short book is divided into four parts. In the first, the hero, Miles Green, wakes up in hospital: after a brief visit from his wife he is left in the hands of a staff sister and a nurse who administer a thorough-going treatment of sex therapy. Part Two begins with the shocking irruption of a female punk rocker who annihilates both sister and nurse and reveals that they were only figments of the hero's imagination. The punk rocker turns out to be one of many incarnations of Erato, the muse of lyric poetry. In the remainder of the book we gradually learn that Erato is herself only a figment of Miles's imagination, though in a paradoxical sense more real than Miles himself, since he (a mere mortal) will die, but she will be immortalised in art. I have not treated *Mantissa* like Fowles's other fictions and given it a chapter to itself because although cast in fictional form, it is clearly not in the normal sense a work of fiction. It belongs instead to the genres of confession (Fowles's revelation of his own creative processes) and critical theory (his pointer to how his works should be read). It is in this latter aspect that it concerns us here. The title of *Mantissa* (glossed in a deprecating footnote as 'An addition of comparatively small importance, especially to a literary effort or discourse', *Mantissa*, p. 185) is apt in more senses than one. Though the work is of no great substance, it bears out its supposed derivation (from an Etruscan word meaning a makeweight) by acting as the final element in the balance, the last little piece missing from the jigsaw, which enables us to see the pattern governing Fowles's fictional treatment of women. What it reveals, or more accurately confirms, is the Jungian assumptions on which Fowles bases his treatment of sexuality. Rather than (or as well as) Miles's muse, Erato is better described as his *anima*, that feminine side (or 'Eve-man', *A*, p. 157) which Jung saw as buried in every masculine personality. The sexual education which every one of Fowles's heroes must undergo can now be seen to consist of two elements. On the one hand he must learn that the girl he is in love with is a real human being, with all that that implies of respect for her rights and identity. On the other hand he must simultaneously learn that his love is not only for another person, but also for an aspect of himself – an intangible that can never be owned, nor shut up in a cellar as if it were in a flesh-and-blood sense 'real'. What attracts men to women in Fowles's fiction is mystery, the fact that they cannot and must not be understood; as Jung puts it, 'All [objective, non-intuitive] understanding . . . has the diabolical element in it, and kills' (Jung, quoted in Kates, 1978, p. 45).

The fourth and final theme mentioned above is that of freedom. Once again the theme is consistently embodied in the working of the fiction. Freedom is at the very core of *The Collector*: deprivation of freedom proves fatal. The endings of *The Magus* and *The French Lieutenant's Woman* show the hero released from dependence into freedom. Moreover the open structure and fictional play which form such a striking feature of all five fictions spring from Fowles's desire to give freedom, not only to his characters (*FLW*, p. 86), but also to his readers, in order that they may become involved actively and of their own free will in the creative process.[4] Freedom in Fowles's work is not the only voice: strong claims are also made for its apparent antithesis, responsibility. But it is my contention that at the deepest level Fowles's fictional practice bears out his early philosophical assertion that 'Freedom of will is the highest human good' (*A*, p. 25).

It will be clear by now that the four strands of Fowles's thought here teased out for analysis are at the same time very densely interwoven with each other. This is particularly true of the theme of freedom. Freedom forms part of the substance of Fowles's treatment of the Few and the Many, since freedom is the evolutionary goal to which the Few are striving; it is an essential part of the domaine, where everything is permitted; and it runs through Fowles's fictional handling of sexual relations, since his male characters are typically faced with a choice between two women, one representing law and the other freedom.

What is required is a critical approach that will group together these four themes and enable us to see Fowles's work as a whole. Given the variety of his output, not to mention (as I shall seek to show in the ensuing chapters) its occasional apparent incoherence, this may seem a demanding task. There is, however, one particular key which seems to me to unlock Fowles's work – one pattern which runs through it. This pattern, which in my view underlies the whole of Fowles's work and gives shape to every product of his imagination, is the romance.[5]

Romance is a difficult term to define, because a bald definition gives little idea of its perennial appeal. Nonetheless I shall try to give a brief account of some aspects of romance, looked at under the headings of form, morality, and atmosphere. The definitions given below are working ones, for use in my analysis of Fowles's work, and though they will be amplified in the ensuing discussion I am aware of how thin and schematic they are. Readers interested in the theory of romance *per se* are therefore referred to Gillian Beer's *The Romance* (1970: the work contains an excellent bibliography) and above all to Frye's *The Secular Scripture* (1976).

'Yes – oh dear yes – the novel tells a story': so writes Forster in *Aspects of the Novel* (1962, p. 49). The reluctance is revealing. The novel uses a story for other purposes: to give insight into character, to dramatise a period of history, to reflect or reform society. The romance *is* story. Narrative, folktale, myth – these are its very essence. Where the novel feels obliged to apologise for its need to use narrative at all and seeks to render its plot credible, to minimise its coincidences, to play down its shape, in Frye's terminology to 'displace' its formulas in the direction of plausibility (or similarity to the formlessness of life), the romance ignores probability and glories in its use of pattern, repetition, and everything that marks its distance from the chaos of everyday life.

The classic story of romance is of course the quest narrative, characteristically expressed in sexual terms as a young man's adventures in search of a bride. This narrative has immense vitality, stretching from *Daphnis and Chloe* to *Peer Gynt*, from mediaeval chivalric romance to Rider Haggard, and from children's fairytales to Hollywood. This is the basic form of all Fowles's full-length fiction. The reference to adventure, moreover, points up the importance of this non-sexual aspect: *The Pilgrim's Progress, The Lord of the Rings,* and much science fiction, are works in which 'the object of the quest serves as the love-object' (Beer, 1970, p. 3), and the ending of *The French Lieutenant's Woman* shows the way in which a narrative can modulate from a sexual to a personal quest without loss of continuity. But complementary to this horizontal movement of the narrative is a kind of spiral movement in which the end of a romance not only repeats, but also in a sense redeems, its beginning: thus *The Lord of the Rings* redeems the initial loss of the ring, Ulysses returns in the end to Ithaca and Penelope, and the Bible itself can be read as a kind of gigantic romance or quest myth in which the risen Christ redeems the fallen Adam. This corresponds to a recurrent pattern in Fowles's work (notably in *The Magus* and *Daniel Martin*) whereby the supposed goal of the quest – the hero's sexual possession of the heroine – is achieved at a very early stage, leaving the hero to work throughout the book to regain something he had had, but disregarded, at the very beginning.

From this introductory account of the structure of romance we must move rapidly to what I have called its morality. Here I would like to look at two aspects: treatment of character, and polarisation of attitudes.

The treatment of character in the romance is something that marks it off once again from its close relative, the novel. As Frye writes:

> The essential difference between novel and romance lies in the conception of characterization. The romancer does not attempt to create 'real people' so much as stylized figures which expand into psychological archetypes. It is in the romance that we find Jung's libido, anima, and shadow reflected in the hero, heroine, and villain respectively. That is why the romance so often radiates a glow of subjective intensity that the novel lacks, and why a suggestion of allegory is constantly creeping in around its fringes.
>
> (Frye, 1957, p. 304)

It follows that balance, complexity, perhaps even consistency and intelligibility, are not the primary criteria of characterisation in the romance. What the romancer is after is intensity and mystery: and in looking for them he will find himself seeking to polarise. He will thus inevitably tend to exaggerate features that make people (and notably the sexes) different, and of necessity play down those features that hero, heroine, and villain have in common as fellow members of the human race. This polarising tendency, with its attendant emphasis on the mysterious and ineffable, we have already seen at work (pp. 5–7 above) in Fowles's treatment of his female characters, as indeed in all his statements about women.

The same tendency to polarise and heighten recurs in the third feature of romance, its distinctive quality or atmosphere. The world of romance is an idealised world, still trailing the clouds of glory of its close association with myth and magic. This idealisation is evident in its treatment of character, where it focuses on the adult privilege of aristocracy (or its modern equivalent in Fowles's fiction, great inherited wealth) and the juvenile privilege of unfallen innocence (*Treasure Island*); it is evident also, as the examples just quoted will show, in its treatment of place, the enchanted islands and faery palaces – in Fowles's terminology 'domaines' – with which it abounds. This is not simply because it is *par excellence* the literature of wish fulfilment: nor is it only because, as Beer rightly points out, 'The romance gives repetitive form to the particular desires of a community, and especially to those desires which cannot find controlled expression within a society' (Beer, 1970, p. 13). It is also an aspect of something referred to earlier, namely the tendency of romance to incorporate a vertical as well as a horizontal movement. The special places of romance are an expression of what would in religious terms be called this redemptive movement.

Characterisations and definitions of romance are provisional and unsatisfactory for many reasons. Gillian Beer writes:

> It might legitimately be objected that the qualities I have defined as characterizing the romance are all to be found elsewhere in literature, and particularly in other types of fiction. This is true. There is no single characteristic which distinguishes the romance from other literary kinds nor will every one of the characteristics I have been describing be present in each work that we would want to call a romance.
>
> (Beer, 1970, p. 10)

To this Frye adds that 'The forms of prose fiction are mixed, like racial strains in human beings, not separable like the sexes' (1957, p. 305). But what I am seeking here, and what I think I have found in romance, is not so much a theory of writing as a theory of reading, and in particular a way of reading John Fowles. Romances are particularly vulnerable to misreading. They demand surrender to the conventions of their world, and appear silly without that consent. Reading Fowles in terms of the conventions of realism has in my view led to misunderstanding and misinterpretation, as much on the part of his admirers as of his detractors. It is time to try an alternative approach.

2   *The Collector*

When she was home from her boarding-school I used to see her
almost every day sometimes, because their house was right opposite
the Town Hall Annexe. She and her younger sister used to go in and
out a lot, often with young men, which of course I didn't like. When I
had a free moment from the files and ledgers I stood by the window   5
and used to look down over the road over the frosting and
sometimes I'd see her. In the evening I marked it in my observations
diary, at first with X, and then when I knew her name with M. I saw
her several times outside too. I stood right behind her once in a
queue at the public library down Crossfield Street. She didn't look   10
once at me, but I watched the back of her head and her hair in a long
pigtail. It was very pale, silky, like burnet cocoons. All in one pigtail
coming down almost to her waist, sometimes in front, sometimes at
the back. Sometimes she wore it up. Only once, before she came to
be my guest here, did I have the privilege to see her with it loose, and   15
it took my breath away it was so beautiful, like a mermaid.

(C, p. 5)

Thus begins *The Collector*, the first of Fowles's novels to be published.
It is written throughout in the first person (a pattern Fowles uses in all
but one of his subsequent full-length fictions). Consequently we have
no external source to give us either factual information or moral
guidance: we have only what the text itself provides. As far as this
extract is concerned, it provides in the first place what we may call
'foreground information' – the obvious fact that it is written by a
person, presumably a man, who is in love at a distance with a beautiful
young girl with blonde hair. This simple situation, at once trite and
archetypal, forms the mainspring of the action which ensues.

Slightly less prominent, but still clearly visible, are several items of
background information. First, it is clear that she – or her family – has
money, while he does not: she goes to boarding-school (line 1), he
leads a life of drudgery ('When I had a free moment') as a local
authority clerk among 'files and ledgers' (lines 4–5). Secondly, he is

jealous of her ('often with young men, which of course I didn't like', line 4), even though she is as yet only a schoolgirl, and even though he shows no inclination to strike up an acquaintance when the opportunity occurs. And thirdly (consistent with the readiness to let the relationship remain a distant one) the lover seems to be some kind of bird- or animal-watcher: 'I marked it in my observations diary' (lines 7–8). The title of the novel at once begins to come into focus.

Moving still closer to the passage we become aware of its very distinctive style. The writing has the flavour of a conversation, and a rather flat one at that: the juxtaposed adverbial phrases ('almost every day sometimes', 'over the road over the frosting', lines 2 and 6), the use of 'too' in line 9, the frequent joining of clauses and sentences with 'and', the colloquial 'a lot' (line 4). The writer assumes with a curious lack of self-consciousness that his reader will be familiar with every detail of the banal world which his language reveals – 'the Town Hall Annexe' (line 3), 'the frosting' (line 6), 'the public library' (line 10), the latter specified with dreary precision as 'down Crossfield Street' (line 10). Yet the minute familiarity with which such details are enumerated contrasts oddly with the lack of information about the girl, introduced only as 'she', and about the nature of the writer's feelings, which the reader is assumed to understand ('of course I didn't like', line 4) before he is actually told that they exist. The humdrum language of the opening heightens the lyrical force of the final sentence, which is worth closer attention. 'Before she came to be my guest here' – what is the meaning of this rather stilted phrase, carefully avoiding as it does both the mundane 'came to stay with me' and the sexually ambiguous 'came to live with me'? How can it describe a relationship between what we have hitherto assumed to be potential lovers? 'Did I have the privilege to see her with it loose' – this sentence is beautifully constructed to partake at once of the respectful, the euphemistic (in reply to a greeting, 'I don't think I've had the privilege' is a roundabout way of saying 'Who are you?') and the ungrammatical (to my ear it should be '. . . of seeing her'). 'It took my breath away ' – in everyday use such a trite phrase, yet one which in the context, and followed as it is by the moving final simile, resonates with unexpected freshness and force.

The style of this paragraph, then, achieves a number of effects. It suggests that the writer is poor not only in status but also in education; it hints that there is something out of the ordinary about the combination of very ordinary factors which go to make him up; it tempts us to read on by the well known but none the less effective device of prolepsis, referring the reader forward to events occurring later on in the book. (I shall come back to the wider issue of the temporal standpoint from which the account is written.) Its hints of privilege, of class resentment, and of jealous possessiveness, prepare us for the part these factors will play in the book as a whole. But above all it creates a very curious mood. On the one hand there is much in this extract to alienate the reader: the narrator's ignorance, his timidity, the dullness of his life and the prissiness of his prose style. But on the other hand there is a suggestion of grandeur in the precision and wonder of the last five lines which directly awakens the reader's sympathy. It is this combination of attraction to and repulsion from the character, of admiration and contempt, which gives the book its curious and distinctive flavour.

The story of the novel can be summarised as follows. A meek young clerk, Ferdinand Clegg, falls in love with an art student, Miranda (the 'M' of the passage above), whose wealthy parents live near his place of work. He assumes that feeling to be unrequited and hopeless, but when he unexpectedly wins a massive sum on the pools he realises that he could make his fantasies real. He buys a secluded house and fits out the cellar to accommodate 'a guest'; then he kidnaps the girl, and keeps her as his prisoner. The relationship between them forms the moral core of the novel. Gradually he shifts from admiring her to despising her: finally she catches a cold which turns to pneumonia, and since to go for medical help would mean discovery, he doses her with useless patent medicines and sits by helplessly while she dies.

This (barring a final twist, of which more later) is the plot. Even such a bald summary reveals it to be extremely rich. Perhaps its most conspicuous feature for a reader already familiar with Fowles's work is the way in which in structural terms it reverses the pattern of romance and fairy tale whereby the hero releases the heroine from captivity: in this book hero *is* captor, and his castle her prison. This parody-romance aspect is pointed up by the epigraph, *que fors aus ne le sot riens nee* (roughly, 'no one but them knew about it'). It is taken from the thirteenth-century French romance, *La Chastelaine de Vergi*, and to the reader alert to its implications it can only sharpen the way in which the narrative harshly contradicts our expectations. But the story works on other levels too. In emotional terms it offers us the pathos of a doomed and innocent heroine, and the tragic irony of a lover who in Wilde's phrase 'kills the thing he loves'. In philosophical or political terms it offers a bitter commentary on the theme of the wish come true; and in terms of detective fiction and thrillers, it gives us the perfect crime.

The principal device Fowles uses to present and develop his plot is, as we have already seen, the first-person narrative; but it is used with a difference. Fowles – possibly, as David Walker suggests (1980), unconsciously influenced by Gide's *La Porte étroite* – gives us not only Clegg's narrative but Miranda's as well, the two overlapping throughout the period of her captivity and thus providing a kind of binocular vision of the main events. Though Clegg's account makes up less than half the book by quantity (139 pages in the paperback edition to 141 of Miranda's), its position allows it to dominate: there are three Clegg chapters to Miranda's one, and hers (Chapter 2) is contained by his (Chapters 1, 3, and 4).[1] This containing and indeed claustrophobic effect is markedly increased by the sharply focused monotony which characterises Clegg's narrative. Apart from a few background details about his childhood and adolescence he has no interests and no topics outside Miranda: his memories are of her, his preparations are for her, his joys and his sorrows are caused by her, and even his butterfly collecting is seen in relation to her ('it was always she loving me and my collection, drawing them and colouring them', p. 6) rather than for itself.

The fact that Clegg's narrative encloses Miranda's is of course highly appropriate to a novel of imprisonment, and there is indeed an increasingly claustrophobic direction to the plot: from suburbia to a single isolated house, from the house to a bolted room, and from the room, finally, to a coffin. Clegg himself picks this up: 'It was like a joke mousetrap I once saw, the mouse just went on and things moved, it couldn't ever turn back, but just on and on into cleverer and cleverer traps until the end' (pp. 281–2) – though, characteristically, it is himself rather than Miranda whom he sees as the doomed mouse. A more subtle effect of containment is achieved by the use of circularity and repetition. As Wolfe notes, Miranda's first moments as Clegg's prisoner (half-conscious and unable to breathe) resemble her last, a circular pattern which makes the thematic point that their life together is a closed circle (1976, pp. 62, 64, 65). This pattern is set in its turn inside the overall circular structure of the novel. For this we must examine Chapter 4 in which the 'final twist' referred to above takes place. In this brief chapter (only three pages) Clegg describes how he abandoned his suicide plans and decided instead to bury Miranda's body and live. Typically, Clegg presents the motives for this decision in a very entangled form, but a major factor is his chance viewing of a blonde shop-assistant strikingly similar to Miranda. With horror the reader sees the same pattern re-asserting itself ('as a matter of interest I have been looking into the problems there would be with the girl in Woolworths', p. 287), and the book ends with the chilling promise of repetition ('I only put the stove down there today because the room needs drying out anyway', p. 288). But what is equally horrific are the stylistic parallels with the opening pages. The stilted 'I had the good fortune to see her' (p. 287) recalls 'did I have the privilege to see her' on p. 5, 'guest' on p. 287 echoes the same word on p. 5, and the 'la-di-da' quality which on p. 6 was attributed to Miranda's mother now becomes in embittered retrospect (and in contradiction to p. 16) an aspect of Miranda herself – 'her la-di-da ideas and clever tricks' (p. 287).

The book as a whole contains a number of literary parallels and allusions, some implicit, some (in Miranda's diary) explicit. The most conspicuous references are to *The Tempest*, in which lovers named Ferdinand and Miranda meet upon an enchanted island: Clegg tells Miranda that his name is Ferdinand (p. 40) and Miranda notes that it is a 'vile coincidence' (p. 131). The *Tempest* parallel continues when she tells him that 'They should have called you Caliban' (p. 65); on p. 255 Miranda is actually reading *The Tempest*, and adapts the enthusiasm of her earlier effusions ('A new age is beginning . . . I love, I adore *my* age', p. 244, emphasis in original) to the sadder 'O sick new world'. The mingled pity and contempt which Prospero feels for Caliban recur as the extremes of Miranda's reactions to Clegg; and – though here the allusion is not made explicit – the role of mentor and father-figure played by Prospero in *The Tempest* is filled in *The Collector* by the artist George Paston.

Only slightly less prominent are the references to two of Jane Austen's novels, *Emma* and (less frequently) *Sense and Sensibility*. Here the structural parallels – 'Caliban is Mr Elton. Piers is Frank Churchill. But is G.P. Mr Knightley?' (p. 230) – are less important than the question of moral growth: Miranda feels that while she suffers from the same faults of arrogance and bossiness as Emma, she also shares Emma's virtues of self-critical honesty and capacity for development and change.

The effect of these explicit references is rather laboured: the analogies are real, but Fowles spoils his case by overstatement. Much more effective, precisely because understated, is the parallel with the dim, Bluebeard region of folktale horrors barely touched on in the text itself beyond such glancing remarks as 'I kiss the beast' (p. 248). At one point Miranda does spell out the analogy at some length (p. 199), but she rightly condemns her own version, which altogether lacks atmosphere, as 'silly' and 'fey': far more frightening is her remark, reported by Clegg, that 'What I fear in you is something you don't know is in you' (p. 75), or the incident after her attempt to feign appendicitis when she runs out of the cellar and into 'all the daylight' only to find 'he was there ... Waiting ... [with] something (a hammer?) in his hand' (p. 214). The suggestive and sinister quality of these moments helps to bring out the full irony of the seduction attempt: the frog is indeed transformed by the princess's kiss, but what steps out is emphatically not Prince Charming.

Clegg's narrative may be circular, but it is not static. On two occasions the narrative makes a decisive change of direction. The first of these turning points is the celebration supper at the end of a month's captivity, after which Clegg requires as a precondition for release that Miranda should marry him. When she refuses – and rashly gives her reasons – he withdraws his offer of release: she tries to dash away, but he intercepts and overpowers her and takes her, chloroformed, down to her cell. There as she lies unconscious he partially undresses her and takes a number of photographs. It is clear from what each writes that both perceive this to be a turning point – Clegg writes that 'Things were never the same again, in spite of all that happened' (p. 95), and Miranda that 'There is a great rift between us now. It can never be bridged' (p. 232) – though in fact they are not talking about quite the same thing, since what Miranda is really upset about is neither the withdrawal of the promise of freedom, nor the photographs (of the latter she knows nothing), but rather the indignity of being undressed by a stranger while unconscious. What has happened for Clegg, as he dimly but only intermittently perceives, is that the façade has cracked, revealing the gulf between the two aspects of his attraction to Miranda – his desire to love her and his desire to control her. By stating that she doesn't love him and will never be able to because 'We don't have the same sort of heart' (p. 92) she makes it impossible for him to continue with the pretence that they are or will one day become a happy couple, that she is a guest rather than a prisoner; all that remains is the desire to possess and control, which will progressively dominate his behaviour (as it immediately begins to do: 'It was like I'd showed who was really the master', p. 94). Only at the end of the story, with Miranda securely in his power because of her increasing weakness, can he once more allow a tide of protective affection to submerge his will to dominate.

It might seem from this that there is no room for a second substantial turning point in the book. This would be mistaken. Karen Lever remarks that 'the Fowles protagonist . . . suffers from that infamous Victorian problem, the madonna/whore complex. He separates love and sex, dividing women into two types to match' (Lever, 1979, p. 90), and Clegg represents this tendency in its most extreme form. On the one hand there is Miranda, 'elusive and sporadic and very refined – not like the other ones' (p. 6); on the other hand there are 'vulgar women such as 'Crutchley's girl from Sanitation' (p. 9) or the prostitute he visits in London (pp. 11–12), both of whom are 'all Miranda wasn't' (p. 9). There is no middle term for Clegg, and consequently every woman he is attracted to must eventually gravitate towards one or other pole. Miranda, as we have seen, is the main (if not indeed the only) occupant of the madonna slot: but it is a dangerous and unstable position for her to be in. This is partly because of her outspoken (if not entirely spontaneous) views about sex and her occasional readiness to use most unladylike language (p. 60), but chiefly because Clegg does have a sexual drive, albeit of a rather unusual kind, and it is likely to be only a matter of time before he decides that if the madonna in question inspires that kind of temptation in him, she is probably a whore like all the rest. That is what nearly happens in the first incident – but, crucially, it does not: Clegg blames himself rather than her for the photograph episode and does not try to remove her from her pedestal. Nonetheless (to vary the metaphor) he has tasted blood, and the way is to some extent prepared for the devastating switch-over which follows.

This takes place when Miranda, steeling herself to expel 'The last of the Ladymont me' (p. 254), resolves to try to seduce Clegg. She succeeds in undressing the two of them, but he proves to be both unresponsive and impotent, and she makes matters worse, first by offering sympathy (to which Clegg's reaction is 'You'd think she had all the experience in the world to have heard her', p. 110), and then by insisting that 'sex is just an activity . . . It's not dirty' (p. 111). The result, as both realise, is dismal: in Miranda's words, 'We've been naked in front of each other . . . we *can't* be further apart' (p. 112, emphasis in original). But is is clear from the different emphasis given to the episode in the two accounts (over eight pages in Clegg's version as opposed to under three in Miranda's) that Miranda has no real idea how disastrous a mistake she has made. What she has forfeited is not Clegg's love, but something far more serious – his respect. By offending his Puritanism ('it was below me, and below her, it was disgusting', p. 110) she has lowered herself to the level of the prostitute and the category of the whore – 'She was like all women, she had a one-track mind' (p. 113). As Clegg correctly observes, 'All I did later was because of that night' (p. 113).

After the deceit and vindictiveness of the remainder of Chapter 1 ('After that, we got on all right, except that I was pretending all the time', p. 115; 'She got quite gay sometimes. I had to laugh', p. 116), the tenderness of Chapter 3 may come as a surprise: but, as I have suggested, when Miranda is close to death Clegg regains his control over her, and then 'All the part from when she took off her clothes and I no longer respected her, that seemed to be unreal . . . her being ill and me nursing seemed more real' (p. 272). It is thus opportune for Clegg to find the diary in Chapter 4, since it allows him to write off the entire madonna category as what I believe mathematicians call an empty set, and to go in search of a less 'la-di-da', more teachable 'guest' who will not oscillate so awkwardly between the categories: 'this time it won't be love . . . I would make it clear from the start who's boss and what I expect '(p. 288).

Much of what has been written here on the themes of *The Collector* draws for illustration on the diary of Miranda. At times, it must be said, this diary is an embarrassment: but it plays, nonetheless, an important part in the economy of the book.

One reason for inserting it may have been that Fowles wanted to put into practice the existentialist principle (already discussed above) that the free will of others must be respected. To give only Clegg's account would be to allow Miranda to be absorbed: to give her a voice restores her independent existence as a person.

A second function that her diary fulfils is to heighten the pathos of the narrative. This effect could to some extent have been achieved without including her diary (as it is, for example, in *La Symphonie pastorale*, where Gide manages to present Gertrude's moral dilemma very forcefully despite the fact that it reaches us only through the filter of the pastor's diary). But allowing Miranda to present herself directly makes her into a much more fully rounded character and thus accentuates the horror of her death. Moreover Fowles uses her diary to aim at a still greater intensity of pathos and tragic irony by allowing her to get more optimistic in the closing weeks of her captivity, at a time when we already know – having by that stage read Clegg's account of the same events in Chapter 1 – that she has been marked down for death.

Thirdly, allowing Miranda a very substantial part of the book to herself (over half, as we have seen) gives Fowles a vehicle for a number

of ideas of his own. This is done by means of G.P., the 40-year-old
artist (Fowles was 37 when *The Collector* was published) that Miranda
is half in love with and to whose memory she constantly turns for
encouragement and resources during her imprisonment.[2] Miranda
relies very heavily on G.P., not only for his Socratic quality ('he always
makes *me* think . . . he makes me question myself', p. 152, emphasis in
original), but also for a set of injunctions which at one point (pp.
153–4) she actually writes out in the form of a numbered list,
presumably rather more for Fowles's purposes than for her own.

A fourth function of Miranda's diary is to provide an intersecting
viewpoint on Clegg's account of events. Such a 'second opinion' could
theoretically be of two kinds. It could either function as a straightforward cross-check, filling in the gaps in Clegg's account and simply
giving us another angle on an agreed set of events; or, perhaps more
interestingly, it might differ unreconcilably from Clegg's story, leaving
us with no secure point of reference to judge which – if either – was
true. Briefly, Fowles tends to prefer the first alternative: in *The
Collector* he is not primarily interested in showing us the relativity of
truth. Moreover Miranda's diary carries such a moral and didactic
weight that in the event of a direct clash between her account and
Clegg's we could hardly doubt which to trust. Nonetheless there are
some interesting differences of balance. Clegg does not mention
reading *The Catcher in the Rye* (pp. 158, 191, 216–17 in Miranda's
diary), nor does he speak of the CND debate Miranda claims to have
had with him (pp. 141–5, though Miranda admits it is partly invented);
she in turn omits some of her less well judged remarks, as for example
when she tells him bluntly that 'They should have called you Caliban'
(p. 65), or when she recounts her little story about her imaginary friend
(pp. 102–3). Similarly the accounts given by each of the celebration at
the end of a month's confinement show, as has already been noted,
completely different emphases.[3]

The fifth, and I think most important, of the functions that
Miranda's diary fulfils may seem at first sight something of an
anticlimax: it is simply to provide a contrast with what and how Clegg
writes, to afford a yardstick against which we can measure how very far
from normal Clegg himself is. To be sure, there are similarities: both
characters have incomplete relationships with their parents, both are
almost obsessively clean, both – oddly enough – are rather prudish
(Miranda insists on the calling the lavatory 'the place', and just as
Clegg will not record her obscenity on p. 60, so she will not record
G.P.'s on p. 179). But these are trivial when set against the differences

which a detailed comparison of the two accounts reveals. These differences can for simplicity be grouped under three headings.

On the level of style, the opposition can be described as 'educated/ ignorant'. While Miranda's grammar is often free and her punctuation non-existent, she can when she wants to write fluently and without solecisms. Clegg handles words with difficulty, makes frequent errors of syntax, and generally uses a flat and pedestrian style. This *by itself* of course is of no moral importance: but what we consistently notice in Clegg is his use of clichés ('as you might say', 'it was not to be', 'good riddance'), generalisations ('on the grab like most nowadays'), euphemisms ('woman of the streets' for prostitute, 'artistic' for obscene, 'passed away' for died, 'the deceased'), and the revealing 'as they say' – revealing because so often it is not Clegg himself we hear but the mean language of unexamined prejudice speaking through him.

At the level of structure the opposition can be defined as 'spon- taneous/contrived'. This is of course implied in the fact that while Miranda's account takes the form of a diary (that is something written day by day), Clegg's is cast in the form of a memoir, that is something written some way after the events it recounts have taken place. The spontaneity of Miranda's account is brought out in a number of ways. Every entry is dated, and reveals that she writes things down as they happen to her. Much of her diary is written in the present or present perfect tense, emphasising that her understanding of her material is still developing.[4] Her diary is often incomplete (for example the gap from 12 November to 18 November when the immediacy of the events overwhelms her); sometimes it is incoherent, and frequently it is descriptive and impressionistic. Generally speaking it records her thoughts as they come ('I'm thinking hours between each sentence I write', p. 246) and is in fact a means of clarifying those thoughts ('I've got to put it down. Look at it', p. 251). For all these reasons the dominant characteristic of Miranda's diary is honesty, an honesty which leads her to the point of doubting the truthfulness of the diary form (p. 260) and indeed of words themselves: as she remarks with unintentionally prophetic accuracy, 'You can get away with murder with words' (p. 170).

This is just what Clegg does. His account, undated throughout, is couched in the simple past, the tense of completed, closed, safely bygone and chronicled events. The episodes in Clegg's account tend to be more complete, more organised, and more linear than those in Miranda's; they bear the marks of deliberate, albeit unskilful, composition. This in turn throws a rather sinister light on the recurring 'What I am trying to say is' (for example pp. 14 and 125). What we had perhaps taken for a rather appealing confession on Clegg's part that he cannot put his thoughts into words suddenly begins to look like the rhetorical device of a lawyer pleading a case. Where Miranda seeks to inform, Clegg seeks to persuade.

The retrospective nature of Clegg's account raises the rather difficult question of when we are supposed to think that Clegg actually writes it. A tempting hypothesis, given the decisive break after Chapter 3 and the affectionate, almost elegiac mood of much of the writing that immediately precedes that break, is to imagine Clegg writing it during Miranda's last illness: the book would then begin with a flashback to the innocent days before his pools win and a glimpse of the disasters to come ('Perhaps that was when it all started', p. 7) before plunging into what is henceforth an almost perfectly chronological account, written from hindsight and moving towards a known conclusion which after many deviations will finally return to the mood of the opening pages. This is borne out by Clegg's apparent misunderstanding, at the time he is writing, of the initials G.P. (p. 268). This suggestion, however, cannot be right, partly because there is no space in the events of the last few days for him to have written anything substantial, but chiefly because the final pages of Chapter 3 (pp. 283–5) are unmistakably written, as the use of the conditional tense makes plain, in the full knowledge that the plans laid out in them never came to fruition.

We must conclude that Clegg has in his mind the entire sequence of events, from first seeing Miranda, through her captivity and death, to his final revulsion against her, *at the moment he starts to write*. And this ability to compartmentalise his mind, to explore and re-live the stages of his emotional life without perceiving that they are incompatible or learning anything from them, gives us perhaps as chilling a glimpse into Clegg's mind as any we have had.

Lastly, at the level of content, we can formulate the opposition as 'open/closed'. (Another way of phrasing this, taking into account the symbolic overtones of the names and the way Miranda is repeatedly associated with images of light, might be 'airborne/earthbound'.) Miranda's openness to experience comes out in quite little things, such as her attitude to food: distress affects her so strongly that she cannot eat ('I haven't needed food. I have been so full of hatred', p. 231), while he when upset rushes to the kitchen ('I shut her mouth up and got the eyelids down. I didn't know what to do then, I went and made myself a cup of tea', pp. 280–1). In a more general way we notice that Miranda's diary ranges over a wide range of events and memories, backward into the past and forward into 'the mystery of the future' (p. 151), to the point where she can say 'I've not been here for most of the day. I've been mainly thinking about G.P.' (p. 155). This range of interests gives her access to a world of cultural activities and moral and political interests from which Clegg is of course excluded (the only book he mentions having read for itself is *Secrets of the Gestapo*), and also to an emotional life – partly with her memories of her family, but chiefly in her developing relationship with G.P. – similarly closed to Clegg. (So vivid are these memories that one thinks of the remark in *L'Etranger* that *'un homme qui n'aurait vécu qu'un seul jour pourrait sans peine vivre cent ans dans une prison'*, Camus, 1957, p. 123). The moral openness of her world enables her, despite her frequent rages against Clegg, to find it in herself to pity him: with very rare exceptions, the most he can do is to 'forgive' (!) her.

The contrast is more striking still when we come to the audience for which the two accounts seem to be intended. Miranda, as suggested above, writes either for herself, in order to sort out her own ideas, or more frequently for someone she loves (see for example p. 133); her attitude is usually open and often self-critical. Clegg writes always as if on trial: his attitude is constantly defensive and self-justifying ('I was not different, I can prove it', p. 12), as if even when alone he is conscious of some accusing eye fixed upon him. It is hardly necessary to point out that such an attitude – consistent with the carefully prepared, almost rhetorical presentation of his case to which I drew attention earlier – is better suited to concealing the truth than to uncovering it.

It is now time to examine the themes of the book; in so doing, I shall use the framework sketched out in Chapter 1 above.

The first point to look at is the question of the Few and the Many.[5] Miranda sees herself as a member of the Few captured by a representative of the Many (though she later decides more cautiously that 'I'm not one of [the Few]. I *want* to be one of them, and that's not the same thing', p. 220, emphasis in original). Although she begins by wanting to help and to educate Clegg ('I know we're supposed to face the herd, control the stampede . . . Work for them and tolerate them', p. 219) she ends in bleakness: 'It's a battle between Caliban and myself. He is the New People and I am the Few' (p. 242). In this she is following the lead of G.P., who sees life in terms of a clash between the two groups and through Miranda speaks of 'the sheer jealous malice . . . the Calibanity . . . of the great bulk of England' (pp. 172–3).

Behind G.P. in turn stands Fowles: G.P.'s The ordinary man is the curse of civilization' (p. 137) is echoed by his creator's 'I think the common man is the curse of civilization' (Newquist, 1964, p. 219; see also the 1968 Preface to the revised *Aristos*).

If we look closely at Fowles's handling of this aspect of *The Collector* we will find that it falls into two parts, one essential and one peripheral. The essential part is simply the contention that some people are superior to others: this will be discussed at some length in my final chapter, and for the time being must simply be accepted on the narrative level as a structural principle of the fiction. The peripheral part (though one which bulks very large in *The Collector*) consists of a sustained attack mounted through the medium of Miranda's diary on two social groups, the lower middle class that Clegg comes from, and the more diffuse group which Miranda (again under the influence of G.P.) calls the 'New People'.

As we have seen, Fowles views the relationship between the Few and the Many in *The Collector* as one of literally murderous struggle. In the course of the book each side in the conflict becomes identified with the social class of its representative in the book – the Few with Miranda's upper middle class, the Many with Clegg's lower middle class. In one sense this is highly successful. Clegg's stylistic mannerisms make him a convincing (if extreme) stereotype of the petit bourgeoisie at its anxiety-ridden, puritanical, and narrow-minded worst. (One might add that Fowles portrays with insight and sympathy, p. 11, the feelings of a member of this class out of his depth in the world of inherited and accustomed wealth.) But Fowles wants to push his class analysis much further than this. What he is venturing here is the intriguing, but entirely unproven and potentially highly offensive, hypothesis that there is a link between the individual psychology and the class mannerisms, between the psychopathic sadism of Clegg (for such it is) and the values of the lower middle class.

Indeed Fowles wants to take these analogies between individual and class further still. Just (sometimes only just) below the surface of his argument lies an equation of this kind:

Miranda (r) educated, liberal   (r) embattled artists   (r) Few
              upper middle class

Clegg   (r) ignorant, prejudiced (r) besieging hordes   (r) Many
              lower middle class   of ascendant,
                                           philistine New People

(r) = represents

But for a mass of reasons – some of them to be found within the book itself, for example the obvious difference (which Miranda partly realises) between Clegg and Sillitoe's Arthur Seaton (pp. 240–2), or Miranda's ambivalent attitude to the Ladymont ethos – this analogy is utterly unworkable. To begin with, Clegg, emotionally stunted by being effectively an orphan, cut off from his colleagues at work, and without friends, can hardly be taken as a legitimate representative of his (or any) class. But, much more damagingly to Fowles's logic, neither Clegg nor his class can possibly belong to the New People as Miranda habitually asserts that they do, being meek where the New People are aggressive, submissive where they are arrogant, timorous where they are confident, and puritanical where they are indulgent. In fact I think the whole category 'New People' (which is alluded to again in the recent *Daniel Martin*, pp. 425–8) is a phoney one, but this is a matter for social and economic discussion and as such falls outside the scope of a work of this kind. What I can say is that as it stands Miranda's discussion of the New People in *The Collector* radiates a singularly unattractive combination of smugness and paranoia, and I regret very much that Fowles should have included it.

'What she never understood was that with me it was having. Having her was enough. Nothing needed doing. I just wanted to have her, and safe at last' (pp. 104–5). As its title implies, *The Collector* is dominated by the theme of having, possessing, or in short collecting. Fowles's treatment of this question, however, assimilates it to a larger one, that of the contrast between masculine and feminine ways of thinking. Fowles sees collecting as a specifically masculine aberration. For him, one aspect of the opposition between the sexes can be summed up as the contrast between having and being.

Fowles himself, as we saw in Chapter 1, regards the collector mentality as a major evil. By making Clegg a collector of butterflies – a subject, it should be said, which is woven into the book extremely skilfully and convincingly, not least because Fowles himself used to collect butterflies (see for example *The Tree*, p. 12) – Fowles brings out the special paradox of collecting. The collector seeks to possess (and in the case of the butterfly collector to kill) things of value; yet the value of what he seeks resides precisely in the fact that it was free (in the sense of unpossessed) and alive. In the things the collector covets, what can be possessed is not what is valuable: what is valuable cannot be possessed. Butterflies are a particularly apt choice to illustrate this point, not only because they are living things which the collector must kill, but also because of their symbolic overtones: the Greeks used the same word for butterfly as for soul. By contrast the blunt, phonetically closed monosyllable of Clegg's name suggests encumbrance and enclosure ('claggy' [sticky], 'clay', 'clog') while the similarity with the dialect word 'cleg', a horsefly, together with the way Clegg is frequently associated in the early parts of the book with the word 'bug', remind us of the distinction sketched by Stein in *Lord Jim* between earthy, crawling bugs and airborne butterflies.

Clegg, as Miranda is not slow to notice (p. 45), moves on from collecting butterflies to collecting people; the analogy is made, but its implications ignored, by Clegg himself on pp. 41–2. Miranda – 'she who is to be admired' – is a particularly cruel choice of victim, and a windowless cellar a particularly cruel place to shut away a person who is so insistently associated, particularly towards the end of her diary and in the death scene, with light. But Clegg is also caught up in the paradox of the lover as defined in Sartre's *L'Etre et le Néant*. The lover wants to assure himself that his love will be freely returned, but this is impossible, for if he controls the free will of the other then the love will be assured but not freely given, and if he does not control that free will he cannot be sure of being loved at all. Love, Fowles is saying, is like free will, which by definition cannot be submitted to the will of another. You cannot collect people; and if you succeed in doing so, then what you have got will not in any worthwhile sense be a person.

This possessiveness spills over into a second feature which Fowles sees as specifically masculine, namely the ethos of courtly love, with its determination to idealise and shield the beloved, whether or not such protection is wanted. We have already seen an aspect of this in the 'madonna/whore complex' (p. 17 above); we find the same metaphor at work in a political context in the USAF sergeant who sees American nuclear forces in Britain as 'knights of old rescuing a damsel in distress' (p. 144). This kind of 'sinister *Frauendienst*' (Conradi, 1982, p. 94) is seen both as destructive and as essentially masculine. Against it Fowles sets Miranda's growing capacity to overcome her prudishness, first by offering herself to Clegg, and finally by overcoming the physical repugnance she feels for G.P. and resolving to sleep with him (p. 258). One may smile at her rather deliberate passion; but in the terms of the book one must admire the determination with which she seeks to accept both her own physicality and that of other people.

The third area in which male and female reactions are contrasted is that of creativity. A little thought will show that from this point of view, *The Collector* depicts a conflict not between minds but within a mind, and not between characters but between aspects of character. If nothing else, the repeated hints that Miranda is in some sense not only G.P.'s *anima* (for example p. 187), but also Clegg's (p. 257), should alert us to this feature of the book. Viewed from this angle, Miranda is the feminine aspect of both Clegg's and G.P.'s mind. She is embodied, not only as a girl, but specifically (like Diana in 'The Ebony Tower') as a creative and artistic girl, because for Fowles *anima* and muse, physical sexuality and artistic creativity, are intimately linked with each other and with femininity. *The Collector* is thus in part about how men come to terms with their own creativity. Both Clegg and G.P. are in love with Miranda, and in both men this love has artistic repercussions. Clegg's creativity comes out in photography, symbolising (as elsewhere in Fowles) his preference for the safely dead over the dangerously alive. His photographs are sexual, but in a sense which is initially masturbatory (p. 113) and ultimately a kind of sadistic rape: 'I took her till I had no more bulbs left' (p. 122). It is consistent with this that for him both sex and art should be not merely voyeuristic but actually impersonal: 'The best (photographs) were with her face cut off' (p. 122). Clegg's twisted Puritanism and his rejection of everything 'nasty' exemplify Pascal's observation that *'Qui veut faire l'ange fait la bête'*, and lead inexorably from rejecting a part of himself, to imprisoning it, and finally to killing it.

G.P. is not innocent, and Miranda might well have become his victim; there is an image disingenuously placed in her diary of 'two fiendishly excited horsemen chasing a timid little fallow-deer' (p. 186). But the experience would not have been fatal. Where Clegg photographs and depersonalises, G.P. paints (notably portraits), bringing out the personality of his subjects. G.P.'s promiscuity, however irresponsible, represents an acceptance of life and of his own sexuality; his motto, one feels, might be Luther's 'Sin boldly'. Despite his moulding, 'Professor Higgins' side (p. 165) and the social prejudices looked at already (pp. 22–4 above), the main influence he seeks to exercise is Socratic and liberating – 'He makes me question myself' (p. 152). In the symbolic terms we are dealing with here, G.P. can give these lessons *to* Miranda because in a sense he has learned them *from* her – or from the feminine side of his own personality, his own *anima*, of which Miranda (*'une* princesse lointaine', p. 188, emphasis in original) represents one, but only one, embodiment. The different attitudes of the two men – to art, to love, and indeed to their own past selves – are well expressed in the celebrated Blake quatrain:

He who binds to himself a joy
Does the winged life destroy;
But he who kisses the joy as it flies
Lives in eternity's sun rise.

The third and fourth themes mentioned in Chapter 1 need no mention here because they are present by their absence: the domaine of *The Collector* (as the epigraph ironically emphasises) is an anti-domaine, and freedom is transformed into its opposite, imprisonment. But there is one aspect of the book which we must briefly mention here since it represents an important aspect of Fowles's existentialism. It concerns the matter of accepting responsibility for one's actions. Clegg constantly excuses himself from guilt – to the extent that in his diary *he* is constantly forgiving *her*! – and generally regards himself as fixed and unable to change, as witness his refusal to let Miranda teach him about music or art. She on the other hand, as we know from her diary, is changing and developing throughout, unceasingly re-working her past and re-planning her future. She accepts guilt (both in her remembered relationship with G.P. and in her day-to-day life with Clegg) and is ready to apologise: moreover, as we see in her anguished debate with herself about violence (pp. 233–9), she accepts responsibility for what she has done, and in the best existentialist tradition chooses not only for herself but also for humanity. It is consistent with this that while Miranda dies in effect an atheist (the word 'God' progressively vanishes from the three pleas for help that end her diary, p. 267), Clegg retains his religious observances to the last: 'not that I believe in religion, but it seemed right' (p. 281).

In many ways *The Collector* forms a curious beginning to Fowles's writing career. It is not a nice book. Miranda's death is a painful one for the reader, and (as Olshen, 1978, and Conradi, 1982, point out) the use of the diary form makes the reader a kind of voyeuristic accomplice of that death. It is curious too that Fowles should start with such a savage parody of the romance form, an attack which, in revealing the murderous contradictions inherent in sexual idealism, strikes at the very roots of the romance impulse. A curious beginning: but an extraordinarily effective one. At the beginning of this chapter, while discussing Clegg's prose style, I spoke of the distinctive flavour of this book, and it is on this note that I would like to conclude. Miranda's diary shows her many merits, merits which shine exceptionally brightly beside the faults of Clegg. But it is Clegg's account that works. For me the distinction of *The Collector* lies in its pathos, its ability to evoke feeling. This pathos, however, is not chiefly of the Little Nell variety which we might expect the death of Miranda to produce – though the closing pages of her diary are indeed powerful and moving. It is instead the pathos of Clegg, implicit throughout in his banal and simple style and rising to the surface in his account of Miranda's death in Chapter 3. What we experience in this section is not so much her death as the impact of her death on him. She has lost her life, but he has lost everything that made life worthwhile: 'You can't buy happiness. I must have heard Aunt Annie say that a hundred times. Ha ha, I always thought, just let's have a try first. Well, I had my try' (p. 284). The bleak desolation of his prospects throws into relief the warmth with which he reviews the past, and after the bitterness of the end of Chapter 1, this *retour de tendresse* is extraordinarily touching: 'All sorts of nice things came back. I remembered the beginning, the days in the Annexe just seeing her come out of the front door, or passing her the other side of the street, and I couldn't understand how it all happened so that she was there below, dead' (p. 281). It may be (though Fowles himself might deny this[6]) that this emotional force derives from the paradoxical dignity of the inarticulate to which Miranda responds on p. 199; it may be, to quote a later work, because 'The subject's self-pity is projected so strongly on his environment that one becomes contaminated by it' (*M*, p. 513); it may simply be because of what the un-named narrator of *La Chute* teasingly describes as *'la sainte innocence de celui qui se pardonne à lui-même'* (Camus, 1956, p. 153). But wherever it comes from, it starts to work on me the moment I see those familiar opening lines: 'When she was home from her boarding-school I used to see her almost every day sometimes . . .'.

3   *The Magus*

> I was born in 1927, the only child of middle-class parents, both
> English, and themselves born in the grotesquely elongated shadow,
> which they never rose sufficiently above history to leave, of that
> monstrous dwarf Queen Victoria. I was sent to a public school, I
> wasted two years doing my national service, I went to Oxford; and
> there I began to discover I was not the person I wanted to be.
>
> (*M*, p. 15)

Thus begins *The Magus*,[1] Fowles's third published work and the one
which offers the first full-scale development of the themes and
methods of his fiction. The opening brings to our attention two major
features of the book. One is its focus on the central character, who is
also the narrator: we learn right from the start that he is 'not the person
[he wants] to be', a discovery which is in itself a kind of personal
development, and we expect that further development will follow. But
the second feature, one which stands out rather sharply in this brief
extract, is the curious bitterness (not to say exaggeration) of its tone.
There is a lot packed into the opening sentence, as if once started the
narrator could not draw breath until his pent-up feelings had been
discharged: 'middle-class', 'English', 'grotesquely elongated', 'monstrous dwarf' – the epithets, whether neutral or pejorative, tumble out
in an accusing rush, and the prevailing tone seems not so much
regretful as resentful. In the face of such spleen we begin to wonder
how much the narrator really has changed. And we are right to feel this
uncertainty: for *The Magus* is a novel of paradox. On our first reading
of the book, the hero progresses from ignorance to knowledge and
from solitude to fulfilled love, acquiring *en route* a number of
important philosophical truths. Re-reading, however, may cause us to
doubt this first reaction. We begin to wonder just how heroic the 'hero'
is; whether or not he really has changed; if the ending is in fact the
happy one that the book seems to be leading up to. Above all we begin
to see that the prominence which the book allots to its philosophical
element may in fact serve, not to assert, but to question and undermine
these so-called 'truths'.[2]

My argument in this chapter falls into three stages. In the first I shall discuss the plot and design of *The Magus* in some detail, exploring its literary affinities and discussing some of the ideas put forward in it. The second (the 're-reading' referred to above) will try to show how the form of the work calls into question and ironises much of its explicit content. And the conclusion will try to reconcile the first two stages by showing how these apparently conflicting moral ironies and paradoxes can nonetheless serve Fowles's essentially moral purpose.

The easiest way to analyse the story of *The Magus* is to treat it from two aspects, namely 'plot' and 'design'.³ The plot of *The Magus* seems at first immensely complex. But despite its length and its constant changes of setting and direction, it rests upon two very simple patterns. The first is the love story – boy meets girl; boy leaves girl; boy returns to girl. And the second is the quest narrative, in which the hero undertakes a magical journey whose true but more or less sublimated goal is a fuller understanding of himself. The love story of *The Magus* is the tale of Nicholas and Alison, who meet, love, and part in Part 1; who seem definitively separated in Part 2 by Alison's suicide; and who are re-united, the suicide being proved a fake, in Part 3. The quest narrative in the strict sense is confined to the 'fenced' island (p. 7) of Phraxos, in which Nicholas goes through a series of ordeals in his attempt to free a kind of imprisoned maiden (Julie) from the grasp of her evil captor (Conchis); but of course both love story and quest myth come down ultimately to aspects of the same search for self-knowledge, the same attempt to become the person he does want to be, which we saw at work in the first paragraph of the book. The literary form in which love story and quest myth coalesce is the romance, and it does not take a brilliant critical intellect to realise that *The Magus* is a work in this genre. It is, moreover, the work in which Fowles gives himself over most fully to certain other features of romance: its fondness for exotic settings; its leanings towards wish-fulfilment (achieved in *The Magus* through Conchis's apparently inexhaustible wealth); and – unusually for Fowles – its freedom to set aside the constraints of plausibility. Fowles has said that 'In its original form there was a clear supernatural element – an attempt at something along the lines of . . . *The Turn of The Screw*' (p. 5), and although this is no longer prominent, it remains an influence. In the case of some of the Bourani tricks, it is exceedingly difficult to work out how they could be done without the aid of magic.

This romantic substructure supports a number of other plot-types.

There is the *roman de moeurs* or social comedy. Nicholas's experiences in England provide the opportunity for reflections upon the English character, both as something unchanging and as something specifically of the 1950s; the inclusion of types from several social strata (Kemp, Jojo, Mitford, the British Council officials in London and Athens) provides in addition a vertical cross-section of English mores. The fact that Nicholas and his development are very much the focus of attention – and that he tells his own story – gives us the patterns of the *Bildungsroman*, the novel of the growth to maturity of a single principal character, and of the fictional autobiography.[4] And the sheer trickery practised on Nicholas throughout the book, together with his determined efforts to unravel what is happening to him, give us the pattern of the detective story.

All these plot-types are essentially directional: they move towards some kind of discovery or resolution. Other plot-types echoed in the work are more leisurely, more static in nature. The four inset tales which Conchis tells Nicholas give us the pattern of the *roman à tiroirs*, in which the main narrative stops while one character recounts a story which is entirely self-contained; and the space and seriousness allotted to moral and philosophical discussion remind us of the novel of ideas, a literary form in which (albeit for very different reasons) narrative development is not the centre of interest.[5]

The suspension of narrative movement provides a convenient transition to the second way of looking at a story, namely the aspect of design. I want now to examine *The Magus* from this angle and to see what meanings are implicit in its design.

We may begin with its use of tripartite structures. The book as a whole is divided into three parts, marked off as such in the text. The first (Chapters 1 to 9) is set principally in London, finishing with Nicholas on Phraxos but not having discovered Bourani. The second (Chapters 10 to 67) takes place almost entirely on Phraxos; in it the various sequences at Bourani are played out, the villa properties finally dismantled, the trial and 'disintoxication' performed, and Nicholas left jobless and baffled in Athens. The third (Chapters 68 to 78) returns us via Rome to London, where Nicholas after a prolonged and exasperating period of waiting is at last contacted by Alison. This structure parallels the threefold plot-structure referred to earlier (boy meets/ leaves/returns to girl), but with an important difference. The central section, which seems from the plot summary to be little more than a means of keeping the lovers apart, becomes in *The Magus* by far the longest and thematically densest part; and in this (in every way) central section, Alison is entirely overshadowed by the beautiful twins June and Julie (or Lily and Rose).

Part 2 is by any standards an extraordinary piece of writing. This springs partly from the beautifully handled descriptions of the island of Phraxos; partly from the web of magic, eroticism, and suspense woven around Nicholas at Bourani; and, perhaps chiefly, from the almost overwhelming impact of the four narratives told by Conchis himself on Nicholas's successive weekend visits. In the course of these stories Fowles displays the full range of his powers; it could be argued that in organisation of narrative, in mastery of realistic detail, in creation of atmosphere, and in suggestive power, he has never done better.

Yet we have to face the fact that Bourani is a phoney. The stories on which it depends so heavily are revealed to be (at least factually) untrue; the magic which so intrigues Nicholas is for the most part revealed as trickery; its incongruously expensive works of art turn out to be fakes. Nor do the 'cast' fare any better: one of Conchis's final tricks is to reveal his own gravestone (p. 559), and Julie is later said by her own mother to have been 'nothing but a personification of [Nicholas's] own selfishness' (p. 601). The agonising 'disintoxication' in Chapters 59 to 62, and the longer process of withdrawal from sexual and metaphysical enchantment which occupies Part 3, leave us in no doubt: we must not be taken in by 'The godgame' (p. 625).

This raises a substantial problem for the balance of the book as a whole. The Phraxos episode, as we have seen, is subverted and ironised in a number of ways. Yet if it is as false as it is made out to be, how can it be proper for it to play so large a part in the work? And if the true heroine of the book is Alison, how can she be absent from its most seductive part?

The answer lies in Fowles's concept of the domaine. We have seen that the domaine is privileged and special; but it is also by its very nature a place of temporary rather than permanent residence. Its function is to encourage learning and change, but the desire to cling to it, to live always at the centre of experience, is as wrong in Nicholas as it was in Clegg (see Chapter 2 above). Fowles has indicated that he considered *The Maze* and *The Godgame* as alternative titles for *The Magus*: both rest on ideas of instructive play or serious tease which form an essential element in the atmosphere of the domaine. In this, of course, the domaine resembles the experience of reading. Just as characters in literature are at once more and less real than those in real life, so are the characters that Nicholas meets at Bourani, a point glanced at by Conchis in a passage that occurs only in the Revised Version: '[Lily] will make her first valid step back towards normality when one day she stops and says, This is not the real world. These are not real relationships' (p. 282). Nor should we be surprised at the exclusion from Phraxos of a character whose supreme virtue, by contrast with the 'phasality' (p. 577) of Julie, is her 'constant reality' (p. 539). Not for nothing is the resurrection of Alison placed in the same chapter (66) as the death of Conchis.

The presence of Alison is a touchstone in more ways than one. She does not set foot in Phraxos: but she does visit Greece, and a crucial sequence between her and Nicholas takes place on Mount Parnassus, 'Where the muses dash about' (p. 251). The implications of this will become clearer if we represent the design of the novel in the form of a diagram (see p. 47 below). Just as there are three parts to the book, so there are three subdivisions within Part 2 (Phraxos, Parnassus, Phraxos); three further subdivisions within the Parnassus unit (Athens, Parnassus, Athens); and three chapter divisions (39, 40, 41 – ascent, arrival, descent) within the description of Parnassus itself. The ascent of Parnassus is thus structurally, if not quite numerically, the exact centre of the book; a fact that Nicholas himself draws attention to, with a characteristic blend of blindness and insight, on p. 273.

The structural (as distinct from thematic) centrality of the Parnassus episode is emphasised by a number of pointers. It is the middle one of three mountain climbs in the book (up to Hymettus in Chapter 7, down from Monemvasia in Chapter 63); it occurs in between the second and third of Conchis's four extended stories; and it is fitted in to a half-term holiday (holiday, moreover, being etymologically 'holy day').

Such a structurally central position leads us to expect a corresponding thematic intensity. The Parnassus episode develops three key aspects of the book. The first, obviously, is the fact that it is Alison, and not Julie, who is Nicholas's true partner. Her authenticity, her courage, her enthusiasm, and her generosity shine forth from these pages. Significantly she is associated more than once with children (pp. 253–4 and 274), reminding us that it is 'a nauseatingly happy "average" family' (p. 643) which Nicholas comes to recognise as his destiny in Part 3, and of the suggestion in Part 1 (pp. 33–4) that it is the abortion Alison had in Australia which is at the root of her self-destructiveness. Secondly, the treatment of sexuality illuminates the contrasting attitudes of the pair. For Alison it is an aspect of her affection for Nicholas: if she can't have a full sexual relationship with him because of his supposed syphilis, she will do the best she can; she accepts him, disease and all. For Nicholas sex with Alison provides a means of deferring the deeper questions of their relationship and of concealing his lack of affection; their sexual union on Parnassus, a testimony of her self-abandoning love for him, he interprets as a sign of her humiliation and defilement.[6] Simultaneously he hankers after sex with Julie as some kind of mysterious experience radically different from the sweaty reality of intercourse with Alison which he refers to elsewhere with unlovable matter-of-factness as 'spilt semen' (p. 387). The mystery Nicholas longs for is clearly present before him – it is affection and love. But when he finds these emotions stirring within him (p. 264) he resolves to exorcise them in the most cauterising way he can, namely by telling Alison that she has been supplanted, and that he has been lying to her all along.

Lying, and its antithesis honesty, is the third and perhaps crucial theme of the Parnassus episode. It dominates the central chapter of the five under its metaphorical aspect of light:

> then at last, hand in hand, we struggled up the last few yards and stood on the little platform with its crowning cairn.
>
> Alison said, 'Oh my God, oh my God.'
>
> On the far side a huge chasm plunged down two thousand feet of shadowy air. The westering sun was still just above the horizon, but the clouds had vanished. The sky was a pale, absolutely dustless, absolutely pure, azure ... With a splendid classical simplicity someone had formed in small stones, just beyond the cairn, the letters ΦΩΣ – 'light'. It was exact. The peak reached up into a world both literally and metaphorically of light.
>
> (p. 258)

In so doing it picks up and unifies a series of references scattered through the book. Greece is the country of light: even Rome is murky by comparison: in London nothing is seen clearly. And light, bright intense sunlight, carries a powerful moral charge in the book. It stands for the piercing and at times corrosive force of analysis, honesty, and insight which Greece itself, and Conchis as an embodiment of Greece ('I finally assumed my Greekness', p. 434), bring to bear on all aspects of human behaviour. The light of Greece, as seen on Phraxos, enables Nicholas to penetrate some of his own disguises; the same light flooding the peak of Parnassus shows us as readers that Nicholas is still wearing several masks too many.

Looking at tripartite structures in *The Magus* in this way brings out the extensive use in the book of repetition, echoing, and opposition. Repeated elements include the use of twins; Nicholas's two suicide situations (pp. 60–2 and 534); the sequence of candidates for Phraxos (Leverrier, Mitford, Nicholas himself, Briggs . . .); the three failed proposals between Nicholas and Alison (pp. 35, 39 and 275–6); and the way in which, once in each part, Alison appears mysteriously (pp. 22, 561, and 647). Echoes and analogies are far too numerous to list exhaustively: one might pick out the pervasive stress on femininity in the use of names (see note 10 below); the way birdsong and music are woven into the book as symbols of a mysterious hope; the two Latin mottos (pp. 188 and 656); and above all the complex affinities between Conchis's experiences as recounted in the stories and scenes of the masque, and Nicholas's own experiences as recounted in his book. As for oppositions, we may cite the relationship between Parts 1 and 3. In the former, Nicholas loses his parents, treats a girl very badly and leaves her, and learns that 'I was not the person I wanted to be' (p. 15). In the latter, he acquires a kind of proxy mother (Kemp) and sister (Jojo), undertakes to wait with reluctant patience for the return of the girl he dismissed in Part 1, and recognises that she is essentially bound up with learning who he really is.

Although these oppositions may give the ending a one-directional flavour of development, I think they are better understood (along with the repetitions and echoes) as asserting the interrelationship of the parts of this novel: as aspects, that is, not of movement but of pattern, not of plot but of design. As the T. S. Eliot extract rather irritatingly reminds us (p. 69), the book is deliberately circular in construction: it begins and ends with London, and its first important emotional relationship is also its last. As I suggested earlier, this is a perfectly legitimate literary device: the carrot of 'what happened next' is not the only means of luring the reader to continue. But we may reasonably ask in the case of *The Magus* whether we are not dealing with something more radical still. Nicholas begins as an orphan and ends by acquiring a 'parent'; he begins (in a kind of parody of the conventional romance) by sleeping with Alison and ends by loving her. Does this not suggest that the book is neither static nor circular, but actually regressive?

A novel of growth which was actually about decline, a *Bildungs-roman* without *Bildung*, would certainly run counter to expectations. Let us examine the evidence for such a subversive reading.

The Magus is a story. It is also largely made up of stories. Conchis's four great narratives in Part 2 have already been mentioned; we also have the various accounts of themselves given by Lily/Julie and her sister Rose, the elaborate fable of the Prince and the Magician which Nicholas finds in the Earth, the explanations of Lily de Seitas, Mitford's account of his experiences at Bourani, Jojo's pathetic attempt to disguise first her age and then her feelings in order to seduce Nicholas. Nor are all these stories oral: what with the Foulkes pamphlet, Anton's account of the atrocity on Phraxos, Conchis's two pamphlets from the 1920s, and the abundant faked letters and newspaper cuttings, *The Magus* becomes a kind of palimpsest of written and spoken tales.

As we read further these tales are increasingly shown to be unreliable. This is initially a matter of presentation: during the first full weekend at Bourani Nicholas remarks on 'a lack of virginity' in the telling of Conchis's story:

> there was some fatal extra dimension in his objectivity, which was much more that of a novelist before a character than of even the oldest, most changed man before his own real past self.
>
> (p. 133)

After a while it comes to taint everything associated with Bourani, so that Nicholas demands proofs: proofs, specifically, of Julie's feelings for him, which will of course ultimately take physical form. When these proofs are delivered in Chapter 58 Nicholas assumes that both they and the story that accompanies them are genuine: he is roughly disabused of both beliefs in the trial and 'disintoxication' that follow. But even the trial is itself a façade. The analysis of Nicholas is explicitly stated to have been incomplete (p. 627), and even if we did not have Lily de Seitas's word for it, the grotesquely Freudian jargon of the psychiatric reports – not to mention the elaborate mystification with freemasonry, masks, and robes that precedes them – would have warned us not to take them at face value.

Unable to believe any of his senses as far as the godgame is concerned, Nicholas clings to his memory of Alison as totally honest. Briefly he builds upon this honesty a reassuring but mistaken opposition between Greece, deceit, and evanescence on the one hand, and England, truth, and solidity on the other. The shock of finding that Alison too has deceived him, that her suicide had been faked and that she has gone over to Conchis, causes Nicholas to call into question everything that has happened – and will happen – to him, arousing an unlimited suspicion that would seem like paranoia if events did not so frequently confirm it.

All these unreliable tales are themselves part of a tale, the story told by Nicholas himself. There is thus an increasing pressure on the reader to look critically at this continuing narrative, and at the moral and philosophical lessons which it delivers. Subversion of narrative goes hand in hand with subversion of narrator.

This subversion is achieved through a number of devices. The first point to look at is simply the narrator's first name. Taken in conjunction with Alison, it strongly calls to mind the Miller's Tale in *The Canterbury Tales*, where Nicholas and Alison are merely the very ordinary protagonists of a bawdy story. Notwithstanding his university background, Nicholas is intended as something of an Everyman (p. 9): his surname (Urfe) links him with earth (p. 9), and he is described in the final chapter as an 'anti-hero' (p. 645). The disparity between the elaborate mechanism of the godgame and the unworthiness of its beneficiary does not escape Nicholas: in an addition to the first version, Fowles makes him ask Lily de Seitas:

'All right. I treated Alison very badly. I'm a born cad, a swine, whatever you want. But why the colossal performance just to tell one miserable moral bankrupt what he is?'

(p. 626)

But given the importance that both Nicholas and Alison attach to sex, the degree to which their relationship as we have it in the book depends on sex, we would do well to bear in mind the possible deflating ironies that the Chaucerian parallel calls to mind.

The second device is Nicholas's style. I personally find the texture of this book absolutely compelling, but I am aware that what I take for richness might less sympathetically be described as over-ripe and self-indulgent (see Binns, 1977, for a good treatment of this point). It is not just that Nicholas (like his creator) is given to frequent verbless sentences, to using abstract nouns in the plural or with the indefinite article, to an almost *précieux* precision of language ('desipience', p. 160, 'algedonic', p. 178, 'eschar', p. 609) and to a rather irritating generalising use of the definite article to imply that the reader is familiar with what is being described ('the usual hot airlessness of nocturnal Athens in summer', p. 561). Such devices, after all, feature in the work of many serious and thoughtful writers – Lawrence Durrell and Henry James, to name but two. Nor is it the difficulty Nicholas has in composing letters within the novel – the many drafts of his would-be spontaneous farewell note to Alison (p. 48), the painfully insincere

letter in Chapter 43 (pp. 279–80: note her apt criticism of his letters on
p. 53). A more important clue, I think, lies in Nicholas's persistent
references to literature, the arts, and Classical mythology. This
name-dropping is noticeable from a fairly early stage: in Chapter 8 we
have direct or indirect allusion to Antwerp blue, Hokusai, Sciron,
Gide, Emily Dickinson, Descartes, Rimbaud, Catullus, Sartre, Gold-
ing(?), and *Romeo and Juliet*. But at key points in the book it becomes
almost obsessive. One such point is Chapter 42 – the descent from
Parnassus. The pair find a hidden waterfall and swim in the pool
beneath, then lie drying in the sun. Alison, still trying to return to the
sexual and emotional harmony of the first London phase, weaves
herself a garland out of wild flowers and turns to Nicholas, offering
herself invitingly. 'She did not know it,' writes Nicholas, 'but it was at
first for me an intensely literary moment. I could place it exactly:
England's Helicon' (pp. 268–9). This processing of experience through
literary filters is picked up in Chapter 51, when Nicholas hears of
Alison's 'suicide': 'Before I went to bed I took out *England's Helicon*;
turned to Marlowe' (p. 400), and three verses of 'Come Live with Mee'
follow. The best way to describe this is to borrow a phrase from
Nicholas himself: he speaks of edging Alison's death 'out of the moral
world into the aesthetic, where it was easier to live with' (p. 401). But it
is not at all clear whether this comment applies to the poetry reading;
nor whether Nicholas realises just how far this interpretation of
experience through art, this Swann-like aesthetic idolatry,[7] conditions
every aspect of his experience. Judging by the sustained high level of
such references even in the final chapter, one is inclined to answer that
he does not.

Thirdly there is the use of the narrative standpoint: the distance
between the time of the events (notionally 1952–53) and the time at
which they are understood to have been written down. If Nicholas is
playing fair, this gap need cause us no difficulty: as readers of fictional
autobiography we are trained to accept without question such
improbabilities as the supposed total recall of events and conversations
long in the past. But we do expect the narrator to lay his cards on the
table, so that we may have some sense of a fixed standard at work in the
book to judge the events it contains. We expect to know, at least at the
end of the book, who it was (fictionally speaking) who wrote it; and we
expect the narrator to be open about the thoughts and motives of the
one character of whom he has inside knowledge, namely himself.
Nicholas fulfils neither of these requirements. In the first place the
book is planted with tantalising references to a future located between

the time of the book and the time of its writing: 'that pre-permissive time' (p. 21, in the Revised Version only), 'anyone less cerebral and self-absorbed than I was then' (p. 35), 'Years later I saw the *gabbia* at Piacenza . . . And looking up at it I remembered that winter in Greece' (p. 62), 'Years later I discovered that [Mitford] *had* been acting that day' (p. 616, emphasis in original); we should perhaps include among these the fortune-telling episode on p. 195. But from this future, though *ipso facto* past and therefore known to the narrator, we are excluded: 'what happened in the following years shall be silence; another mystery' (p. 645), 'She . . . will . . . never leave this frozen present tense. All waits, suspended' (p. 656). Nicholas is teasing us: and if we do not know his time standpoint, we cannot know his moral standpoint either.

Nor, as I have suggested, is he fully open about his own feelings. In Parts 1 and 2 he is admirably ready (following the precepts of the 'Socratic honesty', p. 17, he claims to have acquired at Oxford) to advance evidence against himself: and the lamentable chronicle of his lies and deceptions is made all the more damning by the elevated moral and philosophical reasoning with which it alternates. But in Part 3 there are hints that the crafty reserve of the English – the only English characteristic that he seems even intermittently to admire – is beginning to intrude between us and Nicholas: for though we continue to have what we must perforce presume to be a faithful record of his actions, his thoughts at key moments are concealed from us. Chapter 72 begins, 'I didn't feel angry at first' (p. 594) and goes on to record in direct speech a long argument with Lily de Seitas in which Nicholas gives every sign of being very angry indeed. It is thus something of a shock to read at the beginning of Chapter 73, 'Yet even then I knew I was pretending to be angrier than I really was' (p. 606). The same external treatment is used for much of Nicholas's behaviour in the second, friendlier interview with Lily de Seitas (pp. 624–31), concealing in particular what lies behind two key questions – the 'why me?' (p. 626) referred to above, and the inquiry as to Alison's exact involvement in the godgame (p. 628). And the last passage in the book that can definitely be attributed to Nicholas – the last two paragraphs on p. 655 – is likewise in a mixture of direct speech and external observation.

Discussion of the final chapter of *The Magus* brings us to the fourth way in which the credibility of Nicholas is subverted. The first three and the last paragraphs of that chapter can hardly be written by Nicholas, since the text speaks of 'the anti-hero' (p. 645) and later seems to address, not the reader, but the writer – 'Suspend the autumn trees' (p. 656). But if Nicholas doesn't write them – who does? Whether it is the 'implied author', in Wayne Booth's phrase, or the real author, or just an anonymous voice of the text, it reveals – as did the footprint to Robinson Crusoe – the presence of another intelligence where Nicholas had seemed to reign unchallenged.

Once we start to cast a critical eye on Nicholas himself, some of his actions as well as aspects of his style begin to seem suspicious. It would be naive at this stage to dwell on his selfishness and dishonesty: these qualities he explicitly and repeatedly condemns himself. But certain little occurrences are very revealing when closely examined. A case in point is the incident between Nicholas and Demetriades in Chapter 64 (pp. 540–1).

What happens is simply an unprovoked attack by Nicholas on a fellow member of the Lord Byron staff: an attack preceded by a humiliating insult, and consisting of a blow delivered without warning so that the victim has no chance to defend himself. But the account of it is heavily slanted to cast scorn upon all those participating except Nicholas. The noise in the room as Nicholas enters is compared to 'a pool of croaking frogs'; the masters stare at Nicholas 'as if [he] had committed the final crime'; stress is laid upon the way in which Demetriades deviates from the English public school ideal of manhood, that is on his timidity, on his dandyism, on his sweet tooth, and above all on the inappropriate way ('like a child', 'like a parody of Oedipus', 'like an old woman') he reacts to the cumulative series of insults and the final blow that Nicholas delivers. The intolerant and chauvinistic *machismo* (however discreetly it is expressed) is strikingly reminiscent of Mitford, a parallel driven home with some force by Mitford's own admission on p. 44 that he 'Gave [Demetriades] a black eye one day'![8]

At various points in the book Conchis uses the term 'elect' (in the sense of 'chosen' or 'selected'). The idea of admission to an elect group is perhaps the single most important principle in the book, though in explicit terms it is touched on fairly lightly: Nick dimly perceives the existence of some kind of 'deeper, wiser esoteric society' (p. 519), and Mrs de Seitas seems to offer a functional definition of it when she says that 'Neither I nor my children pretend to be ordinary people . . . We are rich and we are intelligent . . . And we accept the responsibility that our good luck in the lottery of existence puts upon us' (pp. 603–4). However, what does seem clear is that willy-nilly Nick belongs to this group: Conchis tells him after the trial (in what turns out to be their last meeting) that 'you are now elect . . . You have no choice' (p. 531). And the doubts and uncertainties we cannot help feeling about Nick accordingly apply also to the group he has been allowed to join. This is a major difficulty for the reader, applying not only to the elect group but also to its values: for if we can trust neither Nicholas's accuracy nor his judgement, we cannot put much faith either in his facts or in his opinions. To some extent this reflects an aspect of all Fowles's first-person narratives. But one can point to two ways in which our understanding of the matter can be increased. The first is that much of the ritual of Part 2, particularly in the trial scene, is borrowed from accounts of the pre-Christian mysteries of Eleusis. For our purposes the most notable feature of the Eleusinian mysteries was that 'the ritual was absolutely ended [after the initiation ceremony], with *no further requirement of initiates beyond everyday living*' (Huffaker, 1980, p. 63, emphasis added; see also Fleishman, 1976); thus one could continue to be a member whatever one's moral standards. And secondly, it may be useful to locate the question of 'election' in the context of Fowles's other work and to see it as what it really is, namely a special case of the Few and the Many. As such it remains problematic, but (as I shall seek to show in the final chapter) not totally opaque.

The upshot of all this investigation into the personality of Nicholas, as character and as narrator, is not a complete reversal of the naive reading. Nicholas does develop; he is less of a predator, less of an egotist at the end than at the beginning; he is clearly launched upon something worthwhile in his venture with Alison.[9] But the development is irregular and equivocal: as Ronald Binns puts it, 'Nicholas Urfe's narrative reveals a continual rising and falling movement to and from self-knowledge' (1973, p. 327). Like most of us, Nicholas cannot bear very much reality.

This oscillation in the nature and role of Nicholas is matched by a similar dialectic in the themes of *The Magus*. At different times the book seems to propose at one moment freedom, at another love, as the supreme value. (As we shall see, Fowles's later work is increasingly polarised between two extremes, one always being freedom, the other sometimes taking the form of duty.) We must now look at these themes in some detail.

It is difficult to exaggerate the importance in *The Magus* of the theme of freedom. It is particularly associated with the title character, Conchis himself. His narratives build up to a shattering climax in Chapter 53, whose theme – freedom – is emphasised by giving it the only chapter epigraph in the book. A more elaborate device used to highlight the word is to refer to it indirectly before it is explained: thus the Greek resistance fighter bellows 'just one word, but the most Greek of all words' on p. 379, but it is not till p. 425 that we find what this word is in Greek, and only on p. 434 that those of us who have not had the benefit of a Classical education actually get a translation. Chapter 53 explores 'every freedom, from the very worst to the very best . . . The freedom to confront a primitive God . . . The freedom to disembowel peasant girls and castrate with wire-cutters'; and it concludes that 'the annunciation and defence of . . . freedom [is] more important than common sense, self-preservation . . . than the lives of . . . eighty hostages' (p. 434).

The arguments of Chapter 53 spring quite naturally from the underlying principles on which the whole Bourani episode is organised; Conchis remarks rather coldly that 'There is no place for limits in the meta-theatre' (p. 406). In this sense both Bourani and Phraxos itself are special cases of a still larger aspect of the theme of freedom. Even before he discovers Bourani Nicholas remarks that 'Greece . . . made conventional English notions of what was moral and immoral ridiculous' (p. 57), and we remember the strong association, both on Hymettus (p. 49) and on Parnassus (p. 258), between Greece and light. What Greece stands for in *The Magus* is unlimited freedom – the freedom to analyse, to explore, to turn a searchlight on one's deepest and perhaps most anti-social drives and to put them into practice. It represents the world of unfettered desire: a world in which not only the high principles of a Conchis, but also the sensual egotism of a Demetriades, can flourish, and in which a Cretan 'freedom fighter' who is also a thief and murderer can have as his epitaph '*Kakourgos, ma Ellenas*. A bad man, but a Greek' (p. 437).

Counterbalancing this is a range of attitudes and emotions – consideration, respect for others, sympathy, repentance, and of course the 'super-commandment' (p. 641) – which I am grouping under the general term 'love'. (Once again we find the 'pre-haunting' effect, one Fowles seems rather fond of, whereby an idea is introduced before being defined: 'I couldn't say the word', p. 577, 'I understand that word now, Alison. Your word', p. 655.) Love is particularly associated in this work with Alison and with Lily de Seitas, and it is not accidental that both these characters are women. Just as freedom in *The Magus* cannot be discussed without reference to Greece, so love cannot be properly understood without reference to the theme of women. It is of course a work which celebrates women and women's influence. The original version was dedicated to Astarte; Fowles himself wrote in the

Foreword to the Revised Version that 'I long toyed with the notion of making Conchis a woman' (pp. 6–7); Conchis remarks that 'all profound definitions of God are essentially definitions of the mother' (p. 296); and there is a quite extraordinary emphasis in the book on the female line of descent.[10] *The Magus* is entirely open and unashamed in its proclamation of the superiority of women over men (Conchis defines 'a man's world' as 'a world governed by brute force, humourless arrogance, illusory prestige and primeval stupidity', p. 413). And the superiority of women lies precisely in their association with what I am calling 'love', and what Mrs de Seitas calls 'a . . . capacity for attachment and devotion' which is 'the one great quality [her] sex has to contribute to life' (p. 601).

It is not difficult to see the importance of freedom and love in *The Magus*. It is rather harder to define the relationship between the two. It is obviously what Fowles himself might call 'tensional' (*A*, pp. 83 ff), and common sense would lead us to expect some kind of opposition between the two. But there are also teasing hints of a connection. Conchis's philosophy of the smile (see in particular pp. 437 and 531, the latter being his final word to Nicholas) suggests that the apparent opposites can be reconciled, a possibility given concrete form in the narrative by the sexual and emotional relationship between Conchis and Mrs de Seitas, representatives of the two opposing forces (pp. 603 and 629). It may be that the persistent pointers to a Jungian reading whereby Alison is Nicholas's *anima* (see for example pp. 35, 55, 655, and the more or less definitive anagram on p. 266) offer the solution that Fowles himself would like to put forward; thus Nicholas and Alison would be aspects of a single personality, with Nicholas its freedom-loving male element, Alison its affectionate female component, both being essential for wholeness.[11] But what we can say with some confidence is that whether or not freedom and love are complementary, they are certainly distinct.

This distinction is best brought out with the aid of a diagram.

freedom	–	love
Conchis	–	Lily de Seitas
Julie	–	Alison
Greece, esp. Phraxos	–	England
Part 2	–	(Part 1 and) Part 3

exotic	–	familiar
illusion (romance, masque)	–	reality
men	–	women
reason (Conchis/ conscious)[12]	–	insight (Seitas/sight)
death (stories of wars; end of masque; vanishing of Lily; death of Conchis as a childless bachelor; Bourani = skull)	–	life (introduction of Mrs de Seitas, mother of four; return of Alison from 'down under'; beginning of shared life; open ending of book)

Looking down the left-hand column it is not difficult to see that although it contains many attractive and intriguing elements, it is not a match for the column opposite. Another way of saying the same thing is to look at the design diagram (p. 47 below): whether we read up or across, it is hard to avoid the conclusion that the three phases which we find in either reading (London-Phraxos-Parnassus vertically, London-Greece-London horizontally) isolate the middle one as the domaine of illusion, a domaine to which, as we have seen, Conchis is precisely confined, and from which Alison is effectively excluded.

All this seems to undermine the balance of the two poles defined above, and to make love heavily outweigh freedom. And this in turn seems to argue for a quite simple moral for the book, a moral which is trite in itself and whose simplicity turns all the ambiguity and subversion argued for above into mere decoration, formal (and detachable) wrapping for a solid didactic content.

This reading turns *The Magus* into a kind of latter-day *Howard's End*, with Lily de Seitas playing the role of Mrs Wilcox. But such a comparison is only useful in showing up the radical divergence of the two books. Irony is neither marginal nor optional in *The Magus*: it is integral. Irony opens a gap between us and Nicholas, forcing us constantly to question his reliability and consequently that of the text. Through Nicholas's own comments the two magi of the book, Conchis and Lily de Seitas, are themselves called into question (pp. 439 and

633 respectively). Through the structural contradictions and the mythic overtones of Alison ('a kind of human oxymoron', p. 24, 'Eve', p. 269, 'Ashtaroth', p. 566) the book asserts that familiarity, honesty, reality – and by implication love itself – are not only much stronger, but also much stranger, than any simple moral can contain. What after all is the significance of the title? Not, surely, that Conchis's message is the most important in the book in terms of content: but rather that *Magus* and magus have something in common. This something is hinted at in the frequent insistence on the word 'metaphor'; in the glancing reference to June and Julie as 'personification[s]' (p. 601); in a crucial direction to the reader which, being placed so early in the book, can easily be overlooked:

> we didn't understand that the heroes, or anti-heroes, of the French existentialist novels we read were not supposed to be realistic. We tried to imitate them, mistaking metaphorical descriptions of complex modes of feeling for straightforward prescriptions of behaviour. (p. 17)

(This passage is gently alluded to in the 'anti-hero' reference on p. 645.) Whatever it is, this direction points us decisively to Part 2 of the book, and to Phraxos.

On Phraxos an elaborate system of effects, decor, actors, and texts is mounted and then dismantled. Part 2 offers us a message and then withdraws. The theory behind it is elaborated by Conchis on pp. 404 and 406. Bourani is a 'meta-theatre', a form of drama whose essential difference from conventional theatre lies in the fact that *all* the participants – including the audience – are actors, which is why (as we have seen) 'There is no place for limits in the meta-theatre' (p. 406). Meta-theatre and metaphor tell us something about Bourani, but also about the book. French critics[13] have coined the phrase '*mise en abyme*' to describe the reproduction of the overall theme or plot of a work of literature by one element contained within the work itself: a kind of miniaturisation of the larger structure, a story within a story. In this sense Bourani is a *mise en abyme* of *The Magus*: and Conchis (if the extension be allowed) of Fowles himself.

For like Conchis on Phraxos, *The Magus* offers us freedom, not as an element of its content, not as words within it, but as an element of its form. Responsibility and love are its content, its message. But in its multiple ironies it embodies freedom: and in these ironies, as likewise in its open ending, it forces the reader to exercise this freedom, to take up his necessary critical task rather than lazily assenting to a series of ready-made assertions. By placing itself under the sign of the magus, *The Magus* reminds us that it is illusion: and by abolishing itself when it has completed its task, the book, like the godgame itself, demonstrates by its elusive and illusive nature that 'An answer is always a form of death' (p. 626).

Design in *The Magus*

(All events are recounted from the viewpoint of Nicholas; numbers in brackets are page references.)

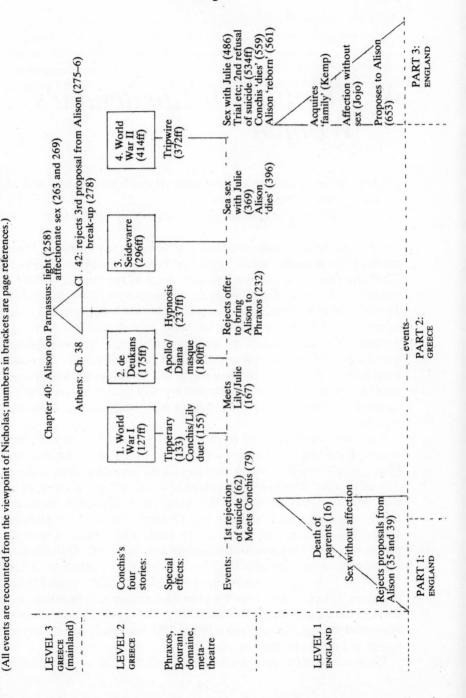

4 *The French Lieutenant's Woman*

> Every emancipation is a restoration of the human world and of human relationships to man himself.
>
> (Marx, *Zur Judenfrage*, quoted as epigraph to *FLW*, p. 3)

As the epigraph suggests, the theme of freedom features even more prominently in Fowles's next book, *The French Lieutenant's Woman*. This is his most successful work to date. Since its appearance in 1969 it has received a string of favourable academic reviews.[1] It has outsold all Fowles's other writings, and – unique among his fictions – it has been adapted to film in a way that has won almost unanimous critical acclaim. It is not difficult to see the reasons for this tremendous popularity, since Fowles has combined the historical novel – the book is set in the years 1867 to 1869 – with the self-conscious work of fiction, thus appealing to a variety of different types of reader and creating an unusual combination of period flavour with anachronism, nostalgia with irony.

The story begins in Lyme Regis in 1867. Charles Smithson and his fiancée Ernestina Freeman are walking along the Cobb, a breakwater jutting into Lyme Bay, when they meet a mysterious woman – 'Poor Tragedy', alias 'The French Lieutenant's Woman' (or whore), later alias Mrs Roughwood, but in fact Miss Sarah Woodruff. Between Sarah, a penniless ex-governess, and Charles, a baronet's nephew, a fascination develops which turns to love, and despite Charles's attempts to hold back and to stay faithful to Ernestina he finds himself keeping an assignation with Sarah in a hotel. They make love. After leaving he writes to her asking her to be his wife, and breaks off his engagement to Ernestina: but his valet deliberately fails to deliver the letter to Sarah, and when Charles returns, she is gone. Twenty months pass – and through the valet she is found. The book ends with Charles's return to London to meet her.

The mechanics of *The French Lieutenant's Woman* – trysts, inheritances, messages delivered and messages undelivered, trickery and deception at all levels – are extremely well handled; the events are both intelligible and plausible, and the plot exemplifies what has been well described as '[Fowles's] seductive narrative drive' (Conradi, 1982, p. 15). As usual in Fowles's work, however, 'design' – patterns and inter-relations within the story – plays a critical part. If we read carefully, and particularly if we come to this work fresh from *The Magus*, we are likely to find that coincidence ('the name we give to a piece of design when we cannot find a use for it', Frye, 1957, p. 99) broods over the work in a very remarkable way. Not for nothing do the characters constantly encounter their own images in mirrors:[2] the book itself constantly throws back to us reflected or distorted images of itself.

At the level of coincidence we may begin with the events of the trial of Lieutenant Emile de la Roncière, borrowed by Fowles from a French text and included as the substance of Chapter 28. At this trial, which took place in 1835, La Roncière was accused of writing a series of poison pen letters to the household of his commanding officer, the Baron de Morell, and of forcing his way into the bedroom of the Baron's sixteen-year-old daughter at night and assaulting her. Despite the flimsiness of the prosecution case, La Roncière was found guilty and sentenced to ten years' imprisonment. The account of the trial itself is followed in *The French Lieutenant's Woman* by an extended extract from a contemporary work written in support of La Roncière's unsuccessful appeal; it gives a number of examples of hysterical illness and self-inflicted injuries undergone by young women, and links these to Marie de Morell's case as similar examples of a desperate striving for attention. It is clear both to Grogan (who uses similar arguments in the preceding chapter) and to Charles (on whom the aforesaid arguments, and the book itself which Grogan lends him, have a devastating effect) that Sarah herself may be such a desperate female, ready to go to any lengths, invent any story, and undergo almost any privation, to escape her predicament. In this sense, the extract, strategically placed near the centre of the novel, serves as a kind of *mise en abyme* for the work as a whole, and reminds us that Sarah's behaviour is as enigmatic at the end of *The French Lieutenant's Woman* as it was at the beginning. My point here, however, is to emphasise, not the deliberate and intelligible structural parallel, but the rather more opaque and apparently accidental set of relationships which binds the Morell case into the framework of the book. La Roncière himself, the luckless though by no means innocent victim of the Baron's daughter,[3] was by 'a sinister

astrology' (p. 204) found guilty and sentenced on the very day Charles
was born. Thus he is linked to Charles as fellow-victim of a designing
woman: but he is also linked to Sarah in a number of ways. Firstly, and
most obviously, he is 'that other French lieutenant' (p. 229) after
Sarah's supposed lover Varguennes. Secondly, his first Christian name
(Emile) is Sarah's second (Emily); thirdly, his surname ('*roncière*'
means 'thick bramble bush') links him yet again with Sarah, who is
similarly named after a wild plant, who constantly associates herself
with thorny wild things,[4] and who deliberately pricks her finger on a
hawthorn (pp. 157–8).

Dates feature in the patterns of the book in several ways. 1867, the
year in which the story begins, is thematically important as the year of
the publication of *Das Kapital*, of the start of Hardy's affair with his
cousin Tryphena, and of the first Parliamentary attempt to give women
the vote. Time intervals, too, recur in the book, reinforced by further
coincidences of name and circumstance. Sarah Woodruff enters
Charles's life in April 1867 after she has been abandoned by a military
man; two years later (May 1869) she re-appears with a daughter; to
support this child she works in the household of a man who
'approached [her] one day in the street' (p. 392). The un-surnamed
'Sarah' whose services Charles purchases in London – a real rather
than a reputed 'whore' – has also been abandoned by a military man
(p. 271); when Charles meets her, she has been on the streets 'Two
years come May' (p. 268) in order to support . . . her daughter. It is
hardly necessary to point out that Charles finds himself in identical
circumstances with both children – one 'lalling' (p. 278), the other
'Lalage' (p. 392) – at different points in the book.

Names carry overtones of all kinds in *The French Lieutenant's
Woman*. Mr Freeman's name may be ironic, but his daughter's –
Ernestina – is presumably intended to indicate something of the
family's dourness. 'Smithson' seems to indicate that Charles is fairly
ordinary: but the existence in America of a Smithson river (p. 371) and
of a Smithsonian Museum reinforces the suggestion on p. 367 that
Charles's real home was, or could have been, America. The abundant
quotations in the text usher in another range of coincidences, namely
literary references. It is, perhaps, mere courtesy for a novel set in Lyme
to include a reference to Jane Austen (p. 12). Other references are less
direct but more suggestive. Thus the structure of the book – above all
the parting of lovers after a single sexual encounter resulting in the
birth of a daughter – recalls Fowles's beloved *Le Grand Meaulnes*,
while numerous features bring to mind Hardy and his heroines.[5]

Not only names but also motifs stitch together the fabric of the book. We have seen the way Charles twice dandles on his knees a child fascinated by a twirling watch: watches feature again, not only in the celebrated final chapter (p. 395), but also (albeit in a non-existent part of the story) in Chapter 44, where Ernestina is knitting Charles a watch-pocket to be adorned, by a particularly piercing irony, with the couplet 'Each time thy watch thou wind, Of love may I thee remind' (p. 291). And just as the three women in Charles's life are linked by the watch motif, so they are by the circulating 'pearl and coral', the brooch bought for Ernestina, sent to Sarah, but received and worn – 'emblem of good fortune' – only by Mary (p. 363).

Even the title (to whose thematic implications I shall return) is reflected and repeated through the structure of the novel. We have seen that not only Sarah Woodruff, but also Sarah the prostitute and Marie de Morell, are in one way or another involved in temporary liaisons with military men. But if we look carefully we find, not three, but five such relationships in the book. In a beautifully placed little scene during his interview with Mr Freeman Charles sees 'a girl . . . waiting on a bench . . . a red-jacketed soldier . . . the eagerness of her turn made it clear that the two were lovers' (p. 247); and, moving up the social ladder, we find that Mrs Bella Tomkins, the destroyer of Charles's hopes of inheriting Winsyatt, is none other (p. 174) than the widow of a colonel in the Fortieth Hussars!

These examples by no means exhaust the range of repetitions, patternings, and connections between events in this book: but many of these are better deferred to a discussion of Sarah. Two areas of design, both apparently more at the intentional than at the coincidental end of the scale, remain to be examined. The first concerns setting; the second relates to chapter organisation.

Characteristically, the settings in *The French Lieutenant's Woman* are brought to life with wonderful vigour and economy: the narrow world of Lyme, the Mediterranean exuberance of the Undercliff, the varied faces of the night life of London, live vividly in the memory. What may be less obvious is the way in which these settings are arranged. In effect they form two groups. In the first, arranged along a scale from closed to open, are respectively the claustrophobic world of Lyme Regis itself; the anonymous, permissive, but fundamentally hypocritical towns and cities of England (Exeter, Weymouth, London) and Europe; and the challenging, problematic, but essentially free 'New World' of the United States. Charles, of course, begins in Lyme, moves through London and a spell of aimless travelling in Europe, and rediscovers in America, to which at the end he seems bound to return, 'a kind of faith in freedom' (p. 373). But there is a second type of setting which does not fit this scale, namely the withdrawn world, the refuge or domaine, which is, as we have seen, a recurrent structural element in Fowles's fiction. The two refuges in question are of course Winsyatt, Charles's ancestral estate in Wiltshire – lovingly described, in a teasing mixture of direct authorial voice and free indirect speech, in Chapter 23 – and the celebrated Undercliff. It is obvious that the first is a false refuge: the logic not only of the plot but also of the evolutionary theme forces us to recognise that it is an ossified, dinosaur world, to which Charles, despite his feeling that he is 'truly entering upon his inheritance' (p. 171), would be as unsuited as he would be to life in the Freeman emporium. The Undercliff, that Eden-like world in which Charles and Sarah conduct the early stages of their romance and hold their increasingly passionate trysts, seems at first a world of which Fowles can only approve: it must surely stand for Nature and Life against the dead world of social convention, the 'hothouse' in which the engagement of Charles and Ernestina is cemented (pp. 74–5). In great part this is true, but we should not forget that as with his acknowledged master Alain-Fournier, Fowles's domaines are usually places of temporary rather than permanent residence. Like Winsyatt (and Bourani) the Undercliff offers a retreat from the stifling air of petty provincialism, and a vantage point from which to get the world into perspective: but it outlives its usefulness, and neither Sarah nor Charles is tempted to return to it.

It remains to discuss a way in which design operates at the chapter level. If we look at individual chapters, we find that Fowles has a habit of quietly balancing one group against another so that each illuminates (or undercuts) the other. Thus in Chapter 14 we see 'a look unseen by [Mrs Tranter and Ernestina] . . . at last pass between Sarah and Charles' (p. 93); we also see Sam and Mary having a 'surprisingly serious' talk in Mrs Tranter's kitchen during which 'Only very occasionally did their eyes meet, and then by mutual accord they looked shyly away from each other' (p. 94). Chapter 19, with a pleasant irony, selects a different pair of contrasts: the male intellectuals Charles and Dr Grogan, 'lords of creation . . . *carbonari* of the mind' (pp. 139 and 141), are juxtaposed with the female figures of Sarah and Millie sleeping side by side in the same bed. And in Chapter 21, the secret meeting of Charles and Sarah – a meeting which despite its secrecy Charles consciously believes to be innocent – is shown up for what it is by the spectacle of Sam and Mary, 'as greenly erotic as the April plants they trod on' (p. 161), and by the knowing smile with which Sarah indicates to Charles (pp. 161–2) that the connection has not escaped her.

When we look at the book as a whole, yet another pattern reveals itself: a symmetrical relationship between chapters as units. Thus, to put it schematically, the last chapter represents a kind of structural transformation of the first:

Chapter 1	*Chapter 61*
Charles with Ernestina approaching Sarah	Charles alone leaving Sarah
Sarah in black	Sarah in brilliant colours
Sarah stands beside 'an old cannon-barrel up-ended as a bollard' (upright, fixed, powerful)	Charles paces behind 'the invisible gun-carriage on which rests his own corpse' (horizontal, adrift, powerless)
scene takes place on land jutting into sea (the Cobb)	scene takes place on sea jutting into land (the Thames at Chelsea is tidal)

(There are other contrasts as well, but these will do.) Chapter 2 contrasts with its structural counterpart, Chapter 60; in the former Charles sees himself as coming to Sarah's rescue ('we can't see you here without being alarmed for your safety', p. 13); in the latter he realises that the tables are turned since 'the damsel had broken all the rules' (p. 381). And in the centre of the book, just as in *The Magus* we find the ascent of Parnassus, so we find the pivotal Chapters 30 and 31 recounting the dismissal of Sarah and the first passionate kiss exchanged between the lovers in the Eden – or Cockayne – of Carslake's Barn. This narrative centre, moreover, is flanked by two supporting thematic pillars: the substantial extract in Chapter 28 on hysteria, and the extended discussion in Chapter 35 of Hardy's disastrous love life and its relation to the whole creative process.

The features of design which we have been looking at could be said to emerge naturally from the plot itself: design (in the sense in which I am using it) is an aspect of all fiction, though its density in *The French Lieutenant's Woman* suggests some sort of deliberate self-reference. The aspects I want to look at next are also features of the handling of the plot, but they concern, not its internal relationships, but the way in which it is laid out – not the order in which things happen, but the order in which they are told.[6] Here, I think, there is no doubt that Fowles manipulates his material quite extensively, and it may be worth looking at some of the techniques he uses. (My argument in the next paragraph may seem trite, but it is to a purpose.)

In the first place, Fowles is very fond of quite crude techniques for heightening suspense. In the centre of the book, the crucial 24 hours during which Charles loses Winsyatt and discovers (through Grogan and Matthaei on the one hand and Sarah on the other) a third dimension of depth in his hitherto two-dimensional stereotype of women, a great deal is happening: but Fowles constantly intercuts his material so as to defer the required information. The first part of Chapter 23, liberally supplied with pointers to what is to come, describes Charles's ill-omened visit to Winsyatt: but instead of the dénouement, we are given the first part of Sarah's own 'fall'. The chapter ends with both incidents unresolved: Chapter 24 takes up Charles's story, but *after* the Winsyatt incident is concluded, so that we are left for a page to wonder what the 'monstrous' event (p. 173) was, and for two and a half chapters (till p. 184) for a full account of how it took place. A second 'event' also takes place in Chapter 24 – 'Mrs Poulteney has dismissed Miss Woodruff', p. 175 – but for a full account of how *this* event happened we have to wait no less than six chapters, until Chapter 30 (p. 211). It would be tedious to continue to list the details of this process of delay and intercutting: suffice it to say that in the thematically and structurally central bloc of chapters running from 29 to 39 the process is used repeatedly and to very good effect.

Just as Fowles is not above deliberately creating suspense, so he is likewise prepared to use the technique of deliberate mystification. This may take the form of giving information whose significance will not become clear to the reader until later: one thinks here of Sarah's purchase of nightgown, shawl, and bandage in Chapter 36, or of the cryptic 'Mutiny, I am afraid, was not [Sam's] only crime' on p. 334. It may take the form of collusion, not between author and reader, but between author and character. A case in point would be the reference to 'an event long buried in [Grogan's] own past whose exact nature need not be revealed' (p. 340): Fowles knows what this event is, and so, of course, does Grogan, but they are not going to admit the reader into their shared confidence. And finally there is deliberate deception of the reader, as when we are given the accurate yet misleading information in Chapter 9 that '[Sarah] had not lodged with a female cousin at Weymouth' (p. 50), or when words such as 'he knew' or 'he understood' – words which indicate that the author believes the character's judgement to be correct – are used, as on p. 390 and perhaps on p. 141, where the context more or less directly belies them.

A further way in which Fowles wrong-foots the reader is by his tendency to alternate in style between a nineteenth- and a twentieth-century authorial *persona*. This teasing effect of shifting style and temporal standpoint blends in turn into another and more familiar Fowles technique, that of shifting point of view. Fowles's treatment of Sarah in this book is well documented: he allows himself some insight into her character (see especially Chapter 9), but will not enter her mind to analyse her thoughts (*passim*; for discussion see Chapter 13), thereby seeking to preserve that independence and unplumbable depth which in Chapters 47 and 60 she insists are essential to her happiness and her very life. Whether you feel that 'Sarah is the novel's one thoroughly modern character, and Fowles strengthens her contemporary quality . . . by making her the only one whose mind he will not enter' (Huffaker, 1980, p. 105), or that this rejection of omniscience is a breach of trust between author and reader (Wolfe, 1976, p. 155), it is at least by and large consistent. Where other principal characters are concerned, however, Fowles's method is more unsettling. He may adopt either internal omniscient, external descriptive, or free indirect speech as his mode of narration: in Ernestina's case it is usually the first (Chapter 5) or the second (Chapter 50), but where Charles is concerned Fowles makes much use of the third, a notoriously unsettling type of narration which calls into question the intentions and trustworthiness not only of the character but also of the author.

The reader familiar with the critical literature on *The French Lieutenant's Woman* – and indeed with the book itself – will have noticed that I have so far avoided the question of the self-conscious, experimental side of the book: the authorial interventions and digressions, the triple endings, and the two appearances of the author himself as a character in his own novel. One reason for deferring discussion of this point until some way into this chapter is to show that whatever we think of such strongly self-referential interventions, they are in one sense only a continuation of the kind of reader manipulation which Fowles (and perhaps any author) is already practising. Another reason is simply to suggest that the whole question is of secondary rather than primary importance: that the book has many merits which can be discussed without any reference to its experimental side. Nonetheless at some point this experimental element must be confronted and assessed. Is the book, in the words of a sub-editor of *The*

Times, 'A bold and enthralling experiment in time'? Or is it merely (to quote his Sunday counterpart) 'A middle-brow yarn with egghead knobs on'?[7]

In the first place there is the question of the three 'endings' – only one of which, of course, can be the end – located at various places in the novel. In the first (Chapters 43–4), Charles ignores Sarah's invitation to Endicott's Family Hotel and returns direct to Lyme: he marries Ernestina and eventually enters her father's business. In the second (Chapter 60), having broken with Ernestina, he rediscovers Sarah, finds that she is the mother of his child, and is reunited with her. In the third (Chapter 61) he again rediscovers Sarah, but she rejects him and he her, and he is left abandoned and alone. The first ending is stated in Chapter 45 to have been false; the second and third endings are apparently offered as interchangeable.

Secondly, there are two substantial interventions in the text by what appears to be the author himself. The first of these takes place in Chapter 13, where the narrator explains that he not only will not but actually cannot explain to the reader what is going on in Sarah's mind because she exists independently of him and is therefore outside his control. The second is to be found at the beginning of Chapter 45, where the narrator tells us that the two previous chapters did not ('really') happen, but were merely Charles's indulgence in a habit we all have of 'writing fictional futures for ourselves' (p. 295).

Thirdly, and most celebrated, are the two occasions on which the novelist himself actually enters his own fiction, 'massively bearded . . . a man of forty or so' (p. 346; Fowles wears a full beard and was 41 when he wrote the first draft of the novel). The first and fuller occasion is in Chapter 55, where with something of the 'aggressively secure' air of a 'successful lay preacher' (p. 346) he enters Charles's railway compartment and ostentatiously tosses a coin to decide on the arrangement of the – as yet mysterious – final chapters. The second appearance takes place at the beginning of Chapter 61. Here the character is related to, yet distinct from, the previous author-figure:

> The once full, patriarchal beard has been trimmed down . . . He looks very much as if he has given up preaching and gone in for grand opera . . . There is, in short, more than a touch of the successful impresario about him.
>
> (p. 394)

As we might expect from this linking with what has gone before, he does in fact carry out the programme planned in Chapter 55. By turning his watch back fifteen minutes, he makes it possible for the alternative endings represented in the final two chapters to occupy what is in fictional terms the same space of time.

Needless to say, the nature of these interventions has been widely discussed by critics. The definitive analysis seems to me to have been provided by Elizabeth Rankin (1973), and my arguments in the following pages draw heavily on hers.

Fowles makes his most ambitious claims in Chapter 13. In the course of 'a short but maddeningly perplexing digression on novels and novelists' (Rankin, 1973, p. 193), Fowles asserts, first that his story is 'all imagination' and that 'These characters I create never existed outside [my] own mind' (p. 85); secondly, and apparently contradictorily, that 'My characters . . . exist . . . in a ['real'] reality' (pp. 86–7); and thirdly, following on from the second point, that 'I do not fully control these creatures of my mind, any more than you control . . . your children, colleagues, friends or even yourself' (p. 87). Summing up and unifying these three claims, Fowles argues that 'The novelist is still a god . . . [not in] the Victorian image, omniscient and decreeing; but in the new theological image, with freedom [his] first principle, not authority' (p. 86).

These claims are difficult even to reconcile (notably the first and second), let alone to meet (particularly demanding in the case of the third). But they are perhaps best understood in the light of another quotation from the same chapter: 'a genuinely created world must be independent of its creator; a planned world (*a world that fully reveals its planning*) is a dead world' (p. 86, emphasis added). The key phrase here is italicised. What Fowles seems to be saying is that novelists may, perhaps must, plan: what they must not do is allow their planning to be detected.

Some of this organising and planning – and some selection amounting almost to deception – we have already examined (pp. 54–5 above). A further and pleasantly ironic example of it is the location of Chapter 13 itself. When Fowles, at the beginning of the chapter, pleads ignorance about Sarah, he thereby avoids having to reveal to us (either then or later) what she is thinking – a revelation which would completely destroy, on the one hand the suspense which keeps the plot going, and on the other hand the aura of mystery which hangs intriguingly round Sarah right to the end of the book.

Like conjurers, authors at times require some kind of disguise or diversion to distract attention from the main activity: and Chapter 13 falls into place if we read it as 'a diversionary chapter in which, tossing a bone to Robbe-Grillet and Barthes, [Fowles] ensures the literary acceptance . . . of his actually quite conventional novel' (Rankin, 1973, p. 196). Within the novel this very technique is discussed and then defined, appropriately in Darwinian terms, as 'cryptic coloration' – 'survival by learning to blend with one's surroundings' (p. 127, emphasis deleted). While pretending to blend with the surroundings and assumptions of the *nouveau roman*, then, Fowles is in fact exercising very much the kind of authority which he castigates in the supposedly outdated novelistic techniques of the Victorians.

It is clear why Fowles lays such stress on the freedom of his characters: a major theme of the book is the evolution of an existentialist awareness of freedom in Charles ('Notes on an Unfinished Novel', pp. 140–1), an evolution in which Sarah plays an important part. But the freedom of the reader is equally important, since Fowles is trying to foster the same consciousness in his readers as Sarah does in Charles. And such an educative process must allow for, and indeed emphasise, the reader's free will. The device that Fowles adopts to achieve this end is paradoxically to thrust himself into the text in the form of an intrusive and obtrusive narrator. But these intrusions are very carefully handled so as to fall into two types: manipulators and non-manipulators. The manipulators (Chapters 55 and 61) are made to appear more or less ridiculous ('a bullying . . . lay preacher', 'foppish, Frenchified beard', 'successful impresario'), thereby devaluing the manipulative handling of plot and character that is associated with them; 'the narrator cannot bear to have us think that he is in control of his novel; he must relegate this unpleasant duty to a surrogate' (Rankin, 1973, p. 204). Conversely when a narrator appears whose views we *can* take seriously – for example the narrator-figure of Chapter 13 – he is not localised, not embodied in a character, and not in any way ridiculed or ironically undermined. The structure and very existence of the intrusions in Chapters 13, 55, and 61 say in effect that while every novel has to have some measure of authorial control, it is a regrettable and trivial part of a novelist's job; the task of both characters and readers is to escape this domineering aspect of the author and to lead their own independent lives.

We are now in a better position to understand the three endings of the book. As we have seen, a major theme of *The French Lieutenant's Woman* is the evolution of Charles's existentialism. The three endings show the three directions in which he could evolve (or not evolve, as we shall see) from his dawning existentialist awareness of 'the anxiety of freedom' (p. 296). The first is to reject freedom: to yield to his conformist self, to return to Ernestina and to creep back into the closed Victorian ideology. This is obviously not a possibility Fowles approves of, but it is a possibility nonetheless, and if the novelist is to allow his characters their freedom this must include the freedom to do things he heartily disapproves of. The second ending, in which Charles is re-united with Sarah, then becomes a second response to the anxiety of freedom. Charles, having rejected conformism and obedience to social convention, chooses the figure who has consistently personified freedom from convention to the extent of being for much of the book a social outcast. It might be thought that this represents an answer which the narrator could support: but although he does not explicitly direct us how to treat it, as he did in the case of the earlier ending, there are a number of implicit pointers as to how it should be read. The repetition of the child-and-watch incident refers us back to a failed attempt at 'connection': the reference to God ('it had been in God's hands, in His forgiveness of their sins', pp. 392–3) comes oddly after the definitive rejection of God in Chapter 48; and the richness of the language in the closing paragraphs looks a little awkward in the light of the ironic conclusion ('high time indeed . . . a thousand violins cloy very rapidly without percussion', pp. 392–3). It is, in short, another kind of wish-fulfilment, the triumph of the Victorian-romantic side of Charles's personality.

Only Chapter 61, in which Charles is shown alone, outcast, but independent, fits the internal logic of the book; for it shows the triumph, not of either of the Victorian aspects of Charles's personality, but of the 'existentialist *avant la lettre*' side to him which was really at stake in his relationship to Sarah and in all the thematic pointers from the author about evolution, ammonites, and survival. This structural and thematic logic is backed up by two important stylistic features. The first is the return of the 'non-omniscient author' first seen in Chapter 13 ('There are tears in her eyes? She is too far away for me to tell', p. 398) and associated with important statements about freedom – understandably so since he represents an attempt to enact freedom in the way the characters are handled. The second is the reference in the last line to Arnold's 'To Marguerite', a poem which Fowles has already told us (p. 365) is 'perhaps the noblest short poem of the Victorian era'.

The three endings, then, show the alert and responsive reader both the wrong and the right ways to respond to the realisation that one is free. But the author is not the only person giving lessons in freedom.

What Fowles is trying to teach the reader, Sarah is trying to teach Charles; and her methods, like those of her creator, depend very largely on stories. The first one she tells (that she had been seduced by Varguennes) is a deliberate lie intended to seduce Charles. Her second story, the confession of her earlier lie, 'corresponds to the second ending of the novel in that both appeal to the romantic sensibilities of their audiences' (Rankin, 1973, p. 206). It is her third story, which can be summed up in a single quotation – 'The rival you both share is myself. I do not wish to marry' (p. 385) – which must be accepted as the truth, for the same reasons of faithfulness to theme and character which caused us to accept the same ending from Fowles himself.

I set out in this section to itemise and then to try to understand the self-conscious, experimental aspects of *The French Lieutenant's Woman*. We have seen, I think, that they are less radical than Fowles seems to want us to believe. But 'seems' is the operative word here. We must not forget that the 'I' in a novel is not the novelist, but the narrator: and that 'What is actually exposed when the narrator's *persona* is dropped' is not Fowles himself, but 'simply another *persona*' (Rankin, 1973, p. 197).[8] Perhaps the nearest we can get to Fowles's intentions in this book is to remember that in the notorious Chapter 13, for all his talk of freedom, he admits that 'The novelist is still a god' (p. 86).[9]

Discussion of the thematic implications of Fowles's self-conscious narration brings us on to the whole question of the themes of *The French Lieutenant's Woman*. Once again we shall find that the four themes isolated in Chapter 1 are of primary importance. One, the domaine, has already been considered; I shall turn now to the question of the contrast between the masculine and the feminine mentality.

The view of the female character which underlies *The French Lieutenant's Woman* cannot be discussed in isolation from the character of Sarah herself. As we have seen, Fowles believes that women think intuitively and emotionally rather than intellectually, and that they are in touch with a deeper and warmer level of thought and feeling than men ever penetrate to. A male writer creating female characters is faced with a logical problem if he tries to carry out this programme, since his characters will have depths he himself cannot plumb. One aspect of the narration of *The French Lieutenant's Woman* already touched on can be seen as an ingenious solution to this problem – the famous or notorious refusal to enter Sarah's consciousness and tell us what she is thinking. (I say 'consciousness' because of course in Chapter 9 we have quite a full analysis of her mind and character.) This refusal on the part of what Fowles thinks of as the intuitive female to open her mind to the intellectual probings of the male becomes in the closing pages a refusal on Sarah's part to submit her actions to any kind of analysis at all: 'I am not to be understood even by myself' (p. 386).

It would be wrong, however, to think of Sarah as some kind of sub-intellectual Earth Mother figure. The book makes this clear in a number of ways: in the metaphor that 'she was born with a computer in her heart' (p. 50); by the fact that she works herself up by her own efforts during the course of the book from rags to comparative riches; by the way that she impresses Charles as being his intellectual equal. To say – correctly – that Sarah thinks with her heart is not to deny that she also thinks with her head.[10]

The danger for any author trying to make such a character credible is that he will seem to be placing her beyond the reach of criticism: dissatisfied readers will simply be told that they are male chauvinists incapable of understanding the profound mysteries of the *Ewig-Weibliche*. Fowles tries to get round this problem in his books in a number of ways. In *The French Lieutenant's Woman*, where Fowles makes his most ambitious claims for his heroine, he also undercuts them with the most savage of his ironies, the inset tale of Marie de Morell. The (deeply pathetic) examples of female scheming in the pages of Matthaei's archive throw into quite a different relief Jung's description of certain kinds of characteristically female behaviour (see note 10 above) as 'never naive, but mixed with unacknowledged purpose'.

Male intellection, the counterpart to female intuition, is represented in the book by the scientific pursuits of Charles and Grogan. These pursuits require rather careful examination. Charles begins as an avid collector of fossils: in Fowles's work activities such as collecting and classifying register strong danger signals, and we are warned to be on our guard. But all is well. Charles serves, not the static, classificatory, *nulla species nova* system of Linnaeus, but the evolutionary method of Darwin which breaks up and supersedes that of Linnaeus. Thus in so far as any of Fowles's works can be said to support any masculine and intellectual (as opposed to feminine and intuitive) approach, *The French Lieutenant's Woman* supports Darwinism; the point is clinched by the adherence to Darwinism of Charles's early mentor Grogan (pp. 140–1). Yet in the last analysis Darwinism itself is only another intellectual system, even if it is one that foresees its own demise. It is when out hunting dead and classifiable fossils that Charles finds the living and unclassifiable Sarah, and under her influence loses interest in fossils for ever (p. 364). Charles and Grogan are linked at two points (Chapters 19 and 53), one before and one after Charles's escapade with Sarah, in a kind of masculine freemasonry of the intellect which is as undermined as its female counterpart by various kinds of irony ('Charles ... was pure intellect ... understanding all. All except Sarah, that is', p. 142). And the *Parallelgeschichte* to all this, which serves to reinforce Fowles's proposition that women live 'much closer to real values' than men, is the story of Sam and Mary. Here Sam, rather than Mary, is the schemer and manipulator; but we are left in no doubt (see especially p. 115, from which the phrase above is taken) that the rock on which his career is built is Mary.

The second thematic grouping is that of the Few and the Many. We have seen that for Fowles humanity is divided into an unthinking mass and a detached, responsive inner group, a kind of 'self-questioning, ethical élite' (p. 256) – Conchis's 'elect' in *The Magus*, G.P.'s 'Few' in *The Collector*. A central question in both those works is whether or not a female character who is already a potential member of 'the Few' will persuade a male character to cross the threshold and join her. This choice recurs as a fundamental theme of *The French Lieutenant's Woman* with the conflict in Charles between Ernestina and Sarah, and Fowles is clearly saying that in choosing Sarah, Charles has applied for membership of the Few.

In referring to this group as 'detached' in the previous paragraph I was thinking rather specifically of *The French Lieutenant's Woman*, for it is noteworthy that a part of Charles's 'emancipation' (see epigraph, p. 48 above) is a release and detachment from some of the more usual kinds of bond that link a man to his society. Freud somewhere defines normality as the ability to love and to work: Fowles would clearly go along with the former, but it is very doubtful what moral value he attaches to the latter. Charles is offered leadership and responsibility – qualities, as we shall see, of fundamental importance for the Few – both as heir to Winsyatt and as future manager of the Freeman empire, but in one way or another he contrives to escape both and to end up on his way to a lonely exile. We have seen that the book is far from expressing an implacable hostility to commercial values: the rise in Sam's fortunes which matches the fall in those of Charles is described with admiration and some relish. What Fowles seems to be saying is that for the Few – and only for the Few – work, profit, compromise, political and economic involvement, are, as Pascal would have it, 'distractions'. In *The French Lieutenant's Woman*, because of the period in which it is set, Fowles has the perfect category to hand with which to define this aspect of the elect, namely the concept of the gentleman. In his extended discussion of this topic in Chapter 38 Fowles argues that the Victorian gentleman was a re-incarnation of the *preux chevalier* of the Middle Ages, and is in turn re-incarnated in our own times as the pure (as opposed to applied) scientist. (I shall pass over for the moment certain inconsistencies in the argument of the chapter in question.) The distinguishing characteristic of each of these incarnations, when viewed from a purely material point of view, is its utter uselessness. This pleasantly Wildean argument has a moral corollary in the theory that in the sphere of values such an elite is very far from useless. In evolutionary terms, Fowles suggests, the Few think out and put into practice the kind of ideas that the rest of humanity is only just struggling towards: they are 'leaders', not in the sense of playing some kind of statesmanlike role in marshalling and guiding political forces, but in the sense of being 'in the lead' in the gradual evolution of humanity. And this in turn imposes on them a tremendous responsibility, the task of neither abrogating nor abusing their freedom but of using it for the highest ends. At this point, of course, we come to the familiar question of the balance between freedom and responsibility (or duty).

In one sense *The French Lieutenant's Woman* is a book obsessed with duty. Throughout the earlier part of the book Charles is very much under the sign of duty; it is for some time the cement that holds together his crumbling relationship with Ernestina, and curiously it is the governing idiom of his first post-coital conversation with Sarah. It is even the lever Sarah uses to split him off from her – 'I know she must love you . . . She is worthy of you. I am not' (p. 306). Charles's disastrous decision to sort things out with Ernestina before he returns to claim Sarah is similarly based on duty. The quotation from George Eliot is exceedingly apt – 'God is inconceivable, immortality is unbelievable, but duty is peremptory and absolute' (pp. 45–6).

If, as the epigraph suggests, the central theme of the book is emancipation, we must examine how the characters escape into freedom from under this dead conventional weight. The principal method Fowles uses to achieve this end is to split the apparently monolithic concept of duty into two parts: duty to others, and duty to oneself. As far as Charles is concerned, duty to others takes a number of forms in the book: duty to Ernestina in the form of the obligations of engagement, duty to Winsyatt in the form of the obligations of inheritance, duty to the economic process in the form of the proposal to exchange the comfortable idleness of a *rentier* existence for productive work in the Freeman emporium. In the novel, all these duties are resoundingly rejected as forms of irresponsibility. What is approved of is duty to oneself, symbolised in personal terms by Charles's relationships with the two Sarahs. The fact that these relationships are not mere self-indulgence is supported in narrative terms by the fact that both involve Charles in less pleasure and more suffering than he had bargained for: with the prostitute Charles reflects gloomily that 'his fate was sealed. He wished it so' (p. 268), and where Sarah Woodruff is concerned he describes himself (in the earlier, unsubverted part of Chapter 60) as 'a ghost, a shadow, a half-being for as long as he remains separated from [her]' (p. 384). Duty, then, is very far from what Fowles seems to think the Victorians thought it was (see for example the Clough epigraph to Chapter 44, p. 290); but in Fowles's own terms it is still 'peremptory and absolute'.

The first obligation that this duty to oneself forces upon us is to think for ourselves. This in turn unifies a number of themes in the book which are built around contrasting pairs. We must prefer innovation over tradition; we must prefer (or at least see the merits of) the United States over the United Kingdom; we must prefer hazard, that familiar god of Fowles's, to the anxious or repressive control exercised both by omnipotent gods and by omnipotent authors; we must prefer Darwinian change and evolution to the static, classificatory system of Linnaeus.

Such assertions have not only moral but also theological implications. In Chapter 48 a kind of alternative theology is put forward through a dialogue between Charles and what appears to be (significantly) not God the avenging (or absent) Father, but Christ the incarnate and suffering Son. The bases of this theology are twofold: on the one hand freedom, emancipation from slavish adherence to social convention; on the other hand the recognition and acceptance of man's physical nature. The first principle seems to liberate the believer from the super-ego: 'Duty is but a pot. It holds whatever is put in it, from the greatest evil to the greatest good' (p. 313). But the second immediately restores this moral imperative in the form of a duty 'to bring about a world in which the hanging man could be descended, could be seen . . . with . . . the smiling peace of a victory brought about by, and in, living men and women' – in a word, 'To uncrucify' (p. 315). This duty, as we have seen, devolves upon the Few, and Charles's final emancipation from all social ties will paradoxically confirm that he is fulfilling this higher duty.

In the last few pages I have been trying to break down the concepts of duty and responsibility and to show how they can be made to yield a theory of freedom. But if we approach the problem from the other side, it can be shown that freedom in turn can be made to yield a theory of duty and responsibility. The opening epigraph, presumably intended to govern the book as a whole, is an assertion of freedom. But it joins hands across the book with the concluding epigraph, ostensibly only to Chapter 61, Arnold's 'True Piety is *acting what one knows*' (p. 394, emphasis in original). Between them these epigraphs contain Fowles's meaning: that we have an obligation to emancipation; that we have a duty to be free.

The previous section was devoted to an exposition of the principal themes of *The French Lieutenant's Woman*. Many readers, however, may feel as I do that the argument of the book is in many ways uneven: that while parts of it are profound and challenging, other parts are inconsistent, self-contradictory, or simply nonsensical. Without wishing to challenge the basic assertions of the book, I would like to single out and briefly examine three areas where Fowles seems to me to be doing himself and his case less than justice. The three topics concerned are evolution; the concept of the gentleman; and the relationship between the nineteenth and the twentieth century.

Many critics have noted the effectiveness with which Fowles binds the theme of evolution into the narrative and descriptive structure of *The French Lieutenant's Woman*. By making Charles an aristocrat by birth and a fossil-hunter by inclination Fowles seems to tie him in with the *status quo*; but the loss of Winsyatt cuts him off from the administrative functions which would have given meaning to his baronetcy, and stumbling upon Sarah gives him something other than fossils to look for on his expeditions. His loyalty to Darwin, his friendship with Grogan, his choice of Sarah over Ernestina seem ultimately to place him on the side of evolution. So far, so good. For evolution, read existentialism: one must change to meet change: Charles's fate, we assume, will not be that of the ammonite or the dinosaur, but instead the more successful strategy of adapting in order to exploit a new ecological or economic niche.

The principal difficulty about accepting this interpretation of the theme of evolution in the book is simply that the chief expounder and most successful exemplar of the theory is none other than Ernestina's father, the business magnate Mr Freeman: 'if one does not . . . change . . . then one does not survive . . . progress is like a lively horse. Either one rides it, or it rides one' (p. 250). Not surprisingly, this proposal fills

Charles with gloom. He has no real point of contact with Mr Freeman; he loathes both the idea and the reality of business; he does not even like the kind of success that doing well in business brings ('The abstract idea of evolution was entrancing; but its practice seemed . . . fraught with ostentatious vulgarity', p. 251). Yet this last quotation only heightens the paradox: if this is evolution, isn't it better to turn one's back on the whole nasty affair?

Fowles's solution, propounded in Chapter 38, seems to me to run something like this. History is an anonymous, impersonal process that forces change upon us: if we do not change then like the ammonite we die. But 'If one had to change to survive . . . then at least one was granted a choice of methods' (p. 258). The Freeman method is a sell-out – a surrender of one's higher self to the meaningless process of commerce. A better method is to develop some sort of analytical power, the gift of the observer rather than the participant; and the aim and upshot of this second method is to constitute a kind of self-questioning, ethical elite (namely the Few). But this involves the members of the elite in the very opposite of what one might have expected. Charles is described as *'a man struggling to overcome history'* (p. 257, emphasis added) – yet the ammonite was condemned to extinction for doing exactly that!

Fowles's treatment of evolution, then, though complex, interesting, and extremely successfully woven into the literary fabric of the book, is in my view incoherent when extracted for analysis on its own terms. The theme of the gentleman can be dealt with much more briefly, on the one hand since it is less central to the book, and on the other because much of what has been said above about evolution applies to this matter also. Two points remain. The first is that we should not allow to pass without comment Fowles's assertion that the modern gentleman, the descendant of 'the parfit knights and *preux chevaliers* of the Middle Ages', is 'that breed we call scientists' and especially 'computer scientist[s]' (pp. 256–7). I am on friendly terms with a number of computer scientists and indeed have good reason to be grateful to them, but I would argue that their personal merits have nothing whatsoever to do with their choice of profession; Fowles's whole notion of science seems to me romanticised and entirely at variance with the competitive and politicised realities of business and research. The second point concerns the divergent fates of Charles and Sam. As fast as Charles flees position and fortune, Sam seeks them, and not by the nicest of means: as the master falls, the man rises. It is the same business – the Freeman empire – which offers the opportunities for worldly success. Yet while Charles is praised for refusing these opportunities, Sam is congratulated for accepting them. Of course this can be easily explained: Charles is one of the Few, Sam one of the Many, and as one of the Few Charles must live up to a higher and more exacting set of standards. But it is hard not to see a scarcely-veiled snobbery at work in this modern version of *noblesse oblige*, and one longs for the day when Fowles will choose his *aristoi* from somewhere other than the aristocracy.

The final problem concerns what Fowles has to say about historical change and progress. Despite certain areas of nostalgia (notably pp. 233–4), *The French Lieutenant's Woman* seems to look back on the nineteenth century from something of a position of superiority, and to reach out to Charles and Sarah as two characters who in the process of outgrowing their own age have almost grown into our own. One feature of Victorianism that Fowles condemns is its self-confident conviction of its own superiority. There is a paradox inherent in condemning an age from a position of secure self-confidence on the grounds of its security and self-confidence; it could be argued that the only acceptable weapon against smugness is irony, and that Fowles's general pronouncements on the Victorians all too frequently lay themselves open to the very objections they are advancing.[11] But the point that I think lies deepest is a questioning of the whole developmental approach. The concept of 'the universal parity of existence' (p. 208) gives us the idea that at any one time all forms of life are of equal value and experience life with equal intensity: elsewhere we find Fowles speaking of history as 'horizontal' ('Notes on an Unfinished Novel', p. 142) and declaring that 'In the scale of happiness evolution is horizontal, not vertical' (*A*, p. 58), thus asserting that this equality extends over time as well as over space. Nor are these random or contradictory assertions, one-off remarks which can be shown to have no organic connection with the rest of Fowles's writing. On the contrary: they spring, firstly from his resistance to classification – a process integrally linked with ranking – and secondly from his insistence on the mysterious and unknowable element in all forms of life. Thus both Fowles's general theory of evolution and his application of it in the form of a theory of history seem to contain fundamental contradictions. As I shall try to show in the final chapter, there are possible ways of rescuing the theories; but it is difficult to accept them as they stand.

Much of the early part of this chapter was devoted to demonstrating the existence of a variety of patterns in *The French Lieutenant's*

Woman; thereafter I looked at some of the external, referential, centripetal uses of these patterns to serve the philosophical and didactic purposes of the book. It is time now to turn back from questions of theme and ideas to more literary and inward-directed matters of form and texture. I shall begin by examining *The French Lieutenant's Woman* in the light of my contention that the basic form of Fowles's fictional works is the romance.

In the romance, as opposed to the novel, we are likely to find what Frye calls an 'undisplaced' plot notable for strongly schematic outlines; use of repetition and coincidence; a tendency to create opposed pairs of characters; focus on the hero and heroine in preference to an even-handed treatment of all the characters; and the appearance of certain set roles (the parent, the helper) and motifs (the journey, the test). We have seen in an earlier part of this chapter the enormously intricate pattern of repetition, coincidence, and parallelism that Fowles builds up in *The French Lieutenant's Woman*. His heroines conform to the familiar romance pattern of contrast, not only in colouring – Sarah dark of hair and dress, Ernestina pale-skinned and clothed in brilliant colours – but in other ways too: Sarah far-sighted ('her stare . . . aimed like a rifle at the farthest horizon', p. 13), Ernestina the reverse (p. 12); Sarah inscrutable, Ernestina transparent; Sarah associated with nature and wilderness, Ernestina with culture and civilisation; Sarah forbidden, sexual, even faintly incestuous, Ernestina lawful and chaste.

We have already seen, in the course of discussing Fowles's attitude to his characters, that he accords to Charles and Sarah a treatment that no other characters receive: in the case of the first by setting him much higher standards to come up to, and in Sarah's case by the much-discussed refusal to enter into her thoughts. (This strongly hierarchical attitude to character is brought out by Fowles's readiness to treat minor characters in a very cavalier way indeed: see p. 69 below.) Where set roles are concerned we may point to the 'heavy father' in the shape of Mr Freeman (who significantly appears to Charles immediately after the latter has made love to Sarah, p. 305) and the faithful helper turned scheming servant, Sam, on whose manipulations the plot hinges. As for motifs, there is the ubiquitous reference to 'tests' – literally a type of fossil, but symbolically much more; the hero's all-night vigil before he sallies forth to rescue the damsel in distress (Chapters 28 and 29); the 'ordeals' of expulsion from society (Chapter 56) and prolonged waiting (the twenty months which ensue) that Charles must undergo; and above all the structurally and thematically central position of the Undercliff as a domain removed from everyday experience in which the decisive trials of the hero's mettle, and his fight to win the princess, can take place.

   Though the minor characters in *The French Lieutenant's Woman* can be interpreted in romance terms, the romance is not on the whole the most rewarding pattern to apply to them. Fowles uses his privilege as omniscient narrator to enter into the minds of a number of his minor characters, and in thus illuminating them with his gaze he correspondingly robs them of the extremes of shadowy depth or of stereotyped flatness with which romance habitually works. This is not to say that the minor characters are particularly rich: Mrs Poulteney, for example, is very close to what Forster would call a 'flat' character, and the animus with which Fowles set her up and then (Chapters 30 and 44) knocks her down perhaps tells us more about him than about her. (It also gives the lie to his protestations in Chapter 13 about allowing all his characters their freedom, 'even the abominable Mrs Poulteney'.) But in one or two cases Fowles's characterisation deserves analysis in the terms used by the traditional critic of the novel. The friendship and mutual respect between master and man in the early part of the book work to humanise both parties to the relationship: the rupture between them is correspondingly double-edged, with Sam on the one hand acting as a kind of moral yardstick, bringing out the sheer cruelty of Charles's treatment of Ernestina ('I don't fancy nowhere, *sir*, as where I might meet a friend o' yours', p. 334, emphasis in original), and on the other hand being revealed in what follows as a crafty – though not conscienceless – schemer. (All this depth is ironed out of the film version, as is the 'vice versa' exchange whereby Sam, wiser in his generation than the children of light, grasps the opportunity that Charles has rejected of a prosperous position in the Freeman empire.)

   A similar flattening-out process takes place in the film where Ernestina is concerned, notably in the marvellously handled Chapter 50 where Charles breaks off his engagement. Up to this point Ernestina has had a distinctly bad press: criticised in Chapter 5 for her timid refusal to confront her own sexuality and in Chapter 24 for her shrewish response to the loss of Winsyatt, she seems destined to act merely as a foil for Sarah. But in Chapter 50, her final appearance, she shows her true mettle, and in a genuine and deeply touching speech fully worthy of Sarah – a speech, moreover, which shows that both she and Sarah had ferreted out the same weakness in Charles's nature and were in their differing and unequal ways engaged in the same effort to put it right – proclaims that she had wanted to make her real bridal present to him 'Faith in yourself' (p. 327). It can hardly be accidental that the same phrase recurs at an even more crucial point in the book, namely the final paragraph – 'he has at last found *an atom of faith in himself*, a true uniqueness, on which to build' (p. 399, emphasis added).

The titles of Fowles's fictions refer, not necessarily to the focus of attention in the book, but rather to the source of power. In *The Collector* and *Daniel Martin* the two (more or less) coincide: in *The Magus* and *The Ebony Tower* they are distinct. Similarly in the present work Sarah, the French lieutenant's woman, is not the heroine in quite the same way that Charles is the hero. In the last analysis she is a figure from myth and romance, just as he is a figure from history and the novel. We are told as much in Chapter 1 ('a figure from myth', p. 9); it is reinforced in Chapter 58 ('he became increasingly unsure of the frontier between the real Sarah and the Sarah he had created in . . . dreams', p. 367); Sarah herself hints at it in Chapters 60 and 61. Moreover Fowles's views on the whole creative process emphasise that for him the metaphor whereby the muses are female is very much a living one. Nonetheless he has gone to great lengths to give this ultimately intangible figure a set of quite concrete moral attributes, and we shall miss much of the pleasure and subtlety of the novel if we do not try – albeit in the knowledge that we shall fail – to comprehend Sarah and her behaviour.

Sarah is a mysterious character, but much of her mystery is associated with good. Certainly we are asked to believe that she is a wholesome, if bitter, medicine for Charles. In its original Hebrew her name means 'princess'; her initial nickname, 'Poor Tragedy', and her frequent (almost too frequent) tears show the profoundly serious side of her nature. Her perceptiveness in human relations is praised without reserve. She assumes and defends the role of the outcast (Chapter 20) in a way that ties in with the central existentialist themes of the book, its belief that ultimately everyone is an island and that the only honest people are those who admit their isolation. She 'makes herself' in an appropriately existentialist way, beginning, literally and symbolically, an orphan, and ending as a committed member of an intellectually revolutionary group, the Pre-Raphaelite Brotherhood. So far is she the heroine indeed that she is associated at various times with the Virgin Mary and with Christ.[12] And this mystery, as we have seen, is constantly made concrete for us by the author's refusal to probe his character's thoughts: 'Who is Sarah? Out of what dark shadows does she come? I do not know' (pp. 84–5).

But mystery is very close to mystification. Sarah's appellations also include 'whore', and a number of pointers in the book alert us to the dual nature of the female stereotype – the extract from *The History of the Human Heart* in Chapter 39; the presence of another Sarah who is a prostitute (and also claims to have been abandoned by a military man); the whole question of hysterical illness that surrounds the Marie de Morell trial and the Matthaei collection of case histories. Like Marie, Sarah deceives. She lies about Varguennes; she invents a sprained ankle when Charles comes to see her in Exeter, and indeed (as Chapter 36 indicates in retrospect) goes to some lengths to set up a seduction trap for Charles; having manipulated Charles from their first meeting, she continues to behave secretively by not answering the advertisements he puts out for her (p. 387) and by seeming to conceal her knowledge of his broken engagement (p. 380). Is she a hysterical Marie de Morell? Is she, more unpleasant still, a scheming gold-digger? – for, in yet another suggestive parallel, while Sarah the prostitute earns only five sovereigns (p. 278), Sarah the governess gets ten (p. 242).

We do not know; neither does Charles – and, if we are to believe her, nor does Sarah herself.

I suggested earlier that Sarah was not the heroine of *The French Lieutenant's Woman* in quite the sense that Charles was the hero. This statement may perhaps benefit from a little expansion.

The great power and influence that Sarah exerts in the book which bears her name should not blind us to one essential fact: that, in terms of character at least, she does not develop. Throughout the story Charles is travelling hopefully: from the very first chapter Sarah has arrived. In the field of literature a character who develops will always steal the show from one (however splendid) who merely marks time, and in this case Sarah cannot hold the place of importance because she is merely the means. It is Charles who is the end.

There is a second limitation upon Sarah's qualifications for the role of heroine. Right from the start her distinguishing feature is the fact that she doesn't fit in, and her plea for the necessity of isolation – 'What has kept me alive is my shame . . . I think I have a freedom [other women] cannot understand' (p. 153) – is enormously effective both for the reader and for Charles, who is thereby persuaded that unorthodoxy of Sarah's type is not lower than common sense but actually higher. It is therefore somewhat paradoxical that at the end of the story she should be accepted and find her niche. 'If I leave here I leave my shame. Then I am lost', she asserts (p. 157); but she does leave behind both Lyme and shame, and perhaps in a sense she is lost. The person who inherits the mantle of the outcast (and in a sense fulfils the task she has begun) is Charles – all the more reason for assuming him rather than her to be the principal character.

Finally one must add a small ironic footnote. Whatever one's feelings about the importance of the role of the outsider, one can only rejoice that Sarah should have found a congenial home in London after her miserable childhood and early adult years. But by choosing a historical setting, the Rossetti household, in which to place his fictional character, Fowles relates Sarah to a world whose existence continues after 1869 and can be verified in documents other than *The French Lieutenant's Woman*. Such documents inform us that in 1869 Rossetti was already in decline as an artist, and that by 1872 he would be dead from continuous and almost systematic overdoses of drink and drugs. The role of the outcast may be closer at the end of the book than Sarah thinks.

As we have seen, the many merits of *The French Lieutenant's Woman* should not blind us to its occasional defects. These defects, it seems to me, are almost entirely on the level of theme: they occur, that is, when Fowles is trying to use the book as a mouthpiece through which to address the reader, forgetting that literature, though constructed of words, is in the last analysis silent. However, to say that literature has no message is not to say that literature has no meaning. *The French Lieutenant's Woman* is full of meanings: but they are not always those that the author intends. The successes of the work are always to be found when its themes are securely embodied in narrative. I should like to conclude by trying to illustrate these points of contact between story and theme which constitute in my view the high points of the work.

Some of these successes are to be found when theme and story are not only in contact but also in agreement. A good example is Chapter 19. Here, in an entirely plausible scene, Grogan and Charles round off a dinner at the White Lion by returning to Grogan's rooms for a drink and a talk, and in the course of their talk touch first upon Sarah, and then upon Darwin. In so doing they allude to two great unexplored continents, the human mind and the human (and pre-human) past. They do not claim to have fully mapped these continents: indeed, where the first is concerned they are emphatic that they have not done so. But a meeting of minds, of rational surveying intelligences, takes place, and every reader will know that such experiences of intellectual kinship are unexpectedly warming ones.

Intercut between these scenes of intellectual brotherhood is the description of what Sarah is doing at the same time: lying asleep in bed with Millie, the upstairs maid. This wordless, and at the time indeed mindless, communion is entirely distinct from the intellectual affinity between the two men. It is physical; it is female; its members are of the oppressed; in short, it is in the modern sense a kind of sisterhood. In all these ways it brings out the unthinking patriarchy of Charles and Grogan: not just the fact that they represent 'cold idea' against 'warm fact' ('Notes on an Unfinished Novel', p. 146) but more crudely that they are in the terms of the novel the oppressors, and women the oppressed (or repressed). In the novel the balance is very nicely held. Sarah, from the position of inferiority, controls Charles: Charles, in the position of control, is himself controlled – yet, as we have seen, in being controlled he retains our interest and occupies the central role. *Qui perd gagne*. Underneath all these ironies, moreover, lies the central narrative irony that all this female-oriented debunking of male modes of thought is the work of a male novelist.

Another beautifully effective synchronisation of theme and expression is presented in Chapter 36, where Sarah is seen (the operative word) in her room in Exeter. We learn later what she is about: at the time we have (in a scene that cries out for a leisurely screen adaptation) an extended and loving account of her actions with no indication as to what it is she is about. In narrative terms this scene is perfectly justifiable as a method of raising suspense and – retrospectively – as an indication that the apparently spontaneous seduction of Chapter 46 had in fact been carefully planned. In thematic terms, however, its external description of precise yet incomprehensible actions gives Sarah something of the mysterious and obsessive intensity of a sleepwalker; it is as if the reader were in the place of Sarah's conscious, ratiocinative mind, observing and marvelling at the methodical actions of another part of herself, and reminds us of Jung's suggestion (see note 10 above) that the deep purposes of women may remain a secret even to themselves.

A third example of the harmonious working of theme and story is the dual ending. We have seen that one of Fowles's central preoccupations is the problem of how to reconcile freedom and responsibility. In *The Magus* the terms are embodied in the fiction in relatively familiar terms: 'freedom' for Nicholas is the Don Juan life of freedom from responsibility, and responsibility is exercising his freedom in order to surrender it and choose Alison. In *The French Lieutenant's Woman* the terms are used quite differently. Freedom and responsibility are not contrasted but merged: Charles has been busy trying to accept responsibility and thereby to evade his freedom all through the book, Chapter 60 being only one more effort to do so, but it takes Chapter 61 to pull the rest of the book into focus and confirm that for Charles his greatest responsibility is to freedom. (The contrast with *The Magus* here is instructive. In the latter the hero is offered a choice of heroines and chooses the less exotic Alison, 'homely as wheat'; in *The French Lieutenant's Woman* on the other hand the hero, faced with the familiar romance alternative of a dark and a light heroine, chooses the dark one, always of ill omen for romance heroes, and comes to what is in the terms of the conventional romance a suitably sticky end.) The Marx epigraph which introduces the book – wonderfully appropriate, unlike so many in *The French Lieutenant's Woman* which seem to be chosen almost flippantly – succinctly prefigures this reconciliation of freedom and responsibility by suggesting that every one of us carries some responsibility for the emancipation, the releasing into freedom, of the whole human race.

The themes discussed so far have been ones which the text itself was doing its utmost to make explicit. The book is also strikingly successful in presenting certain other themes which are not so much embodied in the narrative as embedded in it and which require a little more effort to pull them out.

A case in point concerns the relationship between love and fiction, a theme discussed, but by no means exhausted, within the novel. We might begin by looking at Sarah herself. As Rankin suggests, Sarah is herself a creator of didactic fables in much the same way as her creator; Charles asks in Chapter 60: 'Shall I ever understand your parables?' (p. 393). These fables are in every case linked to love: she lies to get Charles, and lies (or at least evades) when she has got him. What the plot rather persuasively hints, however, is that Sarah's fabulation is pathological rather than merely purposeful, the point being that not only her fabulation but also her love is intensely fictional in nature. The logic of the plot is that she can only love what she cannot get. She loves Varguennes because he is married and Charles because he is engaged, and when Charles breaks his engagement she flees him and joins the household of a man who by reason of age and infirmity can never make a marital or sexual partner for her. Whether or not she is herself unattainable, it seems that the unattainable is all that she can love: to the end (as the title reminds us) she belongs to her 'French lieutenant'.

Nor is Sarah the only fabulator in the book. Charles's inability to distinguish between two Sarahs, 'the one Eve personified, all mystery and love and profundity, and the other a half-scheming, half-crazed governess from an obscure seaside town', is presented as a choice between 'the real Sarah and the Sarah he had created' (p. 367). But we must remind ourselves that not one but both alternatives may be figments of Charles's imagination, projected onto rather than derived from the 'real' Sarah. Once again we see the emergence of the rather Proustian implication that love may be an emotion which distorts the vision and makes it impossible to see the beloved clearly. This in turn adds weight to Chapter 61, with its suggestion that the mystery which Charles found in Sarah, whether real or false, was above all misplaced, being in effect a projection of the workings, whether imaginative or imaginary, of an aspect of his own personality.

If we reverse our terms and look at the relationship, not between love and fiction, but between fiction and love, we come to an area that Fowles has explored quite fully already – the link between (male) creator and (female) character. Fowles's views on this matter, and the Freudian theory on which they are based (see especially 'Notes on an Unfinished Novel' and 'Hardy and the Hag'), are well known; the upshot is that the process of creating a work of fiction is simultaneously erotic and obfuscatory in nature. Once again love and fiction, fiction and love are inseparably interwoven.

This theory is intriguingly developed by an uneven but highly suggestive article which appeared some years ago in an American psychological journal (Rose, 1972). Rose's arguments bear on two relationships: that between Charles and Sarah, and that between these two characters and their creator.

We have seen (p. 50 above) that there is a striking parallel between Sarah Woodruff and Sarah the prostitute – the parting from a lover, the two-year absence, the presence of a daughter. Rose points out that these facts and figures recur in the case of Charles's mother, who, we are told on p. 16, had died tragically young in childbirth along with 'the still-born child who would have been a sister to the one-year-old Charles' – a birth taking place 21 months after Charles's conception and thus giving us a very plausible duration for the marriage of about two years. From this Rose deduces that Charles in both his Sarah encounters is trying to restore or reconstruct the past and to engender a daughter who will replace his lost sister. Among other things this explanation accounts for an otherwise inexplicable parallelism, the repeated use of a watch as a toy to pacify a crying child. Playing with a watch, Rose suggests, stands in the novel for the effort to annul or reverse time, in order to replace the dead child of 1836 by the living child, first of 1867, then of 1869 (the narrator's similar use of a watch on p. 395 supports this interpretation). Furthermore, the reference to 'his dead sister' on p. 155, an apparently nonsensical phrase in the context since it can refer only to Sarah, now yields a meaning. The explanation would be that Charles is haunted by the loss of his sister to the extent that he can only love a woman whom he can subconsciously imagine to be that sister: his feelings for Sarah are thus essentially incestuous in the brother-sister sense. (There is support of a structural kind for this theory from the fact that in many romances the dark or forbidden heroine who tempts the hero away turns out to be the hero's sister.) The hypothesis that this relationship with Sarah is essentially incestuous would also provide another explanation for the extraordinary atmosphere of guilt that haunts their lovemaking: 'the most debased criminal caught in his most abominable crime' (p. 217), 'no gentle postcoital sadness . . . but an immediate and universal horror' (p. 305) – as also for Sarah's firm and repeated insistence that 'You cannot marry me, Mr Smithson' (p. 309). This atmosphere of guilt can perhaps be more fully appreciated if we take a step further and suggest that what Charles is seeking is not so much to reconstruct his dead sister as to re-beget her, to make his own mother pregnant with her once more, and that the incestuous aspect of his sexual experiences is not the relatively acceptable brother-sister form but a more deeply taboo variety, namely son-mother.

Rose's argument then takes him on to the relationship between author and text. We have seen the original parallels between the two Sarahs expanded to a third, between the Sarahs and Charles's mother. To these Rose adds a fourth which we can express in the form of a diagram:

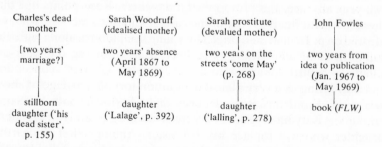

Charles's dead mother	Sarah Woodruff (idealised mother)	Sarah prostitute (devalued mother)	John Fowles
[two years' marriage?]	two years' absence (April 1867 to May 1869)	two years on the streets 'come May' (p. 268)	two years from idea to publication (Jan. 1967 to May 1969)
stillborn daughter ('his dead sister', p. 155)	daughter ('Lalage', p. 392)	daughter ('lalling', p. 278)	book (*FLW*)

This yields the inference that Fowles is in a sense the 'mother' of his own book, it being the fruit of a two-year 'gestation' in much the same way as the children who appear in it.

In his 'Notes on an Unfinished Novel', Fowles remarks (p. 150) that the first draft of *The French Lieutenant's Woman* took him from January to October of 1967 to write – nine months. Drawing on what he calls 'the well-known tendency of the unconscious to play with numbers' (Rose, 1972, p. 167; whether the unconscious in question is that of the patient/author or of the analyst/critic he does not say), Rose produces an argument that can be expressed in a second diagram:

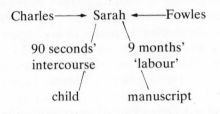

By this argument Fowles is the father of the book and Sarah the mother: Fowles's well documented love affair with Sarah has been consummated and blessed with offspring. This suggestion is borne out by a number of parallels which can be detected between the three men who are in some way loved by Sarah – Varguennes, Charles, and Rossetti. They seem at first to have nothing in common: Varguennes is a French lieutenant, Charles a naturalist and budding existentialist with connections in Lyme, Rossetti an artist. But these disparate qualities are re-united in one man, a man who in his time has studied French, been a lieutenant (in the Royal Marines), acquired an expert knowledge of botany, and written a book of existentialist philosophy; who now resides in Lyme; and who lives by his art. That man, needless to say, is John Fowles.

These, then, are Rose's arguments, supplemented and extended with some of my own. For my part I find them illuminating, not as a comment on John Fowles, whose private urges are no-one's business, but as a comment on otherwise inexplicable aspects, feelings, and moods of the book under study.

Finally there are those parts of *The French Lieutenant's Woman* where theme and narrative are not so much in contact as in collision – where the wordless logic of plot and atmosphere conveys to the attentive reader a message which is exactly the opposite of what the novelist seems to want. Two areas of *The French Lieutenant's Woman* where intention and achievement seem at odds are sexuality and religion.

Fowles's position on the subject of orthodox religion is quite clear, and remains consistent (though not equally prominent) throughout his work. Briefly, he believes in freedom, and consequently rejects the kind of omniscient and omnipotent God that he believes Christians believe in. In *The French Lieutenant's Woman* this brooding and rather cruel figure is erected, the better to be demolished, in a number of quotations from Victorian authors (for example verse four of the Tennyson extract on p. 316, or the last three lines of 'To Marguerite' on p. 366); the argument of Chapter 13 rests on the analogy between an omniscient and omnipotent narrator and a God endowed with such attributes, and understandably opts for both a narrator and a God 'in the new theological image, with freedom [their] first principle, not authority' (p. 86). The conflict between the two views of God is located within Charles and comes to a head in Chapter 48, where after leaving Sarah he 'suddenly [feels] the need for sanctuary' (p. 310) and enters a small church. There he has a kind of conversion *away* from organised Christianity, and leaves the church 'shriven of established religion for the rest of his life' (p. 318). There seems little doubt that Fowles's overt sympathies go with him.

The line of argument here attributed to Fowles is simple, direct, and internally consistent. It is, moreover, entirely compatible with the overall existentialist moral of the book. The problem is that the grain and texture of much of the writing seem to run against it. A pointer is already to be found in *The Magus* in the shape of the Seidevarre episode, to my mind the finest thing Fowles has ever written: if this literary value judgement is soundly based, then it is clear that God-centred religion of a very direct, Old Testament, authoritarian kind engages Fowles's imagination very powerfully indeed. But we do not need to go outside *The French Lieutenant's Woman* to find evidence for this. Chapter 48 seems to me to be steeped, not in agnosticism, but in religiosity, and to bear witness to a 'god-shaped blank' in Fowles of sizeable dimensions. Charles prays before his 'conversion': the conversion itself takes the form of a dialogue, admittedly not with God, but 'perhaps between [Charles] and that spreadeagled figure in the shadows at the church's end' (p. 312); it contains a vision of 'the right purpose of Christianity' (p. 315) which seems to be identical to Fowles's own view of the proper function of existentialism; it is couched in and shot through with religious metaphors, concluding with St Paul on the road to Damascus; and it is followed, just as it was preceded, by prayer. All this could and doubtless should be viewed as part of a legitimate move from Old to New Testament and from God the Father to God the Son: but this does not account for the overall impact of the chapter, which seems to me far more backward-looking and nostalgic than forward-looking and triumphant. The moment I recall from it is not the rather anti-climactic slogan 'To uncrucify!', but instead a passage earlier in the chapter, concluding, by a characteristic Fowles device, with a minor incident left to dangle unexplained:

> He tried to recommence his prayer. But it was hopeless. He knew it was not heard. He began abruptly to cry ... here he was, not weeping for Sarah, but for his inability to speak to God. He knew, in that dark church, that the wires were down. No communication was possible.
>
> There was a loud clack in the silence. He turned round, hastily touching his eyes with his sleeve. But whoever had tried to enter apparently accepted that the church was now closed; it was as if a rejected part of Charles himself had walked away.
>
> (pp. 311–12)

In a sense the lonely figure outside the locked church, like a believer lamenting the impossibility of belief, is far more like Charles's creator than like Charles himself.

The second area where story and preachment seem at odds is sexuality. If I understand him aright, Fowles would like the message of *The French Lieutenant's Woman* on this subject to be something like this: 'sex is a fundamental aspect of love, and should not be thought of as dirty; it is only dirty when it is debased (performed for itself, without love) or commercialised (prostitution); above all it should not be associated with guilt'. This in turn is part of a larger message, particularly forcefully spelled out on p. 319, that we should not split off the soul from the body, the spiritual from the physical, but should treat these as unified. Some of the sexual references in the book bear out this message very well: the gymnastics at Ma Terpsichore's (pp. 263–6), the guilt Charles (rightly) feels at the thought of compensating for the emotional nullity of marriage to Ernestina by teaching her to be fun in bed (p. 229). Fowles is very good at depicting how sex can go wrong: the inconsistencies begin when he comes to the places where it ought to go right.

One couple who do seem sexually fulfilled are Sam and Mary, observed in the Undercliff, 'as greenly erotic as the April plants they trod on' (p. 161), by Charles and Sarah. Indeed, for them everything – sex, marriage, childbirth, even upward social mobility – seems to work

perfectly. But they are in no sense principal characters: their successful
sexual arrangements are implied rather than described; and, if my
argument on pp. 66–7 above is well founded, they belong to the Many
rather than the Few, so that their actions and feelings do not bear the
full stamp of Fowles's authority. For this we must look to Charles.

Charles's principal sexual relationships are with three people:
Ernestina, Sarah the prostitute, and Sarah Woodruff. His relationship
with Ernestina follows the pattern of repression, of separation
between spiritual and physical, noted above, and is understandably
unsatisfactory from the point of view of both parties. His short-lived
encounter with Sarah the prostitute, moving rapidly from the erotic to
the emetic, ends in a singularly revolting fashion with his vomiting all
over the pillow beside her head. But his affair with Sarah Woodruff,
which we might reasonably expect to bring considerably greater
rewards, hardly seems to do so. Reference has already been made to
the disproportionate feelings of guilt which Charles experiences in
Carslake's Barn. When the pair do eventually make love – and we
should note that Fowles displaces their tryst from the rural innocence
of the Undercliff to the seedier setting of the red-light district of Exeter
– their coition is brutish and short, and is once more followed instantly
by an overwhelming reflux of guilt.

There are a number of possible reasons why this might be so. Some,
particularly those bearing directly on *The French Lieutenant's Woman*,
have already been discussed (see pp. 75–7 above); others will be
considered in the final chapter. But whatever Fowles's intentions, the
result is to build into the work yet another layer of subversion and
irony.

When we come to set *The French Lieutenant's Woman* against
Fowles's previous work we can see that it represents something of a
blend of the new and the familiar. By comparison with *The Magus*, it is
new in the importance it allots to its heroine; in its explicit stress on
freedom rather than on responsibility; and in its historical setting. But
if we step a little further back we can see these innovations as
modulations of relatively familar concerns of the author. The extended
treatment of Sarah leaves us in the end knowing no more about her
than we did at the beginning; and the stress on freedom arises from
Fowles's conception of the Victorian age, which he sees as dominated
by duty and guilt. Thus the nineteenth-century setting of *The French
Lieutenant's Woman* is in part a means whereby its author is able to
come to terms with the twentieth century, and the remedies prescribed

for the ills of the past are not those which Fowles sees as appropriate for the present age. In the last analysis *The French Lieutenant's Woman* covers much new ground, but it does not venture beyond the limits of the territory Fowles has already mapped out as his own.

5 *The Ebony Tower*

> The working title of this collection of stories was *Variations*, by which I meant to suggest variations both on certain themes in previous books of mine and in methods of narrative presentation. ... However, *The Ebony Tower* is also a variation of a more straightforward kind, and *the source of its mood, as also partly of its theme and setting, is . . . the Celtic romance*.
>
> (*ET*, pp. 119–20, emphasis added)

Fowles's next published work, *The Ebony Tower*, appeared in 1974. Like *The Collector*, it was produced during the gestation of a longer work; Fowles interrupted his work on *Daniel Martin* and turned out the first drafts in a few days. *The Ebony Tower* is chiefly notable for two reasons. In the first place it constitutes Fowles's first (and so far only) venture into the short story or novella: the collection contains four original pieces, varying in length from 110 pages down to 44. The second striking feature is the prominence given to a piece which is not in fact original at all, namely *Eliduc*, a translation by Fowles of a mediaeval French tale which was itself drawn (as the quotation above implies) from yet older Celtic sources. The tale, translated accurately and self-effacingly,[1] is included in full, and is preceded by an introduction in which Fowles develops both a personal and a general theory of fiction. This theory traces the origins of the novel directly to the influence of the Celtic romance; in an arresting phrase, Fowles remarks that in reading stories such as *Eliduc* '[the] writer of fiction . . . is watching his own birth' (p. 120).

As we shall see, Fowles has interwoven both the structure and the texture of all five tales very closely. But I shall argue that the most important tale, the theme on which (to use Fowles's own phrase) the others are all 'variations', is *Eliduc*. It is referred to directly (pp. 58–9) in the title story (itself both 'a homage and . . . a thumbed nose to a very old tradition', p. 24). Despite its being placed second in the collection, therefore, it is *Eliduc* that I shall consider first.

Of the author of *Eliduc*, supposedly called Marie de France, we know nothing with certainty. The work for which he or she is famous consists of twelve '*lais*', probably composed between about 1165 and 1185.² The last and longest of these *lais*, or '*contes d'aventure et d'amour*' as Mickel (1974) accurately calls them, is *Eliduc*. The story is set in Brittany, and claims to be a re-telling of an older Breton narrative. When the story begins, Eliduc, a Breton knight, is happily married and in the full confidence of his overlord, whom he serves faithfully in return. The trouble starts when evil rumours are spread and Eliduc is dismissed from the court. Unable to persuade the king to take him back, he decides to go abroad, bids a fond farewell to his wife, and crosses the Channel to Totnes, in Devon. There he finds the king besieged, and succeeds after some delay in fighting off his attackers. Unfortunately, however, the king has an unmarried daughter, and she and Eliduc fall madly in love. After various military adventures Eliduc returns to Totnes and he and Guilliadun elope together to Brittany; but when she hears that he is married already, she falls down, apparently dead. Eliduc takes her to a chapel, where his wife discovers her and is able, by means of a healing flower, to effect a miraculous cure. On learning the true facts of the case the wife magnanimously withdraws to a nunnery, allowing Eliduc and Guilliadun to marry. After many years of perfect happiness they too withdraw to lives of contemplation and all three pray for the salvation of one another's souls.

For our purposes *Eliduc* can be considered from two angles. The first is its importance for Fowles; the second, its importance in its context – whether that context is Marie's *lais* or Fowles's novellas. I shall take these points in order.

It is not hard to see why the Celtic romance in general, and specifically *Eliduc*, should appeal to Fowles's particular sensibility. There is, first, the whole aura of the mediaeval past, with its emphasis on a feudal world of solemn contract, of social life highly organised into a system of controlled rank and hierarchy, a world where 'all civilized life' depended upon 'promises sworn between vassal and lord' (p. 123). Secondly, there is the overpowering sense of magic and myth in Celtic romance, a sense which endows quite commonplace events with profound significance. Thirdly, there is the ethos of courtly love, with its grave romanticisation of women, on which many of these romances are based. And finally – a feature particularly evident in *Eliduc* – there is the way in which crises are overcome, opposites reconciled, and contradictions transcended. (We note in particular the harmony between the generations – Eliduc's friendship with Guilliadun's father

– and the final reconciliation between Guildelüec and Guilliadun, wife
and mistress, which Fowles's heroes consistently yearn for.)

In arranging these points I have tried to show how they coincide with
the four themes identified in the first chapter (see above, pp. 3–7).
But there is, I think, a more fruitful and constructive way of analysing
Eliduc. In order to do so we must move away from Fowles's own
interpretation of the tale, and consider it for itself and in the context of
the other works it is grouped with.

In my view the most revealing way to approach *Eliduc* is through the
concept of contradiction. This term may need a brief explanation. As
used here it is borrowed from the anthropologist Edmund Leach,
himself influenced by Lévi-Strauss. Leach suggests that myths are
about fundamental oppositions, or contradictions, in society, and that
the function of myths is simultaneously to conceal and to reveal these
contradictions: 'Myths serve to provide an apparent resolution . . . of
problems which are by their very nature incapable of any final
resolution'.[3]

When we read *Eliduc* we are likely to find our attention focusing on
two points or cruxes. The first is Eliduc's persistent refusal, despite
abundant opportunity and much self-interrogation, to tell Guilliadun
about his wife and vice versa. The second is Guildelüec's extraordinary
act of self-abnegation in first bringing her rival back to life and then
withdrawing to a nunnery to make room for her.

Recent critics have quite properly concentrated their attention on
these two incidents and on the contradictions they bring to the
surface.[4] But they have used them as means to analyse the protagonists: the contradictions they identify are moral ones within the
principal characters. Where the first point is concerned critics agree in
condemning Eliduc's behaviour. On the second problem, Guildelüe's
withdrawal to a nunnery, there is less consensus.[5] But in both cases
critics agree in submitting the tale to the kind of moral and psychological analysis appropriate to real life and real people.

My own view is that if we read *Eliduc* by the conventions of realism,
looking for consistency and depth of characterisation throughout and
seeking to draw moral conclusions, we are bound to be disappointed. It
is much more rewarding to read it as folktale or myth. Marie herself
draws no moral conclusions; indeed, apart from a discreet emphasis on
the importance of the women (p. 125), she leaves the story entirely to
tell itself. Nor, despite its many realistic touches, is the story overall a
realistic one. This can partly be shown by the fact that it contains motifs
(the sacrifice of a sailor to the sea, the 'resurrection' of Guilliadun by

placing a flower in her mouth) which are scarcely, if at all, displaced from their magical origins – motifs which call to mind Auerbach's discussion of the atmosphere of *Yvain*:

> It is from Breton folklore that the courtly romance took its elements of mystery, of something sprung from the soil, concealing its roots, and inaccessible to rational explanation . . *[the] ethical or symbolic significance* [of such adventures and motifs] *can rarely be ascertained with anything approaching certainty.*
>
> (Auerbach, 1953, pp. 130–1, emphasis added)

But more important still is to remember the original context of *Eliduc*, namely the eleven similar *lais* Marie is known to have written. If we replace *Eliduc* in that context and apply to all the tales the kind of drastic structural analysis used in anthropological approaches to myths (see Leach, 1969 and 1970, *passim*), we will find that all the tales, *Eliduc* included, revolve around the conflicts and indeed contradictions inherent in certain kinds of duty: duty to one's parents, duty to one's husband or wife, duty to one's lover, duty to one's feudal superiors and inferiors. The most important point is that these duties are shown to be in many cases *irreconcilable*: the stories explore their contradictions, but are not primarily concerned to apportion praise or blame. Thus in *Le Fresne* a *'seignur'* takes a low-born mistress; in time his knights persuade him that for political reasons he must marry; he defers to their judgement and a marriage is arranged, in preparation for which the former mistress is relegated to the status of a servant. (In the event the situation is resolved, and the contradiction glossed over, by a birth-mystery plot: the low-born mistress is revealed to be high-born after all, and duly marries her lord.) The moral nub of this story might well seem to be the disloyalty of the lord who abandons a faithful mistress simply because of her class origins; but in the story as we have it his action is treated as inevitable and indeed essential. That, the story says, is how things are.

The tales of Marie de France, and to a more marked extent those of Chrétien (we note that Fowles uses five lines from Chrétien's *Yvain* as an epigraph to the title story), have as their 'fundamental purpose . . . A self-portrayal of feudal knighthood with its mores and ideals' (Auerbach, 1953, p. 131) – and, one might add, its internal contradictions. The most important element of courtly romance is summed up in the concept of the adventure: 'trial through adventure is the real meaning of the knight's ideal existence . . . the very essence of the knight's ideal of manhood is called forth by adventure' (Auerbach, 1953, p. 135). But this concept of adventure is itself constructed upon a contradiction which is brought to the surface by marriage: is the knight to go on fighting battles and rescuing damsels? and if so, *what is he to do with the damsels when he has rescued them?* This is the theme which runs through *Yvain*, and in contrasting form through *Erec et Enide*. In the latter, the hero is on the brink of surrendering his knightly pursuits for love of his wife; in the former, it is Yvain's marriage which is almost split on the rock of his incorrigible tendency to fight battles, right wrongs, and never refuse an adventure. In neither case is knighthood and its dual obligations – to men and to women – something that can be honourably renounced.

From this viewpoint, then, the story of *Eliduc* runs something like this:

(1) Eliduc begins at home in Brittany. His knightly duties are honourably discharged (and his need for adventures satisfied) by his loyalty to his overlord and his fidelity to his loving wife.

(2) (The source of all the trouble.) Eliduc is slandered and prevented from carrying out his duties to his lord.

(3) Impelled by the obligations of knighthood, Eliduc decides to seek adventures elsewhere.

(4) In Totnes he finds and succours a needy overlord, thus fulfilling his responsibility towards men . . .

(5) . . . and meets a damsel whom by the obligations of gallantry he cannot but pay court to.

(6) When the time comes for him to return he finds himself saddled with two incompatible obligations – to his wife and to his mistress.

(7) *Only the women can get him out of this.* (We remember Marie's comment that '[the story] is really about the two women', p. 125.) In *Le Fresne* (where once again there is a man, a wife, and a mistress), the mistress solves the problem by turning out to be the wife. In *Eliduc* the older woman gracefully yields place to her younger rival – thus, incidentally, rebuking by implication the jealous old men whose refusal to yield to youth is ultimately responsible for the sufferings of the young in such tales as *Guigemar*, *Les Deus Amanz* and *Yonec*.

The essential feature of this plot summary, crude and reductive as it may be, is to show that Eliduc's failure to tell Guildelüec and

Guilliadun of each other's existence is of no importance structurally speaking (whatever we may think of it morally). From the moment he crosses the Channel, Eliduc is riding for a fall: honour, if nothing else, will force him to be dishonourable.

This lengthy preamble is necessary to my analysis of *The Ebony Tower* because in my view we will indeed find in *Eliduc*, as Fowles implies, the structural features or 'motifs' on which the remaining stories are variations.

The principal motif of *Eliduc*, at least for Fowles's purposes, is simply the situation of one man torn between two women. (It will hardly be necessary at this point to list the other works by Fowles in which this situation recurs.)

The second motif concerns the conflicts between and within what we may call 'gallantry' and 'loyalty'. (Here, as we shall see, the example of Chrétien is instructive.)

The third motif may be termed 'creative withdrawal': creative because it constitutes the removal of a blockage or hindrance. In *Eliduc* the return of the lovers to Brittany produces a crisis which locks the action solid; only the wife's generous decision to abandon a husband she loves and withdraw to a nunnery can clear the jam and allow the action to proceed. The main function of such a withdrawal, whatever one's moral attitude to it, seems to me to be a structural one: it unblocks the impasse into which the characters have got themselves. As I have suggested in item (7) above, the refusal of male blocking characters to get out of the way is a structural element in several other tales in the collection.

The fourth motif is the failure of communication, a heading under which one should include not simply Eliduc's failure to put Guildelüec and Guilliadun in the picture, but the circumstances of slander and exclusion which led him to go abroad in the first place.

The final point concerns the setting of the tale. By placing it in Brittany Marie gives it not merely a location but also an atmosphere and in effect a genre, that of the courtly romance, recognisably linked by a shared moral code to the world of her audience, yet opening into a magical universe in which anything might happen.[6]

We must now turn to Fowles's own contributions to *The Ebony Tower*. The title story concerns a young painter and art critic, David Williams. He has been commissioned to write the introduction to *The Art of Henry Breasley*, and he is on his way to Brittany, leaving behind his wife and family, to interview Breasley, a distinguished but aging

painter who has spent most of his life abroad. When he arrives at the
isolated house in the forest he finds things not quite as he had expected.
'The Ebony Tower' (Breasley's phrase for the isolation and abstraction of modern art) is the story of the three days David spends at the
house; of his sparring with the irascible but deeply committed
Breasley; and above all of his increasingly intense relationship with
Diana ('the Mouse'), one of the two girls who live with Breasley. At a
crucial point in the story David decides not to make love to Diana.
Subsequently he bitterly regrets this decision, feeling that it is part of a
generally second-rate quality about both his life and his art. The story
ends as he meets his wife at Orly.

As we have already seen, Fowles himself indicates (p. 119) that the
tales in this collection are interlinked; and by the time we reach this
suggestion, we have already received what will turn out to be a
considerable number of stylistic signals stressing the connections
between one story and the next.[7] It is thus no surprise to find in 'The
Ebony Tower' all five of the motifs identified in *Eliduc*. The first (one
man torn between two women) is represented by the triangle of David,
Beth and Diana; the second (the contradictions inherent in certain
masculine roles) by the conflict in David between his legitimate
faithfulness to Beth and his obligation as a 'knight errant' (p. 98) to
awaken the 'sleeping princess' (p. 99) of Coëtminais.[8] The third motif
is represented by Breasley's 'creative withdrawal' to allow (and indeed
encourage) the relationship between David and Diana. The fourth
motif, failure of communication, features on two levels. The obvious
reference is to Breasley's verbal inadequacy (p. 59). But that is only
part of a deeper and more serious problem. Throughout Fowles's work
we find the old passing on their knowledge and experience to the
young: Conchis to Nick, Grogan to Charles, Dan to Jenny. In 'The
Ebony Tower' everything is ready for the disciple to learn from the
master. If words fail, there is art (the *Moon-hunt*) and the implicit
message of Breasley's past and present way of life. But the chain of
communication breaks down, and the message does not get through
until too late. The same failure reverses the impact of the fifth motif: a
journey takes place, a magical Breton setting ('the Brocéliande of the
lais of Chrétien de Troyes', p. 58) is reached, but no healing
transformation takes place.

Taking formal analysis a stage further we can show that the sequence
of events in 'The Ebony Tower' is in fact very closely modelled on
Eliduc.

Eliduc	'The Ebony Tower'
(a) married man	....
(b) leaves home and goes abroad	....
(c) visits isolated building	....
(d) where he finds an old man	....
(e) and a young girl	....
(f) man and girl fall in love	....
(g) couple give in to their feelings	X couple resist their feelings
(h) man preserves his self-respect	X man loses his self-respect
(i) girl is rescued	X girl is not rescued
(j) wife discovers	X wife (presumably) does not discover

(X = point of difference between stories)

In this diagram I have written in only those parts of 'The Ebony Tower' which differ from their counterparts in *Eliduc*. The result emphasises that 'The Ebony Tower' is the story of a missed chance; so likewise does the epigraph from *Yvain*, which is perhaps worth a moment's attention.

Yvain, one of five long verse romances by Chrétien de Troyes, is very similar in ethos to *Eliduc* and almost exactly contemporary with it. Indeed much of what Fowles writes in 'A Personal Note' in praise of the female Marie de France applies equally well to the male Chrétien, particularly since two of the latter's romances (*Erec et Enide* and *Yvain* itself) deal specifically with the harmful effects of *desmesure*. *Yvain*, named after the hero (one of King Arthur's knights), tells the story of Yvain's adventures in search of his bride; the epigraph describes his journey to seek her. But a feature of the story is the proportion of it devoted to the hero's jousts and adventures *after* he has found and wed the maiden. These give rise to problems not unlike David's, since Yvain is unable to turn down either a challenge or an appeal and is therefore constantly finding himself committed to rescuing several different damsels from separate crises at the same time. On at least one occasion, moreover, he is the victim of considerable resentment when he turns out (being married already) not to be in a position to marry the maiden whose honour he has preserved. Thus *Yvain* (like its companion piece *Erec et Enide*) is largely about the internal contradictions of chivalry: but of course it contrives to triumph over these problems by presenting a series of successful quests culminating in a victorious return home. To choose it as the epigraph for 'The Ebony Tower' can only emphasise the failure of David's own quest and the emptiness of his reunion with Beth.

It remains to look at two areas of the story which are very much the contribution of Fowles himself. By casting both his male principals as artists, Fowles has thrust art into the centre of the discussion. At first he focuses his attention on the relationship between different kinds of art; later, drawing on hints made in the earlier discussion, he goes on to look at the relationship between art and life.

As artists, Williams and Breasley seem to form the sharpest possible contrast. David Williams is an abstract painter: he has been through a phase of Op Art, and his 'preferred line of descent' runs through 'De Stijl, Ben Nicholson and . . . [Victor] Pasmore'; his pictures '[go] well on walls that [have] to be lived with', that is they are decorative and not too challenging (see pp. 19–22). The first and only painting he actually does during the story consists in '[noting] down particularly pleasing conjunctions of tone and depth' (p. 9). Moreover he has learned to supplement the money he earns from his paintings, first by working as an art teacher, and then by art criticism; the account of the *Moon-hunt* given on p. 24 reads in part like a parody of such criticism, and Fowles himself has said that David speaks 'a kind of smooth language . . . which is losing meaning' (Barnum, 1978, p. 143).

Breasley, on the other hand, has always been at the opposite pole. He hates abstracts ('Obstructs', 'synthetic cubist nonsense', p. 42) and refers to abstraction as 'betrayal' and as '[the] Triumph of the . . . eunuch' (p. 45): its practitioners are as roundly dismissed ('pick-arsehole', p. 32; 'Better the bloody bomb than Jackson Bollock', p. 50). His own work, while not exactly realistic, is in a sense representational: its roots and essence, at least as it is described on pp. 18–19, seem to lie emotionally in a dream-like, Celtic, archetypal world and stylistically in the 'International Gothic' (a method, according to a standard work of reference, '[whose] realism was confined to details'). Nor does Breasley have any time for art criticism in the normal sense of the word: though he has 'an incredible memory for paintings . . . Almost total recall' (pp. 70–1), he distrusts verbal expression and himself labours under the handicap of 'an almost total inadequacy with words' (p. 59).

It is therefore not surprising that Breasley should take on David over supper and administer a lashing attack on David's philosophy of art (though not, we should note, on his paintings). But Fowles has characteristically slipped into his story a number of unexpected affinities between the two men. Both have Welsh backgrounds, David

Williams by name alone, Breasley through his mother and his early childhood (p. 26). Both, curiously enough, admire Braque: Breasley venerates him (p. 32) and keeps a picture by him over his bed (p. 52); David speaks of his wish to follow humbly in Braque's footsteps (p. 42). Further, despite their differences the two are at least alike in that neither could be described as a realist: Breasley seems to be going beyond the representation of nature, not simply in his increasingly dream-like and archetypal choice of subject-matter, but also in his increasing tendency to move away from form in the direction of colour (p. 31). And finally we must remember that David has been moved to write about Breasley, and that Breasley in turn has been sufficiently impressed by the article to make a deliberate selection of David.

Nonetheless Fowles clearly wants to present the two artists as fundamentally different. Obviously it will not do (as the Mouse recognises on p. 54) to label David 'abstract' and Breasley 'representational'. The opposition must be defined in a different way. It seems to me that instead of dividing art into abstract and representational, Breasley (and Fowles behind him) would like to divide it into what might be called 'decorative' and 'expressive': expressive, that is, in as much as it bespeaks some personal response or inner state on the part of the artist. Thus abstracts can be formal exercises, mere tricks of design – 'high artifice' (p. 21), 'colour records' (p. 87); but they can also be records of significant internal feelings or of a deeply personal response to a visual stimulus. The same is true in turn of representational art, which is able at its best not only to represent but actually to re-create the real world, but which degenerates at worst – so Fowles's argument might run – into the kind of lifeless imitative realism whose final extreme is photography.

This argument would explain why Fowles clearly approves of a work such as Breasley's *Moon-hunt*.[9] In the process of 'refinement away from the verbal' (p. 31), this work has also undergone a considerable shift in the direction of abstraction. It is abstract inasmuch as it moves away from external reality, but representational in so far as it records and represents an internal experience. Conversely David's work – which is qualified by epithets such as 'cool', 'precise', 'small-scale' – seems distanced from his own experience and confined to a rather passive process of recording: to put it very crudely, he paints what he sees, while Breasley paints what he feels.

Diana is well qualified to define the differences between the two since in varying ways she is attracted to both: and she it is who explains to David that Breasley's phrase, 'the ebony tower', refers, not to abstraction *per se*, but to 'Anything . . . he thinks is obscure because the artist is scared to be clear' (p. 54).

By now it has become impossible to confine the discussion to the aesthetic plane: we have clearly moved on to the relationship between art and life. The (three-day) narrative of 'The Ebony Tower' divides into three parts. The first is largely concerned with outlining and developing those aesthetic differences of opinion between David and Breasley which we have been looking at; the second, which we now realise to be what the first was building up to, is the crux, and describes what happens between Diana and David on the second night of his stay. The scene is one of Fowles's best; the isolation and natural beauty of the setting, and the growing mutual absorption of David and Diana, allow him to exercise his genius for creating an isolated and heightened reality. It is in fact Diana who describes herself as 'under a spell' (p. 91), but for much of this part of the story it is David who behaves as if he is not fully in control of his own actions. (In view of the way David has been set up by the 'creative withdrawal', first of Breasley (p. 84), and then of Anne (p. 89), this is not far from the truth.) The scene in effect falls into three parts. The first, in Diana's room, consists very much of a kind of sounding-out process in which, like 'hidden birds . . . secretly shifting position between utterances' (p. 93), each is trying to establish the other's position without revealing his or her own. The second (introduced by an extremely skilful transitional paragraph on pp. 97–8) takes place out in the garden; and the third, a winding-down from the high tension of the second, recounts the return of the couple to separate rooms in the *manoir*.

What is very striking in this scene is the way in which both within and between the three parts the decisive character is not David but Diana. She is the one who puts her own case forward for David to analyse; she suggests the idea of the night walk; she, saying the unsayable, makes it clear that David is the knight errant who in another world would have been destined to rescue her (p. 98); it is her unspoken offer ('she said nothing – or everything. No strings now. If you want') that gives rise to their embrace, and 'She was the one who brought it to an end' (p. 99). In the remainder of that part of the scene she is firm and lucid, able to perceive and to describe the force that keeps her and David apart, and to act in a way that preserves her integrity.

Poor David, on the other hand, is almost entirely passive. In her room he responds to her requests for advice: in the garden he reacts first to her physical encouragement to kiss her, and then to her breaking off the kiss; back in the house his three attempts to persuade her to go to bed with him read much more like belated responses to her earlier initiative than like independent actions on his own part. It is hardly to his credit that he manages to remain faithful to his wife Beth: indeed he seems even to contradict the advice that he himself had earlier given to Diana: 'Surely what you ought to do is what you feel you need. And to hell with everyone' (p. 92).

The third part of 'The Ebony Tower' records the impact of Coëtminais, in terms both of ideas (part one) and actions (part two), on David's understanding of himself. He spends the time between leaving Coëtminais and meeting Beth at Orly in self-reproaches of increasing bitterness. The flaw which he sees as pervading and vitiating both his life and his work is a kind of moral cowardice: 'Henry . . . sinned out of need and instinct; David did not, out of fear' (p. 108); 'his real crime [was] . . . to dodge, escape, avert' (p. 109). This 'fear of challenge' (p. 109) results, in artistic terms, in the safe geometric abstraction of David's work; in his life, he seems to be saying, it is what underlies his married state and the fact that he is still (albeit only technically) faithful.

What unifies art and life here is the assertion that the artist must live his life according to different principles from the ordinary man. David's reflections lead him to the conclusion that conventional moral standards do not apply to the artist, and that only through being prepared to abandon them can the artist achieve the kind of intensity on which great art depends:

> But till then, he knew: *he had refused . . . a chance of a new existence,
> and the ultimate quality and enduringness of his work had rested on
> acceptance* . . . The abominable and vindictive injustice was that art
> is [sic] fundamentally immoral . . . Coët had remorselessly demon-
> strated what he was born, still was, and always would be: a decent
> man and . . . an eternal also-ran.
>
> (p. 113, emphasis added)

In the light of the rather rigorous moral standards that Fowles goes to such pains to elaborate in the rest of his work, David's conclusion may seem surprising, if not indeed nonsensical. It is important, however, to understand exactly what he is saying. He is not rejecting duty and responsibility: he is insisting that the duty and responsibility of the artist are to his work, and that the artist's life is an integral part of his work. Great art demands great risks and great sacrifices: the artist must take those risks and make those sacrifices with the whole of his life if his art, which consists essentially in self-exploration and self-discovery, is to achieve greatness.

Thus one way of explaining the contrast between Henry and David is to argue that the difference lies neither in their art nor in their lives, but in the way each relates art and life. While Henry is entirely committed to his art and puts his whole life – including his morality – at the service of his art, David hesitates, hedging his bets by investing some of his emotional capital in conventional morality – wife, children, job.

This, I think, is the – extravagantly Byronic – view of the artist that underlies the novella: and by such a High Romantic canon poor David hasn't a chance. Either his art does not express his personality, or – worse still, in view of the quality of his work – it does!

After 'The Ebony Tower' comes *Eliduc*, which has already been discussed. The third story is entitled 'Poor Koko'. The narrator, an elderly and rather puny writer, goes to a country cottage to work on his long-planned biography of Thomas Love Peacock. There he is surprised by a young, urban, sophisticated, and would-be politically conscious burglar, who to his amazement and horror ends his search of the house by systematically burning all the notes, files, and texts which the narrator has assembled for his book. Afterwards the narrator reflects on the experience and suggests a possible motive for the young man's actions.

On the surface 'Poor Koko' seems to have little to do with the other stories in this volume. There are trivial cross-references: 'my ordeal' (p. 147) points us back to the mediaeval world; the narrator's rather deliberately given age of 66 reminds us that Breasley is 77; the West Country setting and Cornish epigraph link the story geographically with Brittany and the Celts. More substantially, the story resembles the one that follows it in that both deal with an 'enigma' (the word itself occurs on p. 180). But the main concern of 'Poor Koko', one which binds it very closely into the book and into Fowles's work as a whole, is the fourth motif identified on p. 87, namely failure of communication. As the epigraph (translated on p. 187) implies, this is firstly a failure of language. The young burglar, with his reliance on slang, his quick-fix political theories, his preference for gesture over speech, cannot express himself effectively; this is emphasised by his fondness for Conrad, whose work constantly stresses the inability of language to encompass reality.[10] Indeed the narrator comes to the conclusion that the 'enigma', the young man's destruction of the Peacock biography, was an act of jealousy, the rage that those deprived of words feel for those with a mastery of words.

But underneath the failure of language there is a yet sadder failure of communication. The failure to listen (p. 172) and the ' "refusal" to hand down a kind of magic' (p. 185) are symptoms of something deeper still. As the title implies ('Koko . . . correct filial behaviour, the proper attitude of son to father', p. 186), the story really concerns a breakdown of relations between the generations – a relationship, as we saw in Chapter 1, of great importance throughout Fowles's work. This breakdown pervades the collection. Maurice and Jane, the owners of the Dorset cottage, do not get on with their son Richard; Peter, the son of the Conservative MP Marcus Fielding, is described as 'vaguely . . . New Left' (p. 211); and, overwhelmingly, 'The Ebony Tower' recounts not so much the refusal as the dismal failure of an old man to hand on his 'magic' to a young one.

The next story, 'The Enigma', deals once again with an initially inexplicable event – in this case the disappearance of Marcus Fielding, a prosperous rural MP. The story begins in impersonal, documentary style; later the point of view shifts to that of Michael Jennings, the young detective investigating the case. When Jennings comes to interview his last witness, Isobel Dodgson,[11] he falls instantly in love with her, and the centre of interest shifts from a past enigma (the disappearance of the MP) to a present mystery (the developing relationship between lovers-to-be).

'The Enigma' contains all five of the *Eliduc* motifs, though in varying degrees of importance. Three of them play only a minor part. The pattern of one man in pursuit of two women occurs in reversed form: both Fielding and Jennings, in different ways, have an interest in the heroine of the story. The motif of the conflicts and contradictions inherent in male roles surfaces in the form of a clash between being a public figure and 'being your own man' (p. 232), a conflict which in different ways exercises both the politician Fielding and the policeman Jennings. Finally the fact that Isobel's sister is married to a French film director (p. 212), and that she has just come back from a visit to Paris, provides a discreet nod in the direction of the fifth motif, the Breton setting.

The two remaining motifs are central to the story. The first is 'creative withdrawal'. The driving force behind the entire action is Fielding's disappearance: it is the structural fact that projects the entire action, the initial 'enigma' that is explicitly stated to 'cause . . .

The tender pragmatisms of flesh' (p. 244) with which the story ends. The fact that Fielding's intentions and purposes cannot be deduced only adds impetus to his action: as Isobel remarks in a very Conchis-like phrase, 'Nothing lasts like a mystery' (p. 239).

The second motif is that of failed communication. Fowles's handling of this motif is very subtle. On the surface the failure is straightforward: Fielding simply disappears, thus cutting off any form of contact or message, and if Isobel's analysis of his character and actions is right then that failure of communication reaches right back through his life. Indeed he seems to have failed even in his final gesture: he got to the British Museum, but Isobel (p. 229) wasn't there. Analysing the story a stage further leads us to revise our initial assessment. As interpreted by Isobel, Fielding's disappearance does communicate something – his realisation that his life was hollow – and his visit to the British Museum reading-room, 'that house of fiction itself' (Conradi, 1982, p. 88), constitutes a message to the would-be novelist Isobel (p. 233) which she proves quite capable both of receiving and of decoding. (This interpretation is supported by the burning of the manuscript in 'Poor Koko': in both stories actions speak louder and more clearly than words.) Delving yet further we reach a third level of meaning at which the failure of communication is not Fielding's at all but Fowles's, since his story leads him to a conclusion at which words break down and the author can only 'walk out' (p. 244).

The final story is 'The Cloud'. Here we return to France. A group of English people are on holiday in the French countryside. One of them, Catherine, has apparently lost her husband (perhaps by suicide?), and is in a state of deep depression and withdrawal. During the course of the day Catherine makes various attempts – imaginative, discursive, and ultimately sexual – to break out of her isolation and depression. The unexpected and sinister cloud that looms suddenly out of a clear sky, a kind of 'ebony tower' in nature,[12] suggests that she has failed.

Fowles has described 'The Cloud' as his favourite among the stories in the collection (Sage, 1976); though the tale is a gloomy one, there are good reasons for him to be proud of it. In addition to the virtues we have come to expect from Fowles – precise and evocative natural description, suggestive creation of atmosphere, economical plotting – he deploys a new (if sour) realism in his handling of dialogue and character, notably where the children are concerned, together with a relatively open and experimental handling of point of view and story. He has said that the tale was written as 'a deliberate homage to Katherine Mansfield' (Baker, 1974, p. 7, quoted in Olshen, 1978,

p. 105), and her influence can be seen in the impressionistic, prose-poetry style of much of the story.

In many ways 'The Cloud' echoes 'The Ebony Tower' in presenting a kind of twentieth-century parody of *Eliduc*, though in this case the parody is a much more vicious one. The narrative sequence closely models the ten elements of *Eliduc* listed above (p. 89).

Eliduc		'The Cloud'
(a) married man		(Peter)
(b) goes abroad		(to France)
(c) visits isolated building		(the converted mill)
(d) where he finds an old man		(Catherine's dead husband)
(e) and a young girl		(Catherine, aged 27)
(f) man and girl fall in love		(sick sexual challenge on Catherine's part)
(g) couple give in to their feelings		(sordidly)
(h) man keeps self-respect	X	(woman presumably loses self-respect)
(i) girl is rescued	X	(girl is apparently lost)
(j) wife discovers		(Sally suspects)

(X = point of difference between stories)

Here all the narrative elements of *Eliduc* are present, but in a debased or corrupt form. The same is true of the five motifs. In Peter, Sally, and Catherine we have the one man and the two women; in the reactions of Peter and Paul (notably the latter) to Catherine we have the conflict between gallantry and loyalty. In the absences that haunt the story – Peter's wife has 'vanished', Catherine's husband is dead, perhaps by suicide, and Catherine herself goes missing at the end – we have a debased version of the creative withdrawal which is a feature of other tales in the collection. Catherine's inability to scale the walls of her depression constitutes a disastrous failure of communication; and the tale is entirely set in France, the French setting being emphasised by the importance allotted to the ideas of a French intellectual, Roland Barthes.[13]

Despite the uncertain origin of much of the narrative, 'The Cloud' makes many didactic points which will be familiar to us already. In part this is achieved by constantly comparing and evaluating the two sisters, Annabel and Catherine. Annabel's (reasonably) happy, rather matriarchal marriage is compared with Catherine's somewhat necrophiliac matrimonial arrangements ('Having among Graves', p. 291); Annabel likes *The Scholar Gipsy*, a poem which we are asked to admire presumably because (like 'The Cloud') it rejects the modern industrial world, while Catherine is compared to Hamlet, and both criticised, on the grounds of self-pity. Indeed some quite ambitious claims are made for Annabel: she is described, in phrases reminiscent of *The Rainbow* or *To The Lighthouse*, as a 'presiding mother-goddess' (p. 265) and as 'the quiet hub . . . [keeping] the spokes turning' (p. 270). Clearly we are once again being asked to praise 'feminine' qualities of stillness, perception, and insight ('Only women knew now', p. 270) over such 'masculine' characteristics as verbal skill and analytical reasoning. Equally clearly Annabel, rather than the Barthes-quoting Catherine, best embodies these virtues.

These thematic points are only partly successful. To begin with, the messages do not seem quite consistent. If we are to take seriously the story Catherine invents for Emma about Florio and the princess,[14] we have to see both Catherine and the princess as following the lead of the scholar gipsy and retreating from reality into dreams: yet *The Scholar Gipsy* is supposed to be Annabel's poem, not Catherine's. (Indeed the whole claim that *The Scholar Gipsy* is superior to *Hamlet*, while plausible as we read, is likely to bring us up rather sharply on reflection.) More unsatisfactory is the exaggerated use of 'one', a technique, incidentally, which Fowles condemns when Dan uses it in *Daniel Martin*.[15] In 'The Ebony Tower' we can read this as a gentle mockery of David's rather affected style in which the sententious and the slangy cohabit uneasily ('postgraduate acceptance by the fiercely selective Royal College of Art was not something *one jacked in lightly*', p. 38, emphasis added). In 'The Cloud' it reaches epidemic proportions: not only Peter, Annabel, and Catherine but even (in his fleeting appearances) the un-located narrator seem to use it ('One . . . could see Catherine . . . smiling at Sally across her sister', p. 255; 'if one had been a watching bird . . . one could have seen them disappear', p. 304). The effect is not so much distancing as exasperating.[16]

'The Cloud' aims at many targets. It tries to emulate the impressionistic, 'spirit of place' writing of Katherine Mansfield; it plays with shifting and interchanging points of view and with upsetting the reader's expectations; it seeks to create archetypes after the manner of Woolf and Lawrence; it seeks to re-work and transform elements of the other stories in the collection; it tries also to make quite polemical points about historical and social features of the twentieth century.

Whatever the undoubted brilliance of much of its writing, it could not hope to meet such a divergent set of requirements.

Having looked in some detail at the four original works by John Fowles in this collection, it remains to try to assess their value and to locate them in his output. It has already been argued at length that these stories break very little new ground, but are best read as a set of variations on a theme. This is not necessarily a disadvantage: many writers spend their whole literary careers exploring the same few themes. But when we find a writer restricting his range of topics in that way we are entitled to ask whether there is a compensating increase in the depth, intensity, or clarity with which such themes are treated: whether, in fact, we are dealing with a vicious circle or what we might call, for want of a better phrase, a virtuous spiral.

We have seen that 'The Cloud' falters in its stride through trying to do too much. Conversely the most successful story is the one which is least ambitious – 'The Enigma'. In order to appreciate the full point of the story one must apply the title rather carefully. The disappearance of Marcus Fielding is not in the end an enigma; a very plausible explanation is provided within the story, even though it cannot be verified; in this sense Fowles is relatively cautious and conservative in his fictional practice.[17] What is genuinely enigmatic is the missing period of two hours in Isobel's life on the fateful afternoon when Fielding went missing. Jennings's 'test', an appropriate one for a policeman, is to learn to live with indeterminacy and to accept that 'Nice people have instincts as well as duties' (p. 242). The test is set, and passed, discreetly; the story as a whole, like its final sexual episode, is handled with refreshing reticence and delicacy.

Like 'The Enigma', 'Poor Koko' is most successful where it is most straightforward, namely in its treatment of plot and description. The sinister, almost Wellsian undertones of the confrontation are particularly well handled.[18] The chief difficulty facing the reader of 'Poor Koko' lies in deciding what attitude he should adopt towards the narrator. The problem is particularly acute for anyone familiar with Fowles's other writings. On the one hand, it seems that we should support the narrator's attitudes and endorse his proposed solution. In many respects his views are Fowles's own, as is his way of expressing those views. Where the narrator condemns 'the triumph of the visual' (p. 186), Fowles attacks 'a new kind of intellectual . . . [namely] *visuals*' (*A*, pp. 199–200, emphasis in original). The narrator is 'near the end of a lifetime's ambition – a definitive biography and critical account of Thomas Love Peacock' (p. 149), a writer for whom Fowles has repeatedly stated his admiration. And even if we ignore this external evidence, we cannot get over the fact that we have to rely on the narrator for everything – story, analysis, and finally explanation – and that by capturing the relatively wordless burglar in language, by literally having the last word, the narrator symbolically triumphs over him.

Yet the narrator is not a very attractive figure, nor an easy one to identify with. We can leap quite easily over such hurdles as his puniness and cowardice; we can bypass (though with some puzzlement) such ideological differences between creator and character as the latter's indifference to Nature in general and Thomas Hardy in particular (p. 150), his 'hatred of. . . most kinds of physical contact' (p. 153), and the fact that he is a critical rather than a creative writer. But what are we to make of the terrific egotism that pervades the story? It emerges in the narrator's attitude to people ('I have always found my own faults more interesting than other people's virtues', p. 149); in his attitude to literature (he seeks to 'have [the Peacock biography] to [his] credit', p. 149); in the way he rapidly seeks to turn his experience to selfish ends ('I did begin to feel that I had the makings of a story to dine out on for months to come', p. 160). A byproduct of the narrator's egotism is his confidence that he has found the real meaning of his ordeal. The reader, however, may suspect that the real meaning of the events lies elsewhere, closer perhaps to the lesson learnt by Roquentin in *La Nausée* that a life devoted to biography is a wasted life. When the Peacock biography goes into the flames we feel that the experience may turn out to be a cauterising and salutary one, leading the narrator to re-think what is in many ways a very unsatisfactory life. But nothing of the kind takes place. What is resurrected from the flames is not a new and renovated narrator, but simply the old, reconstituted biography: the narrator, having like Louis's courtiers forgotten nothing and learnt nothing, emerges untouched. Fowles has a habit of using unreliable narrators in his fiction, and the smug pretentiousness of this 'Dwarf in Literature' (p. 149) seems to put him squarely in this category. But 'Poor Koko' depends heavily for its meaning on the explanation provided within it. In this case, the narrator's conviction that he has found the right answer is not one that the reader can confidently share.[19]

It remains to consider 'The Ebony Tower', the longest story in the book and the one Fowles has chosen as title piece for the whole collection. As I have tried to show, it exemplifies many of Fowles's most characteristic strengths: Conradi, by no means an uncritical reader of Fowles, speaks of its 'command and subtlety' (1982, p. 84).

My own view, however, is that the story succeeds only partially. There are two reasons for its partial failure: the first springs from an unresolved contradiction within the story, the second from an ambiguity as to how the story should be read. Both reasons have implications for Fowles's work as a whole.

Coëtminais presents David Williams with a choice: should he make love to Diana, or should he remain faithful to his wife Beth? The conflict between love and marriage presented here corresponds to a fundamental antithesis in Fowles's work between freedom and responsibility. His fiction, though ultimately asserting the primacy of freedom, aims at a synthesis of these apparently conflicting pairs: Nicholas ends by freely accepting his responsibility to Alison, just as in the final chapter of *The French Lieutenant's Woman* Charles voluntarily assumes his responsibility to freedom. But this synthesis takes place in an ideal world; Fowles stresses constantly (most notably in *The Magus* and *Mantissa*) that his work is fiction, a temporary domaine rather than a place of permanent residence. This fictionality is thrown into relief when we come to Fowles's comments in *The Aristos* on real life. Here Fowles finds himself unable to carry through into the domestic sphere his otherwise uncompromising support for freedom; instead he praises marriage, rejects adultery, and offers what is in general a strikingly conservative sexual morality.[20] Freedom and responsibility can find their synthesis. They do so, of course, in a harmonious marriage, which may be one reason why Fowles writes in *The Aristos* that 'Marriage is the best general analogy of existing' (*A*, p. 89). But they can also act (as they do in 'The Ebony Tower') as antitheses; it is presumably not accidental that so much of the world's fiction should be about adultery. The resulting conflict, as I have suggested (pp. 93–4 above), is particularly acute for an artist. David Williams is one such, and the conflict becomes in his case that kind of insoluble problem which I have here been calling a contradiction.

The only way of avoiding this contradiction is through a different method of reading. We have seen that *Eliduc* is also fraught with contradiction. This is a fact about the story that we should not ignore; equally, however, we should not be put off by it. We can only appreciate *Eliduc* properly if we read it for what it is, namely romance, and apply to it the canons and the reading expectations appropriate to the genre. Marriage in *Eliduc* is not the focus of sustained attention: it is a symbol, a structural element, in a narrative principally aimed at exploring on different levels the ethic of knighthood. The most convincing way to read 'The Ebony Tower', I suggest, is to approach it as a comparable exploration of the ethic of the artist, and to see marriage functioning in the story as a narrative device, a structural block, rather than as a realistic element and an object of analysis on its own terms.

Such a reading would account for two notable features, one realistic and one symbolic, of the way in which David's marriage is described. Looked at realistically, it seems a cold affair: we are told that he misses Beth, but find singularly little evidence for this assertion, while as a father David is detached to the point of amnesia. If we approach the marriage symbolically, however, much falls into place: it provides for David an excuse, a pretext for not completing his affair with Diana, and for the reader a symbol of David's fundamentally unadventurous nature: 'He was a crypto-husband long before he married' (p. 54). Thus for 'marriage' in 'The Ebony Tower' we should read 'playing safe', 'sticking to the familiar', 'running away from danger'; and for 'adultery' – or as Fowles calls it elsewhere in a less value-laden phrase, the 'illicit sexual relationship' (*A*, p. 160) – we should read everything that is brave, free, and dangerous. Yet the fact remains that however neatly such a contradiction can be presented on the symbolic plane, it remains discordantly unresolved in the apparently realistic context of 'The Ebony Tower'.

The romantic and symbolic reading proposed here, whatever its truth to life, has at least the merit of consistency. Unfortunately Fowles has done his best to rule out this line of approach. He has described the story as 'a kind of *realistic* version of *The Magus*' (Conradi, 1982, p. 79, emphasis added); he has given it a twentieth-century setting, playing down the very elements which enable us to read (for example) *Eliduc* non-naturalistically; and by giving such weight to the final third, with its solemn reflections on art and life, he has shifted the whole tone of the story away from romance.

On these realistic terms, I do not see that 'The Ebony Tower' can succeed; its morality is too incoherent and its contradictions too obvious. It is impossible to believe, as the narrative asserts (p. 113), that the value of David's art depends on a chance act of intercourse with a girl he will probably never see again. We will fully appreciate the story only if we read the whole Coëtminais episode as 'the symbol, not the crux of the matter' (p. 110). Such a reading pushes us back towards *Eliduc* as the dominant story in the book. It reminds us also of Fowles's assertion, which stands as an epigraph to this chapter, that the mood, theme, and setting of the whole collection spring from the Celtic romance.

6 *Daniel Martin*

'. . . if I could ever hope to describe it, it would have to be beyond
staging or filming. They'd just . . . betray the real thing again.'
'What's "it"?'
'God knows, Jenny. The real history of what I am?'

(DM, p. 20)

[*Daniel Martin*] was an attempt . . . to do a kind of English and
twentieth-century *Sentimental Education*, that is a picture of your
own generation.

(Plomley, 1981)

Fowles's next fiction, *Daniel Martin*, was published in 1977. Placed,
like *The Magus*, in a modern setting, it deals with a wide variety of
contemporary concerns, and ranges geographically from California to
Dorset and from Oxford to the Syrian desert. The fiftyish central
figure, the Daniel Martin of the title, is also the narrator, and the book
recounts with many flashbacks and false starts the various influences
that have led him to write it. As a young man Dan spent a happy and
successful three years at Oxford, then married and started writing
plays; but his marriage collapsed and he took up a career as a
Hollywood scriptwriter. When the book starts, he is summoned from
Hollywood back to Oxford to the bedside of an estranged friend from
his Oxford days, now dying of cancer. Contact having been re-
established and peace restored, his friend commits suicide. The
mainspring of the subsequent action is Dan's growing love for Jane, the
dead man's widow. This love, first experienced in a brief fling when
both were students, ripens in middle age into a force which enables
Dan both to take stock of his own life (which will involve giving up
screen biography in favour of written autobiography) and to rescue
Jane from the sterile self-absorption that threatens to engulf her.

   As the first epigraph to this chapter suggests, the principal aim of
Daniel Martin, in its narrator's eyes at least, is an autobiographical one.
But (as is clear from the second epigraph) the book has wider

ambitions. *Daniel Martin* is crowded with characters: screenwriters and producers, journalists and comedians, gardeners and professors, actresses and country squires. One aim of presenting such a gallery of types is to investigate the difference between the American and the English character, a theme which has long intrigued Dan's creator (see for example 'On Being English But Not British'). A second aim is to give a kind of cross-section of English society at a particular point in history: and this aim in turn feeds back into the autobiographical one, since one of the arguments of the book is that Dan's virtues and failings, especially the latter, are characteristic of the whole of his generation.

A third concern of the book is the contrast between film and the novel, a contrast presented, not surprisingly, entirely to the benefit of the latter (see especially p. 371). It is thus rather paradoxical that Fowles should have chosen to use, in setting out the novel, a number of techniques – flashback, flashforward, intercutting – whose very names indicate their specifically filmic origin. In addition he has adopted a rather unsettling process of shifting tense (from present to past) and person (from first to third) without warning and apparently without consistency; and he has further sought to emphasise static design at the expense of linear plot by making the last sentence of the book refer forwards – or backwards – to its first. The result is a work which cannot easily be read in the rapid, linear, and progressive way in which we expect to read novels. Fowles himself is well aware of this.[1] The technique works unevenly in the book as a whole, but a brilliant example of what it can do at its best (together with a foretaste of many other concerns of the book) can be found in the passage which follows:

Later.
He is alone among the highest beeches, over the stooked and now empty field, the marly combe; where he comes each spring to find the first moschatel, strange little transient four-faces, smelling of musk. Another mystery, his current flower and emblem, for reasons he cannot say. The sun in the extreme west, as he likes it best. Its slanting rays reveal the lands in a pasture-field on the other side of the valley, the parallel waves where an ox-plough once went many centuries before; and where he must pay a visit soon, childish, but another of his secret flowers, the little honeycomb-scented orchid *Spiranthes spiralis*, blooms on the old meadow there about now. He clings to his knowledges; signs of birds, locations of plants, fragments of Latin and folklore, since he lacks so much else. The

leaves of the beeches are translucent in the westering sun. A
wood-pigeon coos, a nuthatch whistles somewhere close above.   15
He sits with his back to a beech-trunk, staring down through
foliage at the field. Without past or future, purged of tenses,
collecting this day, pregnant with being. Unharvested, yet one with
this land; and that was why he had been so afraid. It wasn't death, the
agony in the mower's blades, the scream and red stumps . . . but   20
dying, dying before the other wheat was ripe.
    Inscrutable innocent, already in exile.
    Down, half masked by leaves. Point of view of the hidden bird.
    I feel in his pocket and bring out a clasp-knife; plunge the blade in
the red earth to clean it of the filth from the two rabbits he has   25
gutted; slit; liver, intestines, stench. He stands and turns and begins
to carve his initials on the beech-tree. Deep incisions in the bark,
peeling the grey skin away to the sappy green of the living stem.
Adieu, my boyhood and my dream.
    Close shot.   30
    D.H.M.
    And underneath: *21 Aug 42*.
                                        (p. 16, emphases in original)

This extract consists of the concluding lines of the first chapter, 'The
Harvest'. Daniel, the fifteen-year-old son of the local vicar, is helping
with the harvest on a remote Devon farm. The chapter records the
gradual progression of the day through noon to sunset as the patient
work of reaping and stooking proceeds to its close. It is interrupted by
two violent contrasts. The first is the sudden irruption of a German
bomber which has just carried out a hit-and-run raid on Torquay and
now charges terrifyingly low over the field in order to avoid the fighters
and anti-aircraft batteries on the coast. The second is the organised
slaughter of the rabbits trapped in the diminishing rectangle of wheat
left by the binder. In the course of this, one rabbit is caught in the
blades and has its hind legs sliced off: it is Dan who finds it, finishes it
off by breaking its neck, and 'casually . . . throws the corpse towards a
pile of others' (p. 14).
    As ever when Fowles is describing actual scenes, the chapter is
wonderfully evocative. The sights and sounds, the sensations – the
soreness of tired wrists and scratched forearms, the 'sour green' of
cider – are made intensely real to the reader; traditional methods of
threshing and stooking are explained with unobtrusive precision.
    Descriptions of such rural, traditional activities can hardly fail to

evoke a timeless quality, and this is heightened in the case of a harvest by its cyclical and ritual overtones. What seem to stand out from this tranquil picture are the two episodes of violence. In fact, however, both are essential pointers to what follows. The slaughter of the rabbits occurs between the annual ceremony of the harvest, on the one hand, and on the other the tea set out 'as ritual as Holy Communion' (p. 15); moreover the village poacher who presides over the occasion with his dog is said to 'honour' it with 'an ancient presence . . . quasi-divine' (p. 14). Thus we are reminded of the presence of death, and of the corresponding brevity of life, even in this rural idyll; Dan must harvest his own crop, the experiences of his own life, before it is too late. Similarly the German bomber, though apparently intrusive and incongruous, is not so. It points to the inescapable impact of historical events on the life of every individual, to the unavoidable connections between public and private, and in so doing it discreetly announces the second explicit theme of the book.

Much of the impact of this chapter is achieved through style, as I have tried to show elsewhere (Loveday, 1980). The chapter as a whole features a number of different tenses (for example past on p. 7, present on p. 8, future on p. 9) and a high proportion of verbless sentences (the second paragraph on p. 9 has five sentences but only one verb). One effect of these oddities of tense is to cast doubt on the exact status of the events described. Genette, in his discussion of Proust's use of tenses in *A la recherche du temps perdu* (1972, pp. 145–82), shows how Proust uses the imperfect tense of repeated action to describe events which can only have happened once, thus creating a kind of dream-like intermediate category which Genette calls the 'pseudo-iterative' (1972, p. 152). Here, too, I think, Fowles is seeking in his style as well as his theme to blur the boundaries between what is unique and what is recurrent.

It is against this background that we must see the extract quoted on pp. 104–5 above. It begins ('Later') with a reference to time: the one-word paragraph, acting like a sub-heading, also makes a break from what has gone before and announces a shift of tone. And it ends ('And underneath: *21 Aug 42*') with another reference to time, in this case absolutely precise, locating us in history rather than in ritual. In between, however, the use of tenses continues to be very unusual: to start with, mostly present (despite the obvious pastness of the event being narrated), but by the end – specifically the last five sentences – entirely without tensed verbs of any kind. The aim – one that springs naturally from Dan's autobiographical purpose – is to contrast two forms of experience: first, the intense immediacy of reality, conveyed partly by the present tense, but still more by the unstructured rawness achieved by leaving out verbs entirely; and secondly, the equally intense effort of memory to locate, recapture, and analyse moments of experience and make them yield up their full value.

After its abrupt start, making a shift from the main movement of Chapter 1, this short *coda* develops an increasingly close focus on the central character, so far known to us only as 'Danny' (p. 15), and on the preoccupations which obsess him and his yet-to-be-written book. Dan himself – characteristically, as we shall see – is in a position of isolation (line 2), privilege (line 2), and secrecy (line 23). His knowledge of himself is shown as developing, yet still very far from complete (lines 5–6). What he is watching with such puzzled intensity is the field where the harvest has been gathered in. On the one hand he longs to harvest his own experiences, to fulfil his own creative potential; this, surely, is the significance of the flood of literary, biological, and botanical metaphors in lines 17–21. On the other hand, such harvesting is destructive: defenceless creatures get horribly mutilated and what is left is only an 'empty field' (line 3). These dissonant overtones are amplified in lines 24–9. When Dan carves his initials on a tree, 'peeling the grey skin away to the sappy green of the living stem' (line 28), he is presumably prefiguring what he will subsequently do as author of an autobiography, stripping off the accretions of age to reach his green and sappy youth, the living core of his own personality. But the knife which he uses stinks of violence and death, and the incident is followed, not by a salutation, but by a farewell (line 29). We are reminded of Conchis's aphorism that 'An answer is always a form of death' (*M*, p. 626).

Fowles throws the last three lines into even higher relief by giving each a paragraph to itself. The contrast between these verbless, and thus in a sense timeless, sentences, and the very precise date which ends the chapter, has already been discussed. But a further important question also surfaces here, namely point of view. The chapter began with an unspecified, presumably authorial, dictum on the subject of 'Whole sight' (p. 7): it ends, whether as complement or as contradiction, with 'Later' (line 1), 'Point of view' (line 23), and 'Close shot' (line 30), cinematic terms Dan is unlikely to have known in 1942 and which unsettlingly suggest a narrator contriving to look over the shoulder of his own younger self.[2] Finally, having stayed firmly in the third person throughout, it suddenly shifts twice into the first person (lines 24 and 29) before backing off entirely into an unattributable final sentence.

This lyrical first chapter, with its brooding proleptic conclusion, is followed by what seems at first a total break – a leap to California, night, a flat high above the Hollywood skyline, a conversation between lovers. In theme, however, the chapters are very largely continuous. We are still with Dan (though we do not find out his full name till p. 24); he still wants, not simply to 'capture . . . reality' (p. 19), but specifically to tap his own life, to peel back 'layers of lies' in search of 'the green illusion' (p. 18). Chapter 1 lays out the project: from Chapter 2 to the final Chapter 46, despite many twists and turns, flashbacks and false starts, Dan will be trying to write 'The real history of what I am' (p. 20).

As the first two chapters indicate, Dan must learn about himself: the unfolding of the plot reveals that he must also work upon his character. He needs first to clear up his family background. The long early chapter on Dan's childhood ('The Umbrella', pp. 86–102) is principally an account of his unsatisfactory relationship with his father. Conflict with his father (prefigured by the reference to 'his terrible Oedipal secret' on p. 15) is less important than conflict with what his father stands for – silence, reticence, 'fear . . . of any nakedness of feeling' (p. 88; note also 'do not demonstrate so, Daniel' on p. 89). It is a measure of the success of his father's influence that Daniel cannot combat his father face-to-face; his father dies when Dan is at Oxford (p. 88) and the long campaign to throw off the influence of his father and of the vengeful God who 'had my father's face' (p. 423) must be waged posthumously. Not surprisingly, this attempt to settle accounts with the dead proves infinitely more long drawn out and inconclusive than the alternative course, namely a stand-up fight with the living.

A further problem, particularly well diagnosed in Jenny's contributions, is Dan's infatuation with loss, an aspect of his character which he relates to the loss of his mother when he was only three (p. 539). In practice this comes out in two ways. Firstly, his emotional life follows a consistent pattern of 'seeking . . . for situations that carried their own death in them from the beginning' (p. 644): his relationships are always either doomed (Nancy, Nell, Jenny) or transient (Miriam and Marjory, Andrea), and the early chance of permanence with Jane is not taken up. Secondly, where his working life is concerned he somehow contrives to select not only a job (script writer), but also a medium (film) and a place (Hollywood), which he cordially despises. Once again Dan is choosing failure over success – a strategy which, though more rewarding than it sounds, places him in a long line of passive Fowlesian heroes.[3]

The charms of this lotus-eater world Dan must and does learn to reject. In the world of work he decides that his true vocation is not so much for biography (Kitchener) as for autobiography, not so much for writing as for writing himself. In his emotional life he finally opts for a partner who will be his equal rather than his inferior. And in both (notably in his long Middle East courtship of the unresponsive Jane) he rejects the easy in favour of the difficult and dangerous, thus initiating a fundamental change of behaviour from passive to active.

The book that Dan writes is characterised, as we saw in the extract above, by a number of quite striking features of style and structure (of a kind that Lukacs, whose writings are extensively quoted in the text, would probably dismiss as 'formalistic experimentation', p. 559). Chief among these are the alternation of first- and third-person narration; the shifting use of tenses; and the *dérèglement systématique* of the order of events.

The changing use of person in *Daniel Martin* has caused critics some difficulty. Some of the 46 chapters are almost entirely third person (1–3, 5–6, 17, 32, 36–46); some are almost entirely first person (8, 10, 12–13, 15–16, 18, 25, 27–9, 31 of Dan's; 4, 21, part of 28, and 34 written by Jenny); some are substantially mixed (7, 9, 11, 14, 19–20, 22–4, 26, 30, 33, 35). Beyond the obvious points that as far as Dan's own contributions are concerned, the book begins (Chapters 1–6, pp. 7–71) and ends (Chapters 36–46, pp. 510–704) in the third person, it is very difficult to make anything positive of this oscillation, an oscillation particularly puzzling when it occurs in the course of a single sentence, as in the extract quoted above.[4] One possibility, to which I shall return below, is that Dan is trying to emphasise the way in which he is involved in his own story, so that the third-person objectivity he seeks is inseparably mixed with first-person subjectivity: another is that this fragmented style is an embodiment of the 'balkanized [that is fragmented] consciousness' (Conradi, 1982, p. 95) of Dan's whole generation.

The second feature, the alternation of present and past tenses, is likewise almost impossible to account for in detail, despite the fact that it is discussed at some length in the text. The early Hollywood chapters (2 and 5) are set in the present tense, which seems to stress their link with the film world ('the natural grain of [film] . . . was a constant flowing through nowness, was chained to the present image', p. 371).

Unfortunately for this theory the end of Chapter 8 (pp. 100–2), recounting an incident when Dan was only eleven, is also set in the present, as are occasional episodes from the 'Phillida' chapter (for example pp. 392–3). It seems once again that no single explanation will cover all instances of this technique.

Finally there is the question of the order in which events are related: in Genette's terms, of *récit* as opposed to *histoire* (see Chapter 4, note 6 above). Here again we begin with an impression of incoherence. The first chapter is set in rural Devon in 1942; the second in Hollywood in the 1970s; the third in Oxford in the 1950s; and the fourth, which is written by someone else (Jenny) about someone else (Mr Wolfe), in a jumbled mixture of London and Hollywood. In this case, however, a pattern of sorts begins to emerge. There are five main time strata in the book: Dan's childhood, his adolescence, his time at Oxford, his married and post-married life, and the events surrounding Anthony's suicide. Obviously these are not presented in strict chronological order; but neither are they completely jumbled. We begin in Dan's adolescence (Chapter 1, p. 7), at a time when the main lines of his character and hence of the impending action are already formed. Thereafter the events of the main story make up the increasingly continuous narrative spine of the book (Chapters 2, 5, 7, 10, 12–15, 17–20, 23–7, 29, 31–3, 35–46) interspersed with clusters of explanatory flashbacks: childhood (Chapter 8, pp. 86–102), adolescence (Chapter 1, pp. 7–16, and Chapter 30, pp. 387–428), Oxford (Chapters 3, 6, and 9), and finally marriage (Chapters 11, 14, 16, and 22) and the ensuing purchase of Thorncombe (Chapters 13 and 29).

Yet in a sense all this analysis is misplaced. Rather than distinguishing these three techniques and then probing them minutely to see how they work, we should perhaps be recombining them and then looking at their overall effect. What Dan is seeking, there can be no doubt, is expressed in the first sentence of the book and pre-figured in its last, namely 'whole sight'.[5] The book repeatedly draws a contrast between the 'cramped, linear and progressive' time structure of films and the more relaxed and extended structure of the novel, which is 'dense, interweaving, treating time as horizontal, like a skyline' (p. 371). The three elements under discussion – the identity of the narrator, the time standpoint he is writing from, and the order of the events he is describing – are all aspects of narration rather than of narrative. Jumbling them up as Dan does calls attention to narration, to the process of telling rather than the events themselves. It thereby encourages us to free ourselves from the narrator's grip and to scan his story for evidence of bias.

It is also intended to free us from the tyranny of sequence whereby events are seen only in relation to what happens immediately before or after them: to free us from plot in order that we can better appreciate design (these terms are defined in Chapter 3, Note 3 above). We have already seen this at work in the way Chapters 1 and 2, over thirty years apart in time, are placed next to each other for thematic purposes. Another example is the three chapters which Dan has placed at the centre, numerically speaking, of the book: of the three, 'Hollow Men' and 'Solid Daughter' (pp. 286 and 296 respectively) are in chronological order, but they are preceded by a flashback chapter, 'Interlude' (p. 268), which thereby gains in significance what is loses in plausibility.

But perhaps what is most important about all these stylistic and structural features is not their presence in the novel as a whole but their absence from a certain part of it, that is the final twelve chapters (pp. 510–704), from Dan and Jane's departure for Cairo, through their coming together in the ruins of Palmyra, to the parting of Dan and Jenny on Hampstead Heath. These are firmly and unblinkingly recounted in the past tense and the third person. The possible implications of this return to convention I shall leave for discussion in the conclusion to this chapter.

When we move on from style and structure to characterisation, one of the most striking features of the book is the treatment of Jenny. Like Miranda in *The Collector*, she writes her own text; unlike Miranda, she is actually encouraged to do so. Miranda's story fulfils at least two important functions in *The Collector*: it provides a moral norm, and it acts as a cross-check on the factual accuracy of Clegg's account. Jenny's 'contributions' (Chapters 4, 21, part of 28, and 34), though briefer, are in a sense even more significant. In the first place they give us essential critical information about Dan. Where Dan praises his own Robin Hood mentality, Jenny condemns him as a 'professional melancholic' (p. 264); and his view of the disastrous day at Tsankawi (pp. 361–73) is quite different from the briefer but much more perceptive account by Jenny that immediately follows it (pp. 373–4), the closing sentence of which might stand as the motto of the book – 'You *knew*. You should have said *something*' (italics in original).

But the second function of Jenny's contributions renders them unique in Fowles's work – and, judging by his reaction, in Dan's too. In 'A Third Contribution' (pp. 480–95; it is actually her fourth) Jenny apparently invents a scene on her own initiative. Elsewhere in Fowles's fiction we have characters recording events (Miranda in *The Collector*, Jenny herself in *Daniel Martin*) and even originating action (Sarah in *The French Lieutenant's Woman*). Here we see a character usurping the privileged position of the author and actually creating narrative.[6] Whatever the implications for Fowles, the message for Dan is clear: he has a tendency to treat his female acquaintances, in Jenny's words, as 'something in [his] script' (p. 495) or 'figment[s] in [his] imagination' (p. 699), and to forget that 'cattle' – the word used both by Jenny of herself, and by Dan of Miriam and Marjory – can have 'rather good relationships' (p. 480) of their own.[7] With the obtuseness that seems a hallmark of the Fowlesian hero, Dan entirely misses the point by dismissing Jenny's narrative as a 'little document' (p. 496); thereby of course he bears out all Jenny's criticisms of him.

The chief aim of Dan's pursuit of 'whole sight' – an aim in which he is aided, albeit inconclusively, by the contributions from Jenny mentioned above – is to get his own past into perspective. But the phrase has other important implications. A major purpose of the book, as we have seen, is to arrive at an understanding of Dan's (and Fowles's) whole generation, and to understand the connection between Dan as an individual and the history of his time. This is why *Daniel Martin* includes such a multiplicity of characters; it is also why the book devotes so much attention to two political thinkers, Lukacs and Gramsci, whose works centre on the indissoluble links between the individual and the group.

Fowles has given particular prominence to Gramsci by placing an extract from the latter's *Prison Notebooks* as the epigraph to *Daniel Martin*. The extract, whose theme is picked up on p. 99, highlights the awkward position in which Fowles sees his generation, split between the lost certainties of the Victorians and Edwardians ('the old is dying'), and the laid-back confidence of the generation of Jenny, Caro, and Roz. The other extract from Gramsci which features in the book is similarly placed in a highly significant position, namely in the very chapter in which Dan and Jane learn of Anthony's suicide (pp. 221–2).

Still greater prominence is given to the (rather more approachable) theories of the Marxist critic Georg Lukacs.[8] At Jane's prompting Dan reads the anthology *Lukacs on Critical Realism* during the Nile trip, and is sufficiently impressed to quote from it three times (once on p. 559 and twice on p. 617). The first extract (from *The Meaning of Contemporary Realism*) forms part of an extended argument in which Lukacs examines the work of two writers, Franz Kafka and Thomas

Mann, in order to ask what attitude the writer of prose fiction should adopt towards the history of his own time. In Kafka's withdrawn, 'morbid' writing, on or beyond the margin of the credible, Lukacs detects a surrender to *Angst*. This, he says, is because Kafka views man in isolation from society, so that social and historical events, seen as beyond the individual's control, inevitably appear to him as monstrous and meaningless. The early novels of Thomas Mann, on the other hand, are in Lukacs's view fully realist in the proper sense (or senses) of the word. In the narrow sense they are realist in as much as they are plausible: characters do not (as they do in Kafka) unexpectedly turn into cockroaches. But for Lukacs realism has a special extra meaning. 'Realist' writers are those whose work reflects the 'real' historical forces at work in their society, and embodies these forces in representative (Lukacs's term is 'typical') characters. Such writers do not have to welcome these forces: indeed, Lukacs's favourite realists – Scott, Balzac, Flaubert, and to a lesser extent Dickens and even Mann himself – were for the most part profoundly opposed to the forces of change which Lukacs detects in their work. Lukacs's point is simply that if a writer 'escapes from the life of his time into a realm of abstraction', the consequence will be nothing but 'formalistic experimentation' and '*Angst*' (*DM*, p. 559).

Fowles's determination to confront the life of his time and to turn away from the realm of abstraction is unmistakably clear in *Daniel Martin*. There is, first, the way in which he handles character. It is no surprise to find Dan himself equipped with a very full background – Fowles's heroes are usually provided with all the credentials of realism – though Dan's childhood, adolescence, and early maturity are dealt with in unusual detail. What is new is the creation of a whole gallery of characters intended to serve as 'types', representatives of particular historical or national features. The principal historical situation the book is trying to dramatise is the split between the nineteenth and the twentieth century.

This theme, announced in the Gramsci epigraph and expanded on p. 99, dominates Dan both in his experiences and in the order he tries retrospectively to impose on them. It also dominates the treatment of many of the characters, notably Barney Dillon. But there are a number of other substantial historical themes in the book – national character and political commitment, to name but two – and in each case characters are created whose sole function appears to be typicality.[9]

A second development of the Lukacs line is to be found in the way *Daniel Martin* insists on its right to end happily. Throughout the book –

much to his embarrassment – Dan is blessed by almost uninterrupted good fortune. As his idea for a novel starts to take shape he foresees a conflict between his happy circumstances and the unhappy ending which he feels obliged to provide. In the chapter entitled 'In the Orchard of the Blessed' he comes to what he describes as 'the most important decision of his life' (p. 454). Part of this decision seems to be that he will write about himself rather than, for example, Simon Wolfe. But the remainder of this chapter makes two claims on behalf of this decision: first, that 'though [such a decision] may seem a supremely self-centred one, it is in fact a supremely socialist one', and secondly that it involves a rejection of 'existentialist nausea' (namely *Angst*) in favour of 'the real' (p. 454). In Lukacsian terms, that is, Dan will be a typical character, and *Daniel Martin* will be a realist novel.[10]

The arguments of *The Meaning of Contemporary Realism* are put forward in *Daniel Martin* very much as given. But as readers we are entitled to ask how Lukacs can be so sure that the ultimate criterion of value in contemporary fiction is its correspondence with political reality. Why should Thomas Mann, the historical realist, be intrinsically superior to Franz Kafka, who was not trying to write historically 'realistic' novels at all?

The answer, I think, lies in Lukacs's commitment to Marxism, though not necessarily in the obvious sense. As Frye points out, critics have long sought to ground the study of literature outside literature itself – in morality, in biography, in psychology, or, in the case of Marxist critics, in politics. Such a self-contradictory insistence that literature is worth studying, but only from a non-literary standpoint, is an example of what Frye calls anxiety. Lukacs's concept of typicality, according to which the yardstick of a character's literary value is his ability to provide us with historical and political insights, is a good example of such anxiety at work. So are the arguments put forward in *The Meaning of Contemporary Realism*, since they force Lukacs to measure both Mann and Kafka – both of whom, let it be said at once, Lukacs obviously appreciates and admires very greatly – by the same non-literary yardstick, and to contradict his own literary experience by finding Kafka wanting. An alternative view, grounded within the institution of literature, might argue that Mann and Kafka are not trying to do the same thing, and therefore cannot be judged by the same standards; that since they are writing within different genres, broadly speaking one realist and the other fantastic, it makes little sense to compare them and no sense at all to rank them against each other. The most one could do would be to indicate a preference for one genre over the other: but such a preference, if intended to serve the extra-literary purposes that literature can be turned to, would have no serious literary application.

The rise of the realist novel brought in its train a shift in critical taste, as a result of which romance and fantasy, forms at the other end of the spectrum of prose fiction, fell into critical disfavour. It is thus not surprising that Lukacs should see the literary scene in terms of a struggle between novel and romance, history and fantasy. But it is rather striking that a writer such as Fowles, a story-teller and romancer if ever there was one, should so under-rate his own craft.

Whatever the views of his creator, Dan retains a stubborn belief that public decisions must spring from private convictions. This emerges in two principal ways. The first is Dan's decision to write about himself (and in the related confidence, evidenced in the passage quoted on p. 114 above, that this decision is in itself 'supremely socialist'). The second is the way in which Jane's political aspirations, a recurrent theme in the latter half of the book, can only be realised when her personal life is fulfilled. Political activity for her is not a form of self-sacrifice or self-abnegation but a means of self-expression; she is doing her own thing (to use an appropriately sixties phrase), but in public rather than in private. Both these points are anticipated in the passages from Gramsci which crop up at a heavily charged point in the book, the moment when Anthony's suicide is announced. Gramsci has written, and Jane has heavily underscored, the phrase 'a new ethical political force and a source of new initiatives' (p. 221). The placing of 'ethical' before 'political' – of the personal commitment before its public expression – is obviously crucial.

We have seen that Fowles sets himself two distinct aims in *Daniel Martin*: to give a coherent portrayal of the title character, and to depict, through the use of 'typical' characters, the political life of his generation. Unfortunately it must be admitted that *Daniel Martin* does not achieve these ambitious aims. Indeed its shortcomings are embarrassingly obvious – painfully so for anyone who knows and loves Fowles's work at its best. In the first place it does not begin to match Flaubert's achievement in *L'Education sentimentale* of giving a synoptic view of the political life of a generation. Its principal characters – Anthony, Jane, Nell, Andrew, Barney, Dan himself – may indeed form a representative selection, but what they represent is only a minute slice, the Oxford elite (even Cambridge is omitted), of the generation that grew up after the war.[11] Andrew, succouring his flock and shielding his work-force from the blight of trade unionism (pp. 344–5), seems more like a reincarnation of Charles's uncle than a figure from the twentieth century: Compton is like a miraculously preserved Winsyatt, the familiar evolutionary metaphors recur (p. 346), and even the divorced Nell, the woman Andrew unexpectedly marries, might be described with the same phrase used for Bella Tomkins, 'a thruster' (*FLW*, p. 185).[12] The English characters resoundingly fail to achieve typicality in any sense Lukacs would have accepted, and the guest stars never seem to have any organic connection with the body of the book.

It is equally difficult to make sense of Dan's political position. (Jane's, a Fabian and anti-clerical subspecies of North Oxford liberalism, is much more consistent both with itself and with her low-key lifestyle.) On the one hand, Dan loathes the Tory politician Fenwick, deplores the smug self-centredness of the wealthy European passengers on the Nile cruise, has 'read Marcuse' (p. 440), and ends by becoming 'a fully paid-up member of the Labour Party' (p. 700). On the other, he maintains a steady elitist front throughout the Nile trip against Jane's egalitarianism; he clearly admires Andrew for the dogged way he maintains his feudal grip on Compton (pp. 344–5), and correspondingly attributes much of the backwardness of the *fellaheen* to their 'lack of rural landed gentry' (p. 570); he revels in his privileged freedom as a writer (p. 309); and he praises the political nihilism of the Egyptian comic Ahmed Sabry, a fellow-member of what Dan calls in another context 'one of the most distinctive clubs in the world . . . that of the political cynic' (p. 513). One could pass over these inconsistencies without comment if only Dan would do the same, but he insists on thrusting them under our noses. Despite the 'political cynicism' claimed in the quotation above, enormous stress is laid on socialism throughout the book. The prominence given to Gramsci and Lukacs is presumably intended to show that both literature and politics can usefully be analysed from the same committed standpoint; and certainly Fowles has enlisted powerful forces in his support. Yet how, if he really believes with Lukacs and Gramsci that humanity is one and indivisible, can he approvingly quote Beckett (a writer whose work is totally out of step with everything Lukacs stands for) and claim that 'the bedrock of the human condition' is 'the loneliness of each' (p. 260)?

Nor, alas, can the book be said to succeed very much better in its other aim, that of presenting the 'real history' of what Dan is. Certainly the book amasses huge quantities of material from which a real history might be constructed: but there is no evidence of the kind of sifting and arranging which such a history would require. The chaotic jumble of Dan's political views is a case in point, and brings me on to what is perhaps the greatest of the many difficulties with which this novel confronts the sympathetic and well-intentioned reader. This is the fatal problem of whether Dan is teacher or learner.

Fowles's earlier works keep the two categories well apart. There is no doubt in *The Magus* that Conchis is doing the teaching and Nicholas (at least at the time) the learning; in *The French Lieutenant's Woman* Charles and his creator are sufficiently distinct for one acute critic to have remarked that Fowles really rather dislikes his character (McSweeney, 1978, p. 32); and 'The Ebony Tower', as we have seen, describes a lesson unlearned. So much of *Daniel Martin* is given over to Dan's reflections on what *The Hitch Hiker's Guide to the Galaxy* calls 'Life, the Universe, and Everything', that it seems we are supposed to take him as a teacher. In a number of ways, some of which I shall try to indicate, this is less than satisfactory.

One of the principal themes of *Daniel Martin* is national character. Briefly, the Americans are characterised as open but shallow, the British as secretive but deep. The book seems to be working towards some kind of synthesis of these views. Dan has extensive experience of America, and much of Jane's childhood was spent there (we are reminded that on p. 367 of *The French Lieutenant's Woman* America is described as 'home'). Both Dan and Jane have a lot to discover about themselves (they are deep) but must get to work to bring it all to the surface (they need to be open). Yet the book veers sharply away from this synthesis towards a massive reinforcement of the Robin Hood side of Englishness; it is almost as if what had initially appeared as the disease (one thinks of Dan's sustained attack on his father's reticence) had suddenly been hailed as the cure.

Jane and Dan are quite explicitly settling into a very English, indeed very Oxford, world. It seemed at first that Anthony stood as a symbol of Oxford values seen as an over-refined, rather Bloomsbury ethical system, and that his suicide represented a rejection of that claustrophobic self-regard in favour of a fresh breeze from across the Atlantic. But the references to 'right feeling' strategically sown in the early part of the book and copiously reaped in its concluding pages cause us increasingly to doubt this reading. This in turn calls into question the whole meaning of Anthony's death, and by extension of Oxford itself as it is used in the book. When in the final chapter Dan speaks to Jenny of 'a world of value-systems, prejudices, repressions, *false notions of faith and freedom*, that ... she could hardly comprehend' (p. 698, emphasis added), do we take it that he is moving out of this world – or back into it? Had he been merely mistaken in Chapter 14 when he described Oxford as 'Not a city, but an incest' (p. 170)?

This in turn brings in a yet more damaging ambiguity inherent in Dan's attitude to love. Briefly, the book proposes two alternative attitudes to love. The first, short-term and hedonistic, is embodied in two inset tales: the story of Miriam and Marjory (introduced as 'a fable', p. 270), and the episode between Jenny, Steve, and Kate recounted in 'A Third Contribution' (pp. 480–95). The second attitude is more loving (for want of a better word) and aims at permanence: it is embodied in the 'Phillida' chapter (pp. 387–428) and in the Dan-Jane romance which forms the backbone of the book. For reasons too numerous and too obvious to rehearse, we need be in no doubt as to which attitude Dan ends up by supporting. But it seems either perverse or just plain careless, in a book celebrating the redemptive power of Agape,[13] that the narrator should not have read through his text and deleted, or at least qualified, remarks such as 'love is a sickness of my generation. Not yours' (p. 49), or, more damaging still, 'impermanence adds a zest to experience no fixed marriage can ever achieve' (p. 370)!

It is perhaps worth persevering with the notion that Dan is not so much a bad philosopher as a bad, or careless, writer. Despite its many merits, the style of *Daniel Martin* is terribly uneven. Much of it is grossly over-written (see Conradi, 1982, pp. 97–8, for examples); there is the triviality of the family chitchat exchanged within the 'loose, warm web of clan' (p. 250) and the numbing, sub-*Reader's Digest* banality of the philosophising on the Nile ('They decided it was because the river, like the Bible, was a great poem, and rich in still relevant metaphors', p. 551). Worse still, I think, is the structural redundancy of much of the book. The 'Phillida' episode has much to commend it, but it tells us nothing about Dan that we did not already know; Professor Kirnberger, with his Conchis-like pronouncements and his headbanging jokes, seems to have wandered into the story from another book. Above all it is never clear what function Thorncombe is supposed to have. It is dangled before us throughout the book, alternatively picked up and put down, minutely analysed and then written off, praised as a sacred combe and then blamed as a mere vale of thorns – and the end of this extended preamble is simply that Dan and Jane will 'use it as before' (p. 700)!

I have tried to show that Dan makes an unsatisfactory teacher. Is there anything to be gained by injecting a dose of irony into our reading and treating him as a learner, slowly proceeding across the book towards self-knowledge and 'right feeling'?

In the first place, many of the criticisms of his performance as a teacher apply equally damagingly to any notion that he learns during the course of the book. There just does not seem to be any evidence to bear out such a claim. I do not base this apparently ungenerous judgement on the contradictions in Dan's attitudes to love, to politics, or to 'right feeling', because where all these are concerned there is in the closing pages a change at least in his actions, even if this change does not seem to carry over into the narrator who will then write the chapter that precedes these closing pages. Nor am I basing it on his relationship with Jenny. Certainly they form a rather queasy couple. Jenny begins by asserting that she picked Dan because 'I always felt safer when there was something in lovers I could despise' (pp. 46–7); Dan increasingly admits (to all and sundry, moreover, before breaking it to Jenny) that the relationship has no future, that it is based on mutual exploitation; yet they end by playing a very romantic final scene on Hampstead Heath. This relationship and its puzzling ending (as also the inflated rhetoric Dan uses to describe it) can best be understood, I think, in the light of the penultimate chapter of *L'Education sentimentale*, the farewell of Frédéric and Mme Arnoux: that is, by laying the emphasis solidly on 'playing' and 'scene' ('he also knew she was acting, though bravely: because she must', p. 700).

The real bar to any view that Dan has sorted himself out by the end of the book is simply his persistent untruthfulness. We are caught up in this as early as Chapter 2 ('one falls in love with one's complexity – as if layers of lies could replace the green illusion', p. 18), and we are reminded at intervals by Dan and others that 'everything that went wrong . . . stemmed from . . . The general hide-and-seek that went on' (p. 227). Dan's relationship with Jenny seems shot through with deception from the very first, a fact that becomes painfully obvious when Dan is in England and they can only communicate by telephone. The explanations about Jane that he gives to her in these calls (for example pp. 476–9) are nothing short of lies. Dan implicitly acknowledges this when he says that he 'began to rehearse' (p. 475), and no amount of squirming casuistry about 'half truth[s]' (p. 479) and 'he . . . had not lied, merely exaggerated' (p. 470) can get him off the hook. We wonder when the lies will stop and Dan will have the courage to speak the truth. Not, we find, on the first stage of the Nile trip; 'he was hiding something from [Jane] himself' (p. 549), 'He knew he was not saying what he really felt' (p. 560), and (of his postcard to Jenny) 'He read what he had written. It was a worse lie . . . but now the omissions and ambiguities were so flagrant that he felt his conscience eased' (p. 610). We read the magnificent account of the Syrian excursion and Jane's change of heart at Palmyra. Will Dan's heart be changed? We start the last chapter: Dan, after yet further lies ('I honestly didn't know [what was happening]. You must believe that', p. 690), at last comes clean and tells Jenny 'all his letter had lacked the honesty to tell', '[things] I've never told anyone' (p. 698). At last! We turn the pages: the end approaches: surely this will be all. But no – on the last page but one we find *'He had lied a little to Jenny*, to make it easier for her. But that was his secret now, his shared [sic] private mystery' (p. 703, emphasis added). As I suggested earlier in connection with the Robin Hood motif (p. 117 above), it is often difficult in the case of *Daniel Martin* to distinguish between the cure and the disease.

The problems Dan constitutes for the reader are (as one might expect) very much those constituted by the book as a whole. In a phrase, Dan puts much more energy into his task as preacher (we note that he is the son of a vicar) than into his work as an author. In the former capacity he drives home his messages relentlessly: points are made at great length and often repetitively (we are reminded that sermons were not his father's strong point either). As an author, however, he skimps his task. While the individual parts are over-controlled, the book as a whole lacks organisation. It is difficult to assemble, out of the bundle of discrete (albeit often highly effective) images and events which make it up, any unified pattern or sequence. In the last analysis Dan – if not Fowles himself – has abdicated his authorial role, and left it up to his readers to fit the pieces into an order that makes sense. This would be perfectly proper, if the parts he had left us with would only fit together.

Yet it is possible to detect, beneath this jumble of magnificent ruins, the outline of a possible order. It is to the reconstruction of this order, using as a starting point the four-theme framework outlined in earlier chapters, that the remainder of this chapter will be devoted.

Towards the end of Dan and Jane's trip up the Nile, Professor Kirnberger remarks, with a conspiratorial glint in his eye, that there are 'only two nations' (p. 587); he means, one must presume, the Few and the Many. Apart from a few chance remarks by the Tory MP Fenwick (p. 353), this is almost the only mention of the theme in the book. Yet it is implicitly present in a very powerful way. We have seen how the idea of transition and development, of being accepted into an 'elect' group, underlies Fowles's earlier work, and how the relationship of teacher and disciple plays a vital part in his fiction. Part of the difficulty discussed above in deciding whether Dan is teacher or disciple arises because at an unresolved, deep level of the book, he is both: teacher, mentor, G.P.-figure to Jenny; learner, disciple, Nick-figure to Jane; and, in a sense, teacher also in his relationship as a narrator to the earlier self whose adventures he recounts. The failure to sort out these two roles is a major weakness of the book: the view that they are residually present is supported by the random switchings of tense and person which we have already examined. A systematic distinction between first and third person, present and past tense, is a standard technique for recording the stages in the development of an autobiographical narrator: in *Daniel Martin* both technique and development remain embryonic.[14]

By contrast, the handling of the domaine in *Daniel Martin* represents a considerable development from Fowles's earlier works. A number of such privileged places – Thorncombe, Tsankawi, perhaps Kitchener's Island – feature in the book; yet none affords the enclosure and security (albeit only temporary) of its earlier counterparts. Indeed (as we have seen) these domaines seem to have very little function: they are almost spare parts. There is in the book a pervasive sense of loss: Jane notes that Dan 'has a mistress. Her name is Loss' (p. 264), and senses very rapidly that where Thorncombe is concerned, 'What [Dan] really needed was not the place, but an excuse to talk about it' (p. 40). This redundancy becomes explicable in the light of the Tsankawi episode (pp. 361–74). The failure of Dan and Jenny's excursion reveals that Tsankawi, like all the domaines of *Daniel Martin*, is not so much a place as a state of mind, and that its real creation is not in the world but in the memory. This realisation enables the reader to make sense of Dan's extended meditations on Robin Hood, *la bonne vaux*, and indeed on Englishness in general: they are moves away from the husks of domaines that litter the book, and into the source which invests all domaines with power, namely the creative imagination. Moreover this re-location serves to bring out the enormous importance in this work of the past. Jenny can never replace Jane, not simply because she is not Jane, but because Jane represents and embodies for Dan a section of his previous life. Only Jane can bring alive the ruins of Palmyra, that ultimate anti-domaine, because domaines in *Daniel Martin* are functions of memory, and in possessing Jane, Dan at last finds himself in possession of his own past.

Mention of Jenny and Jane brings us on to the question of the importance of women in *Daniel Martin*, an importance increased rather than diminished by the key role which the work allots to memory. Men do not come out of the book well. The central chapter is entitled 'Hollow Men'; Anthony, before his convenient suicide, has revealed himself to be an archetypal Fowlesian classifier (p. 80); Barney is a 'morbid symptom' (to borrow a phrase from Gramsci's epigraph) if ever there was one; Dan himself, linked in many ways with Barney,[15] often seems little better. Conversely, women are very favourably presented in the book. We have already looked at the novelty and importance of Jenny's first-hand contributions to the narrative; having bullied Dan into taking a grip on himself and writing a book (p.21), she resolves that she 'just won't be *only* something in [his] script' (p. 495, emphasis in original) and walks out of the book. Thereafter Jane, associated throughout the book with the *leitmotif* of 'right feeling', takes over the tasks of guiding Dan both into literary creation and into self-knowledge. Indeed the politics of *Daniel Martin*, like much else besides, become clearer if we focus on Jane's contribution rather than Dan's. The various left-wing positions, ranging from Marxism to membership of the Labour Party, which she adopts in the course of the book have in common only one thing: that they are guided by the emotional compass of her right feeling. In the key quotation from Gramsci mentioned earlier (p. 115 above), it is Jane who draws attention to the precedence of the personal over the political.

When we come to the fourth theme of Fowles's work, the balance between freedom and responsibility, a rather similar picture emerges. Dan toys with all kinds of ideas in this area, and indeed throws up at one point (p. 641) a very attractive resolution of the problem. However, it is soon superseded by other and different formulations, and Dan's final position – as I have tried to show above – does not seem to be a coherent one. Once again it is only when we turn to Jane that things fall into place. Jane is associated throughout with Rabelais (see for example pp. 33, 66–8, 120, 446–7), and twice quotes his injunction *Fais ce que voudras* (Do what you will), the second time (p. 68) immediately before she successfully seduces Dan; she refers to Rabelais às 'the only sane human being who ever lived' (p. 67). She thus begins as an apostle of freedom and free love: but, as Dan notes, she draws back from this into a safe but timid marriage, as if the 'attempt to break out of a myth of herself . . . into that of Rabelais' had proved 'too expensive morally' (p. 120). In Fowlesian terms she, like Charles, has abandoned duty to herself in favour of a supposed duty to others: the 'intense selfishness' which Dan diagnoses as 'the one abiding drive of all [his] generation' (p. 178) does not seem to apply to its female members, and the lesson that Jane must and ultimately does learn is that she cannot help anyone else to be either free or happy until she is free herself.

In looking at the structure of the book we have noted two salient points: first, conscious interference with the continuity of syntax and narrative; second, the use of distinct, and at times dissonant, narrative voices to tell the tale. It may be that both of these are ultimately being used in the service of a thematic point, to wit the uncertainty, what Dan calls 'the ultimate ambiguous fiction', of the past. As befits the work of an author and a narrator just turned fifty, *Daniel Martin*, much more than any of Fowles's earlier works, is about memory. Perhaps its central point is that the truth about the past is in some sense *buried*. The hesitations of voice and direction which characterise the main part of the novel become like the questing of a treasure-seeker with a fragmentary and ambiguous chart, casting about for, and ultimately latching on to, the route that leads to his goal.

In the process of seeking this goal I have tried to re-arrange the work into a thematic pattern derived from Fowles's other works. I would like to conclude this chapter by attempting – using a different metaphor – to disinter from beneath the fragments the living body of the book. The starting point, as has become increasingly clear, must be Jane.

We have seen that Jane exhibits two principal characteristics in the book, one positive and one negative. The positive side, represented in public terms by her deeply felt political idealism and in private terms by her instinctive and almost magnetic sense of right feeling, is fairly familiar to us: like Alison and Sarah, she is to act as a guide and muse for her lover, and to be the *pricesse lointaine* for whom he strives. But the negative side, equally strongly developed, is her obsessive fear of freedom. We have already seen this at work (p. 122 above) in the increasingly despondent references to Rabelais; it is evident also in what might be called her pre-marital adultery which deliberately fobs off the right man so as to leave the field clear for the wrong one; in her subsequent decision to reveal her act to Anthony, thus ensuring that her marriage will be a thorough-going penance; in her flight into the Catholic Church with its conscious *sacrificium intellectus*. All these are in effect forms of distraction behaviour, which is why the sight of the bitch at Palmyra engaged in exactly such an activity (pp. 679–84) moves her so unbearably.

But what is it that this distraction behaviour is trying to preserve? In the romances of an earlier generation we would expect it to be her virginity: Frye remarks that

> In the social conditions assumed [in Classical romance], virginity is to a woman what honor is to a man, the symbol of the fact that she is not a slave.

(Frye, 1976, p. 73)

At first sight this appears ridiculous; there are no virgin heroines in Fowles's novels. But once again we have to dig rather deeper. Virginity in romance is not merely a sexual fact. Nor is it merely an indicator of social status. Ultimately it is a symbol of purity, and, beyond purity, of integrity and identity: it is the sign of a character free from dross and unified in itself. And this perfect self-truth and self-consistency points beyond itself and gives to the heroines of undisplaced romance a suggestion of belonging to another world. The access which all Fowles's heroines have to a world of feeling closed to men is a displaced form of this aura of otherness.

But virginity can only last until marriage, and romances characteristically end with the marriage of the heroine. At this point what has most anxiously been feared – the loss of the heroine's most priceless possession – becomes what is most ardently desired, the 'consummation' of all her hopes. (We note a similar polarity in the use of the word 'chastity': in an unmarried woman it denotes the absence of sexual activity, but in a married woman it refers to its presence, albeit in a controlled form.) These shifts of meaning and attitude are further proof that mere preservation of the hymen is not what is at stake. When we undertake a symbolic interpretation, a pattern appears. Chastity before marriage (virginity) represents, as we have seen, the preservation of the integrity of the self; chastity after marriage (lawful sexual activity, responsibility as wife and mother) necessarily requires the surrender of this physical and spiritual integrity, its merging into a new unit made of two people.

Virginity after marriage is thus as pathological in literary and symbolic terms as promiscuity before it. In the case of Jane, her marriage to Anthony is really no proper marriage at all but rather an 'Eternal marriage to yourself', as Dan calls it on p. 676, since it carefully excludes the possibility of the surrender of herself in a full, living, and sexually harmonious relationship. Indeed with Dan too her promiscuity is paradoxically a kind of virginity. Not only does she give

herself to Dan precisely in order *not* to give herself whole-heartedly to
Anthony: the two sexual episodes with Dan which frame the action are
themselves symbolically almost virginal, since on both occasions she
contrives for them to be as brief and awkward as possible, and follows
them by coolness and emotional withdrawal rather than tenderness
and encouragement. In short, she treats each sexual act as if it was the
end of the relationship rather than a stage in its development. Dan's
exasperation at this wilful misunderstanding ('This is what you wanted
– well, here it is') is very sympathetic: if that was all it was going to be, it
was certainly not what he wanted!

Daniel Martin, then, is the story of the progressive revelation of a
buried aspect of Jane – an aspect she spinsterishly lacks the courage to
face. Dan's task as romantic hero is to uncover this aspect, and to bring
Jane to see it – to release the damsel from the prison of herself. This
accounts for the frequent images of enclosure, immersion, burial, and
disinterment in the book. There is the woman in the reeds, discovered
by Dan and Jane together and 'inextricably associated' (p. 103) with
their lovemaking (indeed Jane may even have been planning to seduce
Dan in the very 'cut' in which the submerged corpse was found). There
is Nancy *Reed*, another female character whom Dan might similarly
have rescued from a life of inauthenticity had he only had the courage
to confront a figure of authority (for the connection between Dan's
father and Anthony see p. 126 below). There is Egypt itself, a land
associated above all else with archaeology and in which Dan and Jane
repeatedly visit tombs and crypts. Within Egypt there is the contrast
between Abu Simbel, hoisted out of reach of the dam to a position of
indecent exposure, and Philae (pp. 611–12), poised intriguingly on the
edge between concealment and revelation. At Palmyra there is the
carefully unfinished quotation from T. S. Eliot which invites us to
ponder the significance of dogs (p. 669; the omitted second line is, of
course, 'For with his nails he'll dig them up again'); dogs recur in the
chapter title (p. 673) and in the recognition scene, where the
self-sacrificing distraction behaviour of a feral bitch alerts Jane to the
way in which she has similarly put at risk her own chances of fulfilled
life.

The complement of this process of bringing to light what should
never have been hidden is concealing what should never have been
made open, and this is the form taken by the climax of the chapter and
of the book itself, namely Jane's decision to bury her wedding-ring.
This act of sloughing off a part of herself (and specifically of a ring)
represents a symbolic and significant, as opposed to actual but

meaningless, loss of virginity, and hence a readiness to merge her isolated self in the joint identity of marriage.

This concern with the development of a female protagonist marks a substantial shift of interest for Fowles, whose normal narrative algebra treats the female as the given and the male as the variable. For the first time he has written a book which can truly – if discreetly – be said to be about a woman's quest for identity. This is not to say that he is no longer concerned with the male quest. But Dan's pursuit of himself, as he gradually comes to realise, cannot be achieved without the success of a similar process of self-discovery in Jane: he cannot recapture his past – the project which he set himself at the start of the book (see p. 103 above) – until she has come to terms with her own.

Nonetheless the book is very largely devoted to Dan's own personal development. I have tried to show that in realistic and moral terms, Dan's progress is rather disappointing. But if we extend the burial metaphor to the story itself and try to disinter the 'real' narrative hidden beneath its Lukacsian mask, we will find that a number of interesting features emerge. These concern in particular the use of family patterns within the work.

As we have seen, Dan is the son of a repressive father, who is in turn associated both indirectly (being a vicar) and directly (p. 423) with a repressive God. Dan's father dies while Dan is at university; but his son is not thereby liberated from the dominance of super-ego figures, for he has already made friends with the sober and puritanical Anthony, towards whom he experiences 'all kinds of buried feelings of inferiority' (p. 107) and whom he subsequently comes to recognise as 'a kind of father-substitute, though we were almost exactly the same age' (p. 80). It is the death of this father-figure, rather than of Dan's biological father, which forms the central episode of the narrative and at last allows Dan to play a truly adult role. What this role is becomes clear very rapidly, as the references to the 'loose, warm web of clan' (p. 250) become more frequent: it is to assume his responsibilities as family member, husband, and father.

It might be thought that this *Bildungsroman* view of Dan was vitiated by the difficulty discussed earlier, namely that Dan does not seem to develop. But at the strictly narrative level of which I am speaking, this does not constitute a problem: we are not concerned here with his character but with his role, and in this rather mechanical sense he can be said to advance from the dependent position of a child to the more responsible situation of an adult.

If the hypothesis of an underlying romance structure of this kind enables us to cope with some of the weaknesses of *Daniel Martin*, it also helps us to appreciate its strengths. Chief among these, in my view, is its triumphant conclusion. After 34 chapters of tergiversation between first and third person, Fowles settles for the final twelve chapters into the style of which he is a master: a single focalising narrator;[16] a sustained and suspenseful story-line; an exotic setting; and a 'romantic' conclusion. After the build-up and deferral of Dan's hopes on the Nile trip, the excursion into the Lebanon and Syria is inevitably charged with expectancy, an expectancy which the events at Palmyra – narrated in the author's most characteristic style – amply fulfil.

On the realistic level, the behaviour of both characters is entirely plausible: Jane's, for the reasons we have already considered; Dan's, because Jane's actions (understandable though they are with hindsight) would baffle and exasperate anyone. Her extraordinary switches between intimacy and distance culminate in her giving herself to him again, but with such marked reluctance ('I feel so cold, Dan', p. 667) and anonymity – 'It seemed to him . . . that someone else was aroused, had taken over her body' (p. 670) – that after it is over it is difficult for Dan to know whether to feel closer to Jane or further away. Revealing and lamentable though the simile may be, it is hard not to feel sympathy with Dan when he glares at Jane the next morning 'like a man before a machine that will not function, although he has followed to the letter all the instructions for starting it' (p. 675).

Yet these scenes, and above all these images, are also intensely effective on the symbolic level. To some extent this occurs because of groundwork laid earlier in the book. Reference has already been made to the burial/disinterment imagery which runs through the book. We note in addition the return of the ravens, 'Dan's totem bird' (p. 677), and the fairly obvious but nonetheless successful device of locating new life (the puppies) where it might least be expected, namely in a dead landscape (the ruins of Palmyra). But over and above this fairly straightforward and decipherable use of symbolism, there is a whole cluster of images which cannot be directly decoded and yet which give the two chapters concerned ('The End of the World' and 'The Bitch', pp. 645–87) an unforgettable resonance. Some are simply functions of the setting – the gloomy power of the Krak des Chevaliers, the barren wastes of the fog-shrouded Syrian desert, the ruins of the once-luxuriant Palmyra. Some spring from the situation in which the two protagonists find themselves – thrown together in a shared isolation by geography, by nationality, by language, yet forced apart by their mutual suspicion and incomprehension. And some seem to work on all levels at once, and to arouse echoes both within and beyond the book, like the 'motionless human figure . . . holding out a dead bird' (p. 649) whom they pass in the fog on the road to Palmyra. At such moments we feel that the true story of *Daniel Martin* – discarding a false mystification in favour of a true mystery – has thrown off its disguises and emerged into the light.

7 The Romances of John Fowles

We have now reached the point at which we can look at Fowles's work in its entirety, and attempt to understand and assess it as a whole. It must be clear by now that I feel Fowles's output to be somewhat uneven; in the course of this chapter I shall seek to account for some of the less successful features of his work, and also for some of its great strengths.

We have seen how Fowles's fiction is built around four major themes: the Few and the Many; the domaine; the contrast between the masculine and the feminine mentality; and the difficult necessity of freedom. It is true also to say that his position on each one has changed little during his writing career: as a guide to what he thinks are the ideas behind his fiction, *The Aristos* remained as valid when it was re-issued (substantially unchanged) in 1979, as when it first appeared fifteen years earlier. Yet for all their constancy, these ideas are by no means free from incoherence and contradiction in the form in which they are applied in the fiction. These contradictions become even harder to avoid when we turn to the non-fiction and to Fowles's comments on literature and on life in general.

THE THEORY VERSUS THE PRACTICE

The obvious place to start is with Fowles's social theories. He takes these very seriously: we remember his wish to be thought of as 'a sound philosopher' in preference to 'a good novelist' (Newquist, 1964, p. 222). In line with this, he has included abundant social commentary and reflection in his fiction, and has consistently indicated his wish to be thought of primarily as a realist. Still more notably, he has asserted throughout his writing career that the political philosophy which underpins this realism is a lifelong commitment to democratic socialism (*A*, p. 8). Does his work bear out this assertion?

129

I take it that when Fowles speaks of *democratic* socialism, he refers to that strand of the socialist movement associated in this century with R. H. Tawney and George Orwell, and in the nineteenth century with William Morris (himself appropriately a writer of romances). Socialism of this kind can be said to rest on three principles. The first principle is that men are fundamentally equal, and that this equality is primary, that it is not merely an adjunct of liberty but actually an essential pre-condition of it. The point here is not that democratic socialism denies the differences between humans, but rather that it looks at humans *from the point of view of their common humanity*, and argues that this common element outweighs the factors that separate and rank them.[1] The second principle is that man is social in much the same absolutely fundamental way that he is air-breathing, and that accordingly his well-being and indeed his very existence are very largely socially determined. (This, of course, is the force of Lukacs's claim that in neglecting the links which bind them to society Kafka's heroes are *ipso facto* condemning themselves to misery and *Angst*.) The third principle concerns social change. I take it that just as conservatism is fundamental to Conservatives, so social change is absolutely basic to Socialists. But the important element in this is not whether things should change, but how. As I understand it, democratic socialism holds that change is institutional; that it springs from conflicts of interest between groups; and that it therefore involves some sort of struggle. (This in turn feeds back into the first two principles, on the assumption that neither full equality nor full selfhood can be achieved in an unequal society.)

In the event Fowles's work seems to me to be based on an entirely different set of principles. In the first place he does not see human society as a whole in terms of equality. One need look no further than the theory of the Few and the Many, already extensively explored, to find evidence for this. Nor is this theory confined to the philosophical pages of *The Aristos*. A case could even be made for using the theory to explain the attitude Fowles takes to his reader: at times he lectures him as if he felt himself to be one of the Few despairingly trying to collar and convince a particularly pin-headed member of the Many. Certainly the theory operates (even when it is partly ironic, as in 'Poor Koko') as a basic organising principle of his fiction.

Indeed Fowles seems at times to be projecting a comparable class system on to nature, or deriving his class system from it. One of the features he disliked about Leigh-on-Sea was its homogeneity, its classlessness (albeit within a containing class system); another thing was its distance from nature. The connection between the two is not accidental. Both defects were remedied in the Devon village his family moved to during the war, and the sentence in which he explains his father's attitude to village life says much also about the son's attitude to nature:

> Things [that is 'the antiquated class-system of village life, with its gentry and its "peasants" and infinite grades between'] were far too transparent in Devon, too close to *unfair value-systems that were in turn too close to nature*.
>
> *(The Tree*, p. 26, emphasis added; the inserted quotation is from p. 24)

The reference to the 'infinite grades' of the village class system recalls the 'infinite gradations' (*A*, p. 9) which Fowles claims to detect between the Few and the Many, and suggests that Fowles sees both the natural and the human order as 'naturally' (even if 'unfairly') ranked, the former in a Linnaean hierarchy of species, the latter in a social hierarchy of classes. A comparable equation of human and natural order occurs when Fowles claims that the superiority of some human beings over others is not just social but also biological (see note 2 below). It is only fair to add that Fowles vigorously rejects the idea that this inequality confers a licence to exploit: 'biological superiority is [not] a state of existence . . . [but] *a state of responsibility*' (*A*, p. 10, emphasis in original). Yet even this (undoubtedly genuine) altruism has more of the rural high Tory about it than of the democratic socialist.

Where the second principle is concerned, the role of society, Fowles once again diverges sharply from democratic socialism. Far from thinking of humans as primarily social, he views them instead entirely in terms of isolated individuals, or at best of isolated communities. The view which Daniel Martin attributes to Beckett, that 'the loneliness of each' is 'the bedrock of the human condition' (*DM*, p. 260), seems very close to that of his creator. Fowles's writing is dominated by metaphors of islands and exile, metaphors which correspond not only to the way he sees human society in his fiction, but also to his view of his own life as 'a sort of exile in Lyme Regis' (Halpern, 1971, and *passim* in Fowles's interviews and autobiographical writings thereafter). The Few are always in retreat, or at best in seclusion, from the world; and when the hero leaves the domaine to return to the life of the Many, he does so only in order to seek a single kindred spirit with whom he may

establish a world apart and once more turn his back on society. For all
Fowles's forays into other cultures, the archetypal human being for
him is the Englishman, because for Fowles the English are supremely a
nation of Robin Hoods, retreating from external vanities into the
solitary inner forest of the imagination. This perhaps is what Fowles
means when he writes that 'the key to my fiction . . . lies in my
relationship with nature' (*The Tree*, p. 46). That key certainly does not
lie (except in a negative sense) in his relationship with society.

Not surprisingly, Fowles differs also over the third principle, the
concept of change and progress. We have seen that tests and ordeals
are essential features of his fiction, and that it is centrally (albeit
problematically) concerned with the moral development and spiritual
progress of his heroes. We have seen, too, that he regards his heroes as
having an essential role to play in society. But in Fowles's work change
is always rooted in the individual: and the direction of change is always
from the individual to the group, and not the other way round. The role
of power relationships and of institutions in promoting or resisting
social change is thus never discussed. All forms of membership, not
just affiliation to the TUC, are rejected (*A*, pp. 8–9 and 212–13), and
the 'function in history' of his 'self-questioning, ethical elite' (*FLW*,
pp. 256–7) seems to be one that they must exercise purely by example.

Fowles's way of referring to social change is a revealing one. He uses
the term 'evolution', a word which implies something gradual;
beneficial; biological rather than social in origin;[2] autonomous; and,
above all, inevitable. It is also revealing to glance at what he considers
the ideal circumstances for this evolution, namely leisure, affluence,
and reduced population (see for example Boston, 1969, p. 54). The
reason why such circumstances provide the individual with the
maximum space for growth is of course because the constraints of
government are minimised and the frontiers of the state have been
rolled back. Despite Fowles's vigorous disclaimer (*A*, p. 8), it is difficult
not to be reminded of the nineteenth-century liberalism of John Stuart
Mill.

A second important clash between theory and practice is to be found
in Fowles's literary theory. One of the reasons for Fowles's critical as
well as popular success has been the open and experimental nature of
his writing. This appeared as early as *The Magus*, in the form of
Nicholas's rather ambiguous narration and of the shifts in stance and
structure of the final chapter. It reached a peak of critical acclaim in
The French Lieutenant's Woman, with the alternative endings and the
appearances of the author in his own work; and it was sustained, albeit

in a muted form, in the 'theme and variations' structure of *The Ebony Tower*, the alternations of tense and person and the circular shape of *Daniel Martin*, and the fictional play of *Mantissa*. As might be expected, Fowles in his interviews and critical writings has consistently supported what he or his narrators have already expressed within the work, namely that the self-conscious aspects of the writing are not accidental, but part of a deliberate policy of handing over part of the control of the work to the reader.

While the existence and indeed the effectiveness of these experimental devices cannot be doubted, there are other forces at work in Fowles's fiction which do not contribute to the reader's freedom, and indeed pull in the opposite direction. Some of these at least Fowles is certainly aware of: throughout his writing career he has stood by his early view that 'writing is a kind of teaching' (Newquist, 1964, p. 220, and *passim* in interviews thereafter), a phrase which would hardly have appealed to such authors (naming only two for whom Fowles has mentioned his admiration) as Joyce and Flaubert. As I have tried to show, the manipulative and didactic side of Fowles's literary personality is always liable to intervene in the smooth running of the fiction.

A relatively minor instance concerns Fowles's use of language. He uses an extensive vocabulary in his fiction, some of it (for example 'batrachian', 'accipitral', 'swaling', or the already-mentioned 'algedonic' and 'eschar') quite obviously beyond the reach of the audience of 'average education . . . average intelligence' he claims to be writing for (Delaney, 1981). Fowles himself consistently maintains that he has 'a duty to language' (Delaney, 1982; see also Delaney, 1981, and Freeman, 1982). This may be so, though despite this laudable aim Fowles's style is alarmingly uneven.[3] It seems more likely, however, that the duty Fowles has in mind is a schoolmasterly one, to share his learning with the reader. This hypothesis is supported by a revealing characteristic of Fowles's style, namely his tendency, first to use a supposedly unfamiliar word, and then to explain it. Thus we find, for example, '*Aut Caesar, aut nullus*. If I can't be Caesar, I'll be no one' (*The Tree*, p. 50); 'a mere psittacism – a mindless parroting' (*ET*, p. 184); 'the stele, the stone epitaph' (*The Enigma of Stonehenge*, p. 53); 'personified – made things into persons' (*The Enigma of Stonehenge*, p. 47); 'they're telepathic – they can read minds' (*Mantissa*, p. 79). Too often in Fowles's writing the author's pedagogical side gets between us and the fiction; while the reader is having his word-power increased, the story is languishing.

When we come to the structure of the fictions we find once again that a rather intrusive didacticism is at work which interferes with their open form and ironic method. Thus while we are not told in so many words that Nick and Alison leave the novel together, we are given a pretty hefty pointer in that direction (provided, that is, that we can read Latin). The 'tyranny of the last chapter' (*FLW*, p. 349) pulls us towards accepting its version of the ending of *The French Lieutenant's Woman*; and *Daniel Martin*, for all its initial subversion of narrative, positively bristles with pointers telling us how we are supposed to read it.

In fact the moral urgency behind Fowles's writing is so intense that it is very difficult for his stories to remain non-aligned; they are pulled into its magnetic field and polarised accordingly. This didactic urge leads him at times not only to manipulate the narrative, to declare 'a preferred aftermath' (*M*, p. 7), but also to insert into some of his narratives sizeable non-narrative elements, undigested chunks of information and argument. Telling the reader what to think in this way cannot be squared with letting the reader make up his own mind – unless, that is, the instructions are subject to irony, encouraging us to read between the lines in the same way as we are urged to read the narrative in which the instructions are embedded. But this, as we have seen at length, is not the case with Fowles. In all his major works we find points at which both narrative and irony are suspended and the author puts his head out from behind the curtain to address us directly: Lily de Seitas and her 'Eleventh Commandment' in *The Magus*, the historical commentaries upon the Victorians in *The French Lieuten-ant's Woman*, the theories of national character in *Daniel Martin*. (This is particularly true when the views being put forward are those of a real rather than a fictional character: one thinks of the prominence given to Barthes in 'The Cloud', or the sizeable extracts from Lukacs quoted verbatim in *Daniel Martin*.) At such moments the only freedom left to the reader who finds himself in disagreement is hastily to turn the page.

I do not want to say that there is nothing open about Fowles's works. But it does seem that there is a part of him which is afraid to leave them open and keeps trying to close them up. The particular way in which he combines recherché words with simple explanations shows a lack of respect for the reader's intelligence. His handling of events, and his insertion of didactic material into the text, show a failure of trust in the reader's judgement, good sense, and ability to come to the 'right' decision unaided (his apparent assumption that such a decision exists at all is itself a loaded one). In fact it is rather as if Fowles, like an over-anxious parent, was reluctant to let his works out of his supervision at all.

This rather well-worn analogy of an over-protective parent may be worth taking a stage further. Fowles hates to publish: publication means giving up control over the book and handing it over to other people who through reading it will in effect re-make it themselves. He likes to mull over a manuscript at great length, and has on two occasions actually gone to the length of issuing revised editions of his works (*The Aristos* and *The Magus*). Each work of Fowles's is a world: while he insists in the sphere of religion that no creator has any business lingering on in the world he has made, it is an argument he seems to find difficult to accept when his own role as author is at stake.

The third area in which Fowles seems frequently at odds with himself is in his attitude to women. His explicit position is absolutely clear. He has always maintained, in both his fiction and his non-fiction, that women are intrinsically better, more authentic, and freer than men. Moreover he has always constructed his fictions upon this principle: women are either the goal of the hero's quest, or (as in *The French Lieutenant's Woman*) the means whereby that goal is achieved. For Fowles, as for Baudelaire, woman is '*l'Ange gardien, la Muse et la Madone*'. However, the picture becomes rather different when we come to look more closely at the way Fowles treats women in his fiction.

The first point that must be made is that Fowles's female characters tend very much to be women first and people second (see Benton, 1983, for a feminist comment on this). The principal reasons for this sexual stereotyping lie in the conventions of the genre Fowles is using (a point I shall return to later in this chapter); but, as we shall see shortly, it is related to a more serious difficulty in Fowles's work. This is his ambivalent attitude to the physical side of sex.

There is every reason to expect that his attitude should be a positive one. Sex is, after all, an aspect of love, and love, both Eros and Agape, is the force that propels his heroes in their redemptive pursuit of the heroine. Moreover Fowles insists throughout his fiction that women have sexual needs, and that they have a right to sexual fulfilment. His heroines assert their freedom quite vigorously: Miranda, Alison, Sarah, Diana, Isobel, Jane – in each case it is the woman who makes the sexual advances. Fowles asserts too that he deplores the reticence and prudishness of puritanical attitudes to sex (Sage, 1976).

Yet it is a curious feature of Fowles's work that the explicit sexual episodes are so frequently described in unequal terms. In *The Magus*, the sweaty reality of Nick's quite frequent love-making with the enthusiastically participating Alison (his equal, or more accurately his complement) is relatively briefly described; what is reported in great detail are the two occasions (pp. 369–70 and 483–7) on which he reaches orgasm with the rather distant and deodorised Julie. In both she is much more like a detached and at times passive professional than a lover. It might be argued that this is perfectly appropriate, given the role she has to play. But it sheds an interesting light on Nicholas that he finds these relatively transitory sexual encounters worthy of such detailed description and such ambitious claims. Sentences such as 'It was not like any other moment of first entry I had ever gained; something well beyond the sexual . . . I knew I had won far more than her body' (p. 486) contrast rather oddly with the discreet one-liner allotted to his first time with Alison (p. 28).[4]

What really turns Nick on, for most of *The Magus* at least, is a girl who holds something of herself in reserve. Well, we say, he gets over that, doesn't he? Surely the book itself is proof of that? Yet Fowles's next hero seems to suffer from a similar problem: he pursues the elusive Sarah for the greater part of the book, and even in their sexual encounter there is a curious distance and detachment about the 'passive yet acquiescent' Sarah, who lies with her face 'twisted sideways and hidden from his sight' and who receives his penis 'flinching' and with 'an instinctive constriction' (*FLW*, p. 304).

Female coldness (verging on contempt), even at the height of passion, continues to excite Fowles's heroes. Peter finds Catherine's way of 'looking through' him (*ET*, p. 296), as she waits passively for him to make love to her, to be 'Very sick; and very sexy' (p. 297), a revealing combination of adjectives. In 'The Ebony Tower' David pursues the forbidden Diana until she turns to him and responds passionately, whereupon he falters and backs down; and Dan, having at various times had the offer of such enviably willing and passionate partners as Nancy, Andrea, and Miriam-and-Marjory, settles for a sexual sphinx in the form of Jane.

It can hardly be unrelated that sex in Fowles's fiction is so unremittingly followed by disaster. This emerges very clearly if we list the occasions on which full sexual intercourse is described. (I am not including the catastrophic consequences of Miranda's failed seduction attempt in *The Collector*, though these in fact support the point I am making.) Once in *The Magus* (pp. 483–7) – followed immediately by kidnap and trial. Once in *The French Lieutenant's Woman* – followed instantly for Charles by 'an immediate and universal horror . . . like a city struck out of a quiet sky by an atom bomb' (p. 305; we remember that two earlier full or partial sexual encounters, on pp. 17 and 274, ended equally disastrously). Once in 'The Cloud' (*ET*, p. 297) – resulting in the disappearance, and almost certainly the death, of Catherine. Twice in *Daniel Martin* (pp. 104 and 669–70); the first time preceded by the discovery of a corpse and followed by the terror of discovery, 'Never so frightened, before or since' (p. 105); the second time resulting only in something impersonal and unsatisfactory, the essence of Jane slipping away from the sexual act as her physical self steals out of the bed early the following morning and leaves Dan to wake up alone. In only two works by Fowles does sex come without a price tag of guilt: in *Mantissa*, where Miles and Erato reach a glorious climax together (pp. 151–4), and in 'The Enigma'. Even here, however, a form of prudishness can be detected – in *Mantissa* embodied in the prurient gaze of the staff sister, and in 'The Enigma' in the simple structural fact that the story ends just before the sexual act takes place.

In the last analysis, therefore, Fowles's attitude to sex (like Baudelaire's) is fundamentally dualistic. On the one hand it involves an element of the sublime and mysterious; but possession (understandably a loaded word for Fowles) does away with that mystery, cheapening the woman by turning her into a possessed 'object', and leaving a residue of guilt and punishment. It must be emphasised that Fowles himself is well aware of some of the artistic implications of this; he has consistently maintained that creation comes out of loss, and that the unconsummated relationships of fiction which preserve the elusive mystery of the loved one are 'more fertile and onward to [his] whole being as a writer' ('Hardy and the Hag', p. 35). But it is paradoxical that this division of women into types, this madonna/whore complex (Lever, 1979, p. 90), should be a basic organising principle of the very fiction in which it is so energetically condemned.

Nor does this dualism work only at the level of structure. As Conradi convincingly shows in his analysis of the 'sexual politics' of Fowles's fiction (1982, pp. 90–4), it also has important consequences for the way Fowles handles narration in his fiction: consequences which bring us back to my earlier point (see p. 135 above) that Fowles's heroines are women before, or perhaps *rather than*, people. For the most part Fowles does not enter into the consciousness of his heroines: the classic case is Sarah, but Alison, Diana, Isobel, and Jane fit the same pattern. Thereby, of course, they retain that 'narratological virginity' (Conradi,

1982, p. 93) which is a symbol of their mysterious otherness. But when
women do take over the story (Miranda's diary, Catherine's stream of
consciousness) – when, that is, the narrator 'penetrates' and symbolically 'possesses' their thoughts – *he kills them*. Here, as in other areas,
Daniel Martin marks a significant advance in Fowles's fiction – Jenny is
allowed, not only to write both factually and imaginatively, but also to
survive the experience.[5] To some extent *Mantissa* sustains this
development, reversing the pattern of *The Collector* and making
atonement for it. Where Clegg imprisoned and killed his muse, Miles
acknowledges his subjection to Erato and gives life to her in his
writing. But from a woman's viewpoint, the victory may seem to be
something of a Pyrrhic one. Erato lives – but only inside someone else's
head, and a man's head at that.

We have seen in this section that in three major areas – politics,
literary theory, and sexual attitudes – Fowles's theoretical and
philosophical statements seem of little use as guides to his fictional
practice. Nonetheless it is my conviction that his work does form a
coherent whole, and that the right critical approach will be one that
demonstrates this unity. The next part of this chapter will be devoted to
reversing my earlier line of argument, and to seeing how far the fiction
can be used to help us understand the theory.

FROM FICTION TO PHILOSOPHY: THE EXISTENTIAL PROJECTION OF ROMANCE

In his *Anatomy of Criticism*, Northrop Frye draws attention to the
familiar fact that different literary forms are based upon different
assumptions about the world. Tragedies depend for appropriately
tragic endings upon misfortune, accident, a hostile fate, and a general
sense that things are against us: consequently the world-view of
tragedy will be quite different from that of comedy, whose upward-
moving dramatic structures and happy endings require a benign fate
and a merciful providence. Frye stresses that these contrasting
world-views are not 'substantial philosophies', statements about life;
they are literary hypotheses, elements of the fictional or dramatic
contract between writer and audience. But he goes on to identify a
tendency, on the part of both writers and critics, to extract these
conventions and to treat them as if they were capable of standing on
their own as statements about the nature of existence: 'It is natural . . .
for tragedy and comedy to throw their shadows . . . into philosophy

and shape there a philosophy of fate and a philosophy of providence respectively' (Frye, 1957, p. 64).[6] To this extension of literary hypotheses into the field of philosophy Frye gives the name 'existential projection'.

The examples given in *Anatomy of Criticism* and quoted in the paragraph above refer to tragedy and comedy. But all genres are conventional, and it follows that the conventions of any genre can be projected as statements about existence. Romance, a highly conventional literary form, is no exception. It is my contention that many of the features of Fowles's philosophy are existential projections of romance: in other words that his philosophy is the expression of his fiction, rather than (as he has always maintained) the other way round.

One of the principal characteristics of romance is its obsession with aristocracy: Frye writes more bluntly of its 'pervasive social snobbery' (1976, p. 161). This is true both in a static and in a dynamic sense. Not only are romances concerned with characters who are by birth superior to those around them; they are also very frequently about the way in which characters who are initially outside the charmed circle – for example the rustics Daphnis and Chloe, or the kitchen-maid Cinderella – are taken up into it in the course of the story, often by the solution of a birth mystery or by marriage.

By a further development of this romantic convention, the aristocratic group may turn its back on the larger society and become increasingly withdrawn and esoteric. This is what we find in Frye's so-called 'sixth-phase' romance:

> The sixth . . phase is the last phase of romance as of comedy. In comedy it shows the comic society *breaking up into small [esoteric] units or individuals*; in romance it marks the end of a movement from active to contemplative adventure. . . . a characteristic feature of this phase is the tale in quotation marks . . . In *The Turn of the Screw* a large party is telling ghost stories in a country house; then some people leave, and *a much smaller . . . circle gathers around the crucial tale*.
>
> (Frye, 1957, p. 202, emphasis added)

Precisely this theme of a kind of elite or aristocracy – the 'elect', the 'Few' – is found throughout Fowles's work, as is the powerful tendency (only partly restrained by the author's rather anxious insistence on responsibility and commitment) to pull away from society into the esoteric sub-groups which are often associated with domains in his fiction. There is even a telling parallel on the level of technique. Fowles has acknowledged the influence of *The Turn of the Screw* on *The Magus* (*M*, p. 5), and the similarity of Frye's 'tale in quotation marks' to Conchis's inset tales – a technique Fowles uses widely in his fiction – is striking. Elsewhere Fowles matches this 'tale within a tale' technique with a comparable method which we may call the 'cast within a cast'. After opening with a fairly large range of characters, he engineers a withdrawal so that the hero is left with only a small circle around him for the crucial episodes of the story. Such circles, moreover, fit very well the definition of the comic society italicised in the quotation above: it would be hard to think of more esoteric groups than the circles at Bourani and Coëtminais, and in *Mantissa* the 'comic society' is contained within the head of a single individual.

One very obvious projection of the 'pervasive social snobbery' of romance is to be found within Fowles's fiction, and consists precisely of the pervasive social snobbery of the fiction itself. We have seen again and again the class bias at work in Fowles's romances. Members of the lower or lower middle classes such as Clegg, Sam, and most of the women that the hero forms temporary liaisons with, are more or less of the Many; conversely members of the Few are mostly from the higher echelons of society, or – like Alison and Sarah – in one way or another outside the class system. It is obvious that Fowles has found it convenient, consciously or unconsciously, to map onto British society the aristocratic ideology and world-view of his chosen literary form. Yet it is equally clear that he has not found the fit between the real and the ideal a particularly close one. In the first place we may note the strong radical tendencies evidenced in his explicit republicanism, his contributions to *Socialist Challenge*, his readiness (were a suitable candidate to offer himself to the electors of Lyme) to vote Communist (personal interview). More importantly, though all Fowles's *aristoi* are (more or less) aristocrats, not all his aristocrats are *aristoi*: Charles must abandon his baronial responsibilities at Winsyatt in order to qualify, and Andrew in *Daniel Martin* is barely a member at all.[7]

In Fowles's non-fiction, the existential projection of this romance convention is of course his concern with the Few and the Many. The title of *The Aristos* – a title which is itself revealing – refers to the author's wish to foster the development of a nucleus of like-minded individuals, *aristoi*, who will form an elite of a new kind: enlightened, responsible, moral, yet at all times detached, not only from the mass of humanity, but even from their fellow *aristoi*. If we look at this elite from any kind of realistic angle, it is difficult to make any kind of sense of it; its members do not exercise any authority, they neither teach nor preach, they have neither mystical nor charitable functions. But it becomes intelligible when we think of it as a projection of the late-Romantic esotericism outlined above in the quotation from Frye. Thus the *aristos*, problematic to say the least as a social and philosophical concept, falls into place when restored to his proper, that is literary, context.

The same process of structural convention becoming a philosophical principle, of things being compared with their own shadows, operates also where the second major theme of Fowles's fiction is concerned. It will scarcely be necessary at this stage to emphasis the overwhelming importance which the romance allots to women. The tendency of the form is to idealise women and to attach intense symbolic significance to them. Campbell does not exaggerate when he writes:

> The hegemony wrested from the enemy, the freedom won from the malice of the monster, the life energy released from the toils of the tyrant . . . is symbolised as a woman. She is the maiden of the innumerable dragon slayings, the bride abducted from the jealous father, the virgin rescued from the unholy lover. *She is the 'other portion' of the hero himself* . . . She is the image of his destiny which he is to release from the prison of enveloping circumstance.
>
> (Campbell, 1975, p. 288, emphasis added)

As the quotation emphasises, the role of women in quest myths is at once a primary and a passive one. This role is precisely the one we find them playing in Fowles's fiction, and the narration aligns itself with this in being about women, but very seldom by them. Nor are we surprised, given that we are in the world of fiction, to find that the narratorial and indeed authorial commentary associates women with emotional subtlety, psychological depth, and inscrutability.

But the world of romance is a symbolic world, constructed for literary and imaginative purposes, and all similarity with real human beings, living or dead, is to say the very least entirely hypothetical. Nonetheless it is extraordinarily tempting to map this symbolic system onto real life, and to start thinking that because one is working with conventions that attribute certain qualities to women, women actually possess those qualities. The classic case of this is *The Aristos*, where Fowles says a number of laudatory things about the association between women and creativity. As historical judgements, these can best be described as provisional (for example the assertion that our own period resembles the Renaissance in being an 'Eve society' in which 'the woman and the mother, female gods, encourage innovation and experiment, and fresh definitions, aims, modes of feeling', *A*, p. 157); as contributions to aesthetics ('There are of course Adam-women and Eve-men; singularly few, among the world's great progressive artists and thinkers, have not belonged to the latter category', *A*, p. 157) they are frankly circular. But they become intelligible as projections of the ideology of romance: when, in this case, we remember the function of woman as *anima* and as muse. Yet again a philosophical superstructure can be traced back to a fictional underpinning.

The third theme of Fowles's work, the domaine, once again connects in a fairly straightforward way with the conventions and *topoi* of romance. Thus the characteristic mediaeval romance involves some kind of symbolic journey, a transition to a place of heightened existence where adventures and ordeals can take place: later examples use the secret garden or (as in *The Tempest*) the remote island. Domaines are of vital importance in the work of such acknowledged precursors of Fowles's as Richard Jefferies and Alain-Fournier. It is thus not difficult to understand why they should form such a keystone in his own fictional structures.

We would expect the existential projection of this aspect of romance to take the form of a concern with something at once special and separate. In fact when we come to look for such an element in Fowles's discursive writing we must go rather carefully. This is because Fowles himself has an intense interest in and love for nature, and it is not my aim at this point to argue that romance determines his life and tastes to quite this degree. However, we can distinguish between the part that nature plays in Fowles's life, and the part that it plays in his writing; while the former is not our concern, the latter is, and it does seem that nature fulfils the criteria put forward above, being treated throughout Fowles's writing as both special (almost to the point of sacredness) and separate. The existential projection of the domaine into Fowles's non-fiction is thus his attitude to nature itself.

This attitude is based upon a premise which is itself, historically speaking, a Romantic projection, namely the conception of man as logically prior to society. This conception underlies the philosophy, not only of *The Aristos*, but also of Fowles's other non-fiction (notably *Islands* and above all *The Tree*). When society is perceived as external to man, it comes to be seen – as it characteristically is seen, both in

romances and in Romanticism – as hostile to man: Fowles writes that
'All states and societies are incipiently fascist' (*A*, p. 115), and the idea
of separation discussed in the previous paragraph takes the form here
of an emphasis on exile which runs not only through his work but also
through his life (see p. 131 above).

Fowles's insistence on being 'English but not British' (see his
1964 article with that title), and his rather defensive fascination with the
Robin Hood myth which exemplifies what he sees as the secretive,
two-faced nature of the English, thus begin to come into focus. Fowles
sees the English in the light of the characters in his fiction, that is as
having one face turned outwards towards the world, but one turned
inwards to a separate, inner world, a domaine or refuge inaccessible to
society. And given the separation between man and society which
underlies the conventions of romance, we are better placed also to
understand the prominence of a Beckettian existentialism in all
Fowles's work: as he writes in *The Tree* (p. 122), 'We still have this to
learn: the inalienable otherness of each'.

Yet in emphasising the way Fowles dwells upon the theme of
separation in his non-fiction, we must not miss the degree to which
nature is also special and even sacred. The quotation above concludes
with a significant reversal: 'the inalienable otherness of each, human
and non-human, which may seem the prison of each, but is at heart, in
the deepest of those countless million metaphorical trees for which we
cannot see the wood, *both the justification and the redemption*' (*The
Tree*, p. 122, emphasis added; we should not overlook the theological
vocabulary). Nature – in which we may include all that man experiences outside society, everything (in Lévi-Strauss's phrase) that is not
culture – is a refuge and sanctuary. Indeed it is more. For Fowles (as for
the conventions of his chosen genre) there is a separation, not only
between society and nature, but between society and human nature:
the two natures come together as the locus of what is extra- or
anti-social, and hence of what is imaginative and creative in man. For
Fowles, as for romance, creativity flourishes in the darker and less
discovered areas of the mind, and thus stands in the same kind of
relationship to society as Robin Hood to the Sheriff of Nottingham.
Romance associates both nature and imagination as aspects of the
same separate and sacred place; and it is this which underlies both the
domaines of Fowles's fiction, and the identification between the two
natures expressed throughout his non-fiction. 'As long as nature is
seen as something outside us, frontiered and foreign, *separate*, it is lost

both to us and in us. *The two natures, private and public, human and non-human, cannot be divorced'* (*The Tree*, p. 106, last sentence not emphasised in original).

The fourth theme of Fowles's work, one which overshadows all the others, is freedom. It is a theme on which the conventions of romance are singularly unanimous. We saw in the previous section (pp. 131–2 above) that Fowles's characters tend to be at odds with their society. In this he is entirely consistent with the ideology of romance, which views the individual as logically prior to society and experiences society as a constraint: the world of romance is that of the conceivable rather than the real, a world of freedom from both social and material laws. Despite its apparently conservative fascination with aristocracy, romance thus has profoundly revolutionary implications: Frye writes that 'an element of social protest is inherent [in its structure]', since in romance it is characteristically 'the individual . . . who has the vision of liberation, and . . . society . . . that wants to remain in . . . darkness' (1976, pp. 77 and 139). But the principal direction of the movement of romance is inwards: the hero has been described as a form of 'idealised libido' (Frye, 1957, p. 306), the characters of romance can be read in Jungian terms as 'aspects of the one mind' (*Islands*, p. 104), and the romantic concept of duty which counterbalances its stress on freedom is principally a duty to the uniqueness and identity of the self.

Freedom is absolutely fundamental to Fowles's fiction, which is based, as we have seen, on a creative clash between system and individual preference, freedom and duty. Freedom is not the only message of his fiction; in their varying ways, *The Collector* and *The Magus* set out to show how dangerous it can be if wrongly interpreted. But it remains a prime force even in these works. In *The French Lieutenant's Woman* and 'The Ebony Tower' it acts as a kind of moral touchstone, and in *Daniel Martin* there is an almost defensive determination to rejoice in the creative possibilities of freedom whether or not it is currently fashionable. (*Mantissa*, one might add, seeks to put itself conclusively out of reach of all systems by being confined to the inside of a mind.) Moreover every one of Fowles's works seeks to embody freedom in its form, whether through tricks of style, shift of narrative voice, open ending, or circular plot.

The chief existential projection in Fowles's work of this formal, generic emphasis on freedom is existentialism itself. Fowles's enthusiasm for this philosophical system has dominated his interviews and his non-fiction from the very start. Existentialism is for him above all a theory of freedom.[8] He wrote in 1968 that 'My chief concern, in

The Aristos, is to preserve the freedom of the individual' (*A*, p. 7); and this concern underlies the urgency with which he has pursued the publication, revision, and re-issue of this longest of his discursive works.

But the subversive potential of existentialism, like the revolutionary potential of romance mentioned earlier, tends in Fowles's hands to turn towards personal rather than social transformation. Robin Hood is a powerful figure in Fowles's mental landscape, not because of what he does for the poor, but because of what he does for himself. Fowles's existentialist *aristoi* are committed to discovering their own identity (see *A*, p. 148) and to establishing 'a sense of [their] own uniqueness' (*A*, p. 116). Yet again we find the fictional practice underlying the philosophical theory: for this commitment to the uniqueness and identity of the self is precisely what we find at the very base of the structure of romance.

TALENTS VERSUS GENIUS: THE PRESSURE OF REALISM

The critical strategy which I have adopted throughout this work is not one that has hitherto appealed to Fowles: indeed, quite the reverse. He has consistently asserted that 'We need a return to the great tradition of the English novel – realism' (Newquist, 1964, p. 220), and has emphasised the importance of the artist's commitment to social commentary and moral judgement (Delaney, 1982). It is true that his works are well supplied with the kind of documentary and historical material to which such 'realistic' judgements can be applied; they contain in equally substantial measure examples of exactly those kinds of commentary and judgement. But, as I have tried to show, most of this essentially didactic material has no genuine connection with the fiction which surrounds rather than incorporates it. If this view is right, then the task becomes one of explaining why Fowles has tried so consistently to disguise from himself and from others the fundamental nature of his genius, and to align himself instead with Leavis's 'great tradition' of 'realism' (Leavis, 1948) and with all that those terms imply.

In this section I shall try to analyse this realist pressure and the influence it has exerted upon Fowles's work. My arguments follow four stages. I shall begin by briefly considering the low status of the romance form itself, relative to the realist novel. Next I shall look at the influence of two forms of social pressure which we may call, first social anxiety, and second moral anxiety. And finally I shall consider the influence on Fowles's work of something more basic still which we may call the anxiety of fiction.

Romance has always been a somewhat embattled genre, constantly under attack from those who see it as little better than sub-literature: the very term itself (which originally referred to tales translated from Latin into the vernacular for ease of access) points to its uncertain position in the literary class structure. The rise of the novel in the eighteenth century was accompanied by a further decline in the reputation of romance, so that it has come to be thought of as if its *True Romances*, Mills & Boon side was all there was to it. Throughout the nineteenth century writers in the genre felt under an obligation both to warn their readers not to expect total plausibility, and to apologise for producing a work which did not match the norms of the novel. Fowles's requests to be read as a realist seem to me to be manifestations of the same insecurity about the status and value of the romance: despite the very recent surge in its academic respectability, it has by no means overcome its second-rate status – a status much more marked in the 1950s, Fowles's formative period as a writer.[9] The writer who takes himself and his fiction seriously is thus under strong pressure to modulate his work in the direction of 'realism', that is documentary accuracy, social engagement, and plausible plot. The effect on Fowles of this realist pressure seems to me extremely clear, pushing him to include in his work steadily greater quantities of social commentary and factual bulk. His assumption seems to be that such sociological grist will render the work more nutritious to the reader: an alternative view would be that it merely makes it indigestible.

The nub of my argument, then, is that in order to conform with the temper of his age, Fowles has imposed upon his essentially free-ranging, patterned, un-'realistic' romances, the disguise of realism.

The second part of my argument concerns the relationship between individual and society in Fowles's fiction. We have seen that there is throughout his work a tension between freedom on the one hand and responsibility on the other. In social terms this takes the form of a clash between rights and duties, between egoism and altruism. The basic message of the fiction, like that of *The Aristos*, is unambiguous: every work consists of a movement towards freedom. Thus if we look from this point of view at Nicholas's development in *The Magus* we can trace three stages. In the first he has very little freedom, since his self-imposed role as Don Juan makes him dependent (not to mention parasitic) on society as a whole. By the end of Part 2 he has reached a second stage, being largely cured of his earlier disease but having transferred his fixation onto the patronage of the Bourani 'elect'. The third stage is reached only in the last chapter, when Nicholas finally makes up his mind to shake off the domination of Conchis and go it alone with Alison. These three stages, then, mark an ascending scale of self-knowledge and liberation. In *The French Lieutenant's Woman* the same stages recur, though the characters do not progress through them in quite the same way. Charles, the aristocratic dilettante, begins like Nicholas as a parasite upon society. With the aid of Sarah he makes a rapid transition to the third stage of full independence, his renunciation of Sarah giving him a freedom more exposed and painful, but also more productive, than Nicholas's. (Sarah, by contrast, having seemed to begin where Charles ends, slips back at the end to accepting a comfortable but sheltered berth in the second stage, namely dependence on the artistic elite which has crystallised around the nucleus of the Rossetti household.)[10]

Freedom of this thorough-going kind cannot be combined with social responsibility.[11] This is obviously something that disturbs Fowles, who has (as *The Aristos* makes clear) a very proper concern with the poor and needy. In *Daniel Martin* he has tried to put the matter right by devoting much of the book to Dan's reflections on socialism (whence Gramsci) and mutual responsibility (whence reading Lukacs and joining the Labour Party). But the separability of these additions from the body of the book proper shows how little they have to do with its underlying message; Dan may assert that giving up script-writing (low-brow mass entertainment) to write a novel (high-brow minority entertainment) is a 'supremely socialist declaration' (*DM*, p. 454), but it is hard to see what he means. A much truer, albeit much tougher, account of the underlying philosophy of these books is provided by Conchis, with his calm acceptance of the inequality and injustice of life (see for example *M*, pp. 146–7, 438). We note that a similar snatching of egoism out of the jaws of altruism sneaks into *Daniel Martin* in the person of the satirical playwright and 'born anarchist' (p. 522), Ahmed Sabry. Both Conchis and Sabry are above all survivors, and their independence and love of life are sustained despite (or because of) the harsh extremes which each in his differing way has had to face. By contrast, Fowles's two most left-leaning characters, Dan and Jane, are both highly prosperous, nor has either ever experienced anything approaching poverty.

Far from advocating charity and Doing As You Would Be Done By (or indeed from actually advocating anything at all), the impetus of romance lies in the other direction altogether, towards the Rabelaisian *Fais ce que voudras* and the indulgence of all fantasies. In their way Fowles's novels, too, strive to this end. The chief desire they indulge is for sex without all those tiresome emotional complications: a recurrent form of this (examples can be found in every one of Fowles's full-length fictions) is the 'pasha' or 'harem' fantasy of two women ministering to the needs of one man. But one way and another most human urges are catered for: for power, for travel and the exotic, even for violence.

Yet this freedom, this fantasy, is nothing to be ashamed of: on the contrary. The romance's thoroughgoing lack of social responsibility, its stress on personal goals, on being a swimming rat rather than a sinking ship, is its glory rather than its shame. Not only does it thereby remind us that in the last analysis society exists for its members, not the reverse: in addition, and more importantly, it provides an opportunity to see what would happen if we took the lid off human behaviour. Sexuality and violence, the principal driving forces of romance, are in every society harnessed, inhibited, or sublimated in some way: in real life even when their indulgence is allowed, as in the Roman circuses or the concentration camps and political prisons of our own time, it is to serve the tacit purposes of authority, so that the behaviour which results is not so much basic as debased. The consequence of this loosening of the ties which bind the individual to society is, of course, the formation of smaller societies; and because the means of severing the original social connection is usually either money or privilege, such sub-societies characteristically take the form of aristocracies or similar privileged groups. This is where we find the central paradox of the relationship of romance to society. Romance is consistently conservative or even reactionary in texture, as we have seen. In addition it is constantly in danger of being subverted by a dominant class or interest in society into serving its ends and expressing its own social mythology (see for example Frye, 1976, pp. 165–8). But the fundamental nature of romance is always revolutionary, because of its freedom to burst through the limits, not only of the permissible, but even (in the form of fantasy) of reality itself. Romance (as we see from the 'magical realism' of Latin American fiction) is thus *par excellence* the genre of dissidence, of internal emigration. It is particularly interesting in this connection to note Fowles's statement that 'Dissidence is for me an important function of the novel' (personal interview): even more noteworthy, in view of this quality of perpetual opposition, is his remark that though he has always voted Labour and would like to see a very left-leaning or even Marxist party in Parliament, if such a party seemed likely to get into power he would have to re-consider his support for it!

My third point, in a sense an extension of the second, rests on a distinction between social and what we may call 'moral' anxieties, using moral to refer to more personal questions of virtue and vice, good and evil. We have seen that Fowles's plots present a movement from constraint to freedom. But they also depict the same movement in a different form, in terms of acceptance or 'election' into an elite. Fowles constantly asserts that this elite is a moral one, and gives a prominence to tests and qualifying ordeals which is reminiscent of the courtly and knightly romances of an earlier date. The effect is not only to highlight the kind of neutral, structural, narrative movement outlined above (the kind of transition I have drawn attention to in *Daniel Martin*, p. 126 above), but also to suggest that there is a corresponding spiritual progress, an inner movement matching the outer one. (Here, as elsewhere, we may detect the pressure of realism, urging Fowles to turn facts into values, quest myth into *Bildungsroman*.)

The key question, then, is what principles govern election to these fictional elites? The author's comments on the matter are highly ambiguous. On the one hand, as we have seen, he implies that selection is by merit: on the other, notably in *The Magus* (for example pp. 87, 109) but discreetly in all the fictions, he asserts that selection is by hazard, that 'darkest, strangest and most omnipotent [sic] god of them all' (*DM*, p. 567). The evidence of the fictions, their narrative logic, seems at first quite clear: not only is election by merit, but only candidates from the upper echelons of society need apply.[12] The obvious inference from this is that only those social strata have the necessary personal qualities; candidates for admission are thus chosen in effect from a screened 'pre-Few' already known, by virtue of belonging to a superior class, to be superior to their fellows. But there are two things wrong with the selection method described here. The first is that it is insufferably smug and incestuous, reducing the mysterious processes of initiation and spiritual growth to the level of a Phi Beta Kappa election. The second, fortunately for us as readers, is that it does not fit the facts. It is true that, for reasons perhaps connected more with existential projection than with literature, Fowles always draws his male *aristoi* from the Oxbridge establishment: true, but fortunately irrelevant. While they may belong to an intellectual elite, they certainly do not have any corresponding moral distinction: Nicholas is snobbish and immature, Dan a thumping liar, and even Charles, in some ways the best of the bunch, is vacillating and at times rather pompous. In other words they are just like anyone else. Election is not selection: it is not by merit at all, but operates instead (like grace in its Calvinist counterpart) by pure chance. Conchis is not joking when he tells Nicholas that 'Hazard makes you elect' (*M*, p. 87), and the only answer to Nicholas's anguished 'Why me?' is Conchis's relaxed 'Why anyone?' (*M*, p. 185).[13]

We thus see that the clash between freedom and responsibility in Fowles's fiction is to a large extent a factitious one. Duty and responsibility do exist, and play a vital role, in romance; but they take the form of duty to private standards, and responsibility to inner imperatives, which are not open to public scrutiny. The essentially social, conformist obligations which Fowles erects in his romances, the moral hoops through which he obliges his heroes to jump, are not integral to the works. Instead they are additions, mistaken attempts to make the romance conform to the ideology and critical norms of the realist novel.

But the realist novel is itself a fiction, a fellow-member of the institution of literature. It is a truism of criticism that the function of literature is both to teach and to please, both to edify and to entertain; it seems to me equally self-evident that the first item in each pair is achieved, neither as well as, nor in spite of, but actually *by means of*, the second. Yet there seems to be in Fowles – whatever its origins, external or internal – a didactic, almost puritanical strain which distrusts the entertaining and pleasurable side of fiction, and indeed views the whole of imaginative literature, the house of fiction itself, as a place of escapism. It is to this fourth area, which we may call the anxiety of fiction, that I wish to turn now.

The evidence for my argument is drawn from two tendencies in Fowles's work. The first is to include an increasing proportion of non-fiction within his fiction; the second – as is clear from a glance at the bibliography – is to move away from fiction completely in the direction of other, supposedly worthier, more instructive, or more scholarly literary activities.

The particular provinces of the romance writer are atmosphere and narrative. In these two fields Fowles is pre-eminent. Yet there is every sign that Fowles has systematically played down the areas in which he excels in order to give rein to areas which he feels to be more important. In the case of *Daniel Martin* we have Fowles's own testimony for this (Plomley, 1981), but the evidence is plain to see elsewhere. Abandoning story-telling, yarn-spinning, spell-binding, he has increasingly taken up social analysis, the discussion of ideas, and the propagation of moral truths. His magical feeling for atmosphere and place has likewise largely been diverted into the writing of photographic essays (*Islands, Shipwreck, The Tree, The Engima of Stonehenge*), while his interest in language and his fascination with the past have gone into translation and editing. It is an uncomfortable – and I hope transitory – fact that since *The French Lieutenant's Woman* in 1969, Fowles has produced only one full-length work of fiction in fourteen years, and that heavily encrusted with non-fictional accretions.

It is not that Fowles is unaware of what he does well. The two things that guide his own reading are a love of narrative[14] and a search for the atmospheric power which he has called 'The capacity . . . to provide an experience beyond the literary' (*M*, p. 6). He knows – and acknowledges – that he likewise has a marvellous knack for telling a story and creating a fictional world. He has often spoken of the dream-like origins of his stories (see for example 'Notes on an Unfinished Novel', p. 136) and of the joy of slipping back into the fantasy world of the creative process. Like Daniel Martin, he is happy in his work – yet like Daniel, he is guilty about this happiness. As Lever puts it, 'he does not seem to realise how great (*and respectable*) his story-telling talent is, nor that it appeals to all' (Lever, 1979, p. 97, emphasis added). It is as if he knew the nature of his talent, but not its worth, and so felt compelled to indulge it only furtively, and as far as possible to eschew the practice of it altogether.[15] It is not that Fowles has no skill at the various non-fictional pursuits he has adopted. It is rather that his ability there is as nothing to his capacity in the field of imaginative literature. In that area his skill is of an entirely different order; and in undervaluing his own marvellous creative powers, he is allowing his talents to undermine his genius.

CONCLUSION

In the course of this study I have tried to bring out the overwhelming importance for the romance genre of freedom. The chief emphasis has been laid on the thematic aspect of freedom. But this thematic side has a structural counterpart. Romance is a highly conventional literary form: but convention does not exclude freedom, and may indeed actually foster it. The more a genre turns in towards its own conventions rather than out towards the imitation of reality, the more it is freed to use its designs in relatively undisplaced forms: in the case of romance, to press on with its story without concerning itself overmuch about whether what is happening is either moral (in the narrow sense) or plausible. In this it enjoys a dispensation not granted to its sister form, the realist novel, which must modify and often disguise its structures both in order to render them plausible, and (because of the convention of originality that governs our reading of realist fiction) in order to conceal their affinities with other works of a similar shape.

This formal licence clearly creates the potential for considerable formal self-reflexiveness, for patternings, echoings, variations, and transformations of the kind made familiar to us by structuralist analyses of myths and legends. This is not to say that traditional narratives of this kind are *consciously* modelled upon each other (or, for that matter, that they are not). It is simply to point out that intricate formal structures of this as of any other kind offer the possibility of equally intricate formal variations and interconnections.

Emphasis of this kind on the radical and revolutionary potential of romance provides what is, I think, something of a new approach to the fairly well-turned field of Fowles's use of literary form. Except for what I have already said in the earlier chapters of this book, I have nothing specific to add to the body of detailed criticism of Fowles's literary techniques which has already emerged. What I believe may be new is my argument that Fowles, in handling his romance structures in ironic, open-ended, or subversive ways, is not so much adding something extraneous to the genre as developing qualities which were already inherent in it.

In fact Fowles's work makes relatively little use of the freedom of romance to dispense with plausibility.[16] Where Fowles's work does exploit the formal possibilities of the genre is precisely in its concern, not only implicit but also explicit, with form. In a rather muted sense this underlies the collection published under the title *The Ebony Tower* but originally entitled *Variations*. But it is chiefly evident in the way Fowles undercuts the linear drive of his plots in order to emphasise the static, formal qualities of the design of his fiction. This is done partly (as we have seen) by the use of the inset tale and the *mise en abyme*, but also by the way he uses endings to call into question the entire preceding narrative: the open ending of *The Magus*, the three alternative endings of *The French Lieutenant's Woman*, the incomplete ending of 'The Enigma', the partially unintelligible ending of

'The Cloud', and the circular endings of *Daniel Martin* and *Mantissa* which return the reader to the beginning. These endings may not be as open as they seem: it may be that the obtrusive way in which they play with the reader's expectations springs in large part from a didactic and manipulative element in Fowles's own literary personality. But such an almost biographical explanation need not exclude another and more formal reading according to which these features, hesitant and incomplete though their openness may be, are explorations of an open and self-referential quality, an awareness of its own literariness, *latent in the genre itself*. As such, these devices function to direct the reader's attention to the constructedness, the artificiality, of what he is reading. Exactly the same effect is produced by the frequent use of unreliable narration in Fowles's work: an invitation, that is, to reflect upon the fact that what we are reading is not self-generated, but rather the end product of a certain process, not nature but culture.

The upshot of all this talk about form is that not only Fowles, but also the form he is using, are trying to encourage us to read actively ('I hate the idea of the passive reader', Sage, 1976). This in turn makes it easier to understand a very marked tendency of Fowles's critical practice, namely his emphasis on process. Whether he is writing about other authors (Homer, Marie de France, Shakespeare, and especially Hardy) or about himself (for example in 'Notes on an Unfinished Novel', 'Hardy and the Hag', or *Mantissa*), he constantly seeks to redirect our attention away from the work as stone-cold finished product, reified and immutable, and back to the artist who created it.[17] Whatever the reasons behind such advice, the effect once again is to remind us that what we are reading is the construction of a writer, and is thus open to the deconstruction of a reader.

If we read the romances of John Fowles in this way – if, that is, we pry them free, both from the anxious grip of their author, and from their consecrated position in the niche of literature – we will find that they hand back to us as readers the ultimate responsibility for their interpretation. Fowles's characters enter and inhabit the domaines in his fictions: but they also leave them, and are forced to accept that in the world outside, their life is in no-one's hands but their own: 'There were no watching eyes. The theatre was empty. *It was not a theatre*' (*M*, p. 654, emphasis added). In a very similar way the readers of Fowles's work enter its magic world, but must also leave it: the artificiality of his endings is a kind of disintoxication, freeing us from dependence both on author and on text. The true heroes and heroines of the romances of John Fowles are not incarnations of their author, however much they may sometimes seem to be. They are his readers. And just as the characters of romance must retain in their everyday life the vision and sense of creative potential that they acquired in the domaine, the knowledge that reality itself is only a fiction, so the thoughtful reader of romance should carry away with him an awareness of the patterns and artifices created by the human imagination, that we impose on life itself in order to make sense (or nonsense) of it. This presumably is what Proust meant when he described his massive work, at once romance, autobiography, novel, and essay, as a kind of magnifying glass which would equip his readers to be 'their own readers of themselves'. And it is to a similar process of imaginative re-creation, of applying a liberated reading to our own lives, that Fowles is calling us when he writes in *The Aristos* (p. 202) that 'the true destiny of man is to become a magician himself'.

Notes

1 JOHN FOWLES: THE LIFE AND THE WORK

1. He did not care for Leigh-on-Sea, his birthplace: 'The rows of respectable little houses inhabited by respectable little people had an early depressive effect on me and I believe that they caused my intense and continuing dislike of mankind *en masse*' (Wakerman, 1975, p. 485, quoted in Conradi, 1982, p. 22).
2. Fowles's only sister is fifteen years younger than him.
3. Fowles uses this French spelling throughout his work, presumably as a homage to Alain-Fournier.
4. 'the power to affect . . . by imaginative means is strictly dependent on precisely that same *active* energy of imagination in the audience [as that which] lay behind the creation' (*Islands*, p. 101, emphasis in original).
5. I am far from the first to treat Fowles's works as romances. What I have sought to do is to follow through the implications of the romance form more single-mindedly (not to say obsessively) than other critics have done, and to try to locate the apparent contradictions and tensions of Fowles's work within his chosen form, rather than in a clash between that form and something outside it.
   It is only fair to add that Fowles has consistently rejected this interpretation of his work. The point is discussed in some detail in Chapter 7 (pp. 145–51) below.

2 *THE COLLECTOR*

1. Though in fact the use of Clegg's story to frame Miranda's was an afterthought and came as a recommendation from Fowles's editor. The author had originally submitted the two accounts in sequence (Olshen, 1978, p. 20).
2. It may be objected here that there is no *a priori* reason to assume that Fowles thinks like G.P. To this I would answer, firstly, that Fowles almost always puts a magus or mentor into his books – G.P. is succeeded by Conchis, Grogan, Breasley, Professor Kirnberger; secondly, that what these mentors have to say varies astonishingly little; and thirdly, that what they say matches very closely what Fowles himself writes *in propria persona*, e.g. in *The Aristos*. Even the Goldberg Variations, favourites of Fowles's fictional characters in *The Collector* (p. 201) and *Daniel Martin* (pp. 627–8), turn out to be Fowles's (unplayed) first choice on Desert Island Discs!
3. There is also one point of flat factual contradiction. Clegg dates this celebration to 11 November, Miranda to 14 November. In view of the details given on p. 49 of the book I am inclined to think that this is merely a slip on the part of author and proof-reader alike, a view which Fowles himself confirms (personal interview).

4. This contrast between the spontaneous and authentic present and the cold and distanced past is one which Fowles returns to frequently in his writing (see *Daniel Martin*, *passim*, and *The Tree*, pp. 70 and 108–22). A most helpful and suggestive discussion appears in Walker, 1980.
5. 'The boy in *The Collector* stands for the Many; the girl for the Few' (Fowles in Newquist, 1964, p. 219).
6. 'I also wanted to attack [in *The Collector*] . . . the contemporary idea that there is something noble about the inarticulate hero' (Fowles in Newquist, 1964, p. 218.)

3 THE MAGUS

1. References throughout are to *The Magus: A Revised Version* (1977). Page numbers are the same in both hardback and paperback editions. My argument (though not, of course, the detail of my quotations) applies equally to the first version, published in 1966 but in fact largely written in the 1950s. For accounts of some of the differences between the two versions, see Binns, 1977, or (more detailed) Docherty, 1981, pp. 122–3.
2. Fowles's comment here runs as follows: 'I find this paragraph slightly perverse. The *donnée* (right or wrong) is that he is trying to represent (or make present again) what he *was* at that age. "In my view *then*" is to be understood. Like everyone else, I think you rather undersell N's "honesty", if we are to treat him as autobiographer.'
3. As used here these terms are borrowed from Scholes, 1968, pp. 15–17, 35–40. Plot is linear, chronological, recounting events in the sequence in which they occur in the book: we speak of 'a plot summary'. Design, on the other hand, is a slightly more elusive term: it covers those aspects of the story which give it shape and completeness, and which we often become aware of only after we have finished – after, that is, we have completed the line of the plot. If we say that an event *follows* another, we are speaking from the viewpoint of plot; if we say that two events (or characters, or situations) are *related* to one another, it is design we have in mind.
4. The classic combination of these forms in English literature is of course *Great Expectations*, and Fowles has acknowledged the influence of this novel by inserting two references to it into the text of the revised *Magus* (see pp. 6–7 of the Foreword, and pp. 347 and 392 of the text).
5. Fowles has often spoken of his admiration for Thomas Love Peacock, whose works are of precisely this type.
6. The act, which is of necessity incomplete and culminates in his ejaculating upon her breasts, seems to Nick 'like being with a prostitute' and makes him think of Alison as 'my mistress and my slave' (pp. 263–4).
7. The allusion (mine) is to Swann, significantly a collector of *objets* and of *amours*, who falls in love with one of his conquests in *Un Amour de Swann* because she reminds him of something from the world of art, a figure in a Botticelli.
8. It is only fair to point out that Nicholas is at least intermittently aware of the affinities between himself and the unspeakable Mitford: 'I disliked Mitford because he was crass and mean, but even more because he was a caricature, an extension, of certain qualities in myself . . . I thought of Lily de Seitas; how to her I must seem as Mitford did to myself. A barbarian' (p. 616).
9. One of the more marked changes in the Revised Version concerns the rewriting of the final chapter so as to tone down drastically its violence of action and imagery,

and thereby to emphasise the positive aspect of Nicholas. See Docherty (1981) for a more detailed discussion of this point.

10. To pick out only a few examples: Conchis is named after his mother (p. 81), as is Mrs de Seitas (p. 596); Alison's mother outlives her father (p. 33), as did Conchis's (p. 171); Conchis has a picture of his mother, supposedly by a mother-obsessed artist (p. 92); and Lily and Rose are so called to placate their grandmother, who was 'a hungry goddess' (p. 595).

11. This view is supported by Fowles's reading of *The Tempest*: 'It has, I think justly, been interpreted as a play with a cast of one; that is, its eleven main parts can all be seen as aspects of the one mind' (*Islands*, p. 104).

12. Fowles himself rejects this: 'Conchis/conscious offends me' (Huffaker, 1980, p. 140).

13. See e.g. Daellenbach, 1977.

4 THE FRENCH LIEUTENANT'S WOMAN

1. Ian Watt speaks of its 'harmonious . . . mingling of the old and the new' (1969, p. 75), and Malcolm Bradbury describes it as 'the best book out of Britain in the 1960's' (Bradbury, 1980).

2. See for example pp. 15, 29, 40, 181, 242, 280, 321, 330.

3. Fowles reveals in a footnote to the English edition (p. 204) that La Roncière was exonerated and rehabilitated in 1848. In the American edition (p. 245) the corresponding footnote is rather longer and gives the full background to the events which led up to the trial.

4. Her coat is caught on a bramble on p. 104, and on p. 158 she compares herself to a thorn tree.

5. Sarah is as elusive as Sue Bridehead; like Eustacia Vye, she is '[a] vivid heroine offered a job reading to an elderly lady', and like Eustacia (though with happier results) she is intimately associated with water. Where Tess worked at Talbothays, Sarah works for a Mrs Talbot (who, by yet another apparently meaningless coincidence, is '[her] own age exactly', p. 148); like Tess, she is the victim of her father's 'obsession with his own ancestry' (p. 51); and like Tess, Eustacia, and other Hardy heroines, her fortunes turn upon an undelivered letter. (For these and other references, see Wolfe, 1976, pp. 127 and 145.)

6. The distinction I am drawing here – between events in their time sequence, and events as they happen in the text – broadly corresponds to Shklovsky's *fabula* and *sjuzet* (Bennett, 1979, p. 23) and Genette's *histoire* and *récit* (Genette, 1972, p. 72).

7. The first comment is from David Robinson, *The Times*, 16 October 1981; the second is from Alan Brien, *The Sunday Times*, 18 October 1981.

8. For Fowles's own comments on this aspect of the work, see pp. 141–3 of 'Notes on an Unfinished Novel'.

9. I prefer to relegate to a footnote a remark made by Fowles in an interview: '*The French Lieutenant's Woman* was a cheat . . . I thought it was . . . obvious' (Sage, 1974, p. 35).

10. It has been pointed out that Sarah's character fits extraordinarily closely into a pattern suggested by Jung, whose influence Fowles has often acknowledged. The relevant quotation is as follows: '[Woman's] moods and emotions do not come to her directly through the unconscious, but are peculiar to her feminine nature. They

are therefore never naive, but mixed with unacknowledged purpose . . . It fits in with her nature to remain in the background as an independently willing and responsible ego, in order not to hinder the man, but rather to invite him to make real his aims with respect to herself. This is a sexual pattern, but it has far-reaching implications in the feminine mind. By maintaining a passive attitude with an invisible purpose in the background, she aids a man towards his realisation, and in that way holds him. At the same time she weaves a web of fate for herself, because whoever digs a pit for others falls himself therein' (Jung, *Contributions to Analytical Psychology*, pp. 168 and 170, quoted in Huffaker, 1974, pp. 233–4).

11. Fowles himself writes that the precise reconstruction of the Victorian age was not his aim: 'I don't think of [*The French Lieutenant's Woman*] as a historical novel, a genre in which I have very little interest' ('Notes on an Unfinished Novel', p. 136). For further comments on the use of literary and historical material in the work see Kaplan (1973) and Mason (1981) respectively.

12. It may be objected that these associations are made by Charles rather than by the author and are thus subject to ironic understanding. In some cases (e.g. pp. 121 and 311) this is true, but in at least one (the various references on p. 54) it seems that Fowles is speaking in his own voice.

5 *THE EBONY TOWER*

1. For a different view see Morse, 1984.
2. The question of whether or not they are properly to be called *lais*, and indeed of what the term *lai* means, is in some dispute: it appears that the views Fowles outlines on pp. 122–3 of *The Ebony Tower* are out of step with current thinking on the subject. Fortunately the debate does not affect the argument put forward here.
3. The reference is to Leach, 1969, p. 54; see also Leach, 1970, pp. 58, 70–1. There are obvious parallels with the work of Althusser and Macherey in France, and Eagleton in England.
4. E.g. Harris, 1930; Mickel, 1974; Hieatt, 1977. Hieatt offers a particularly perceptive analysis of the theme of betrayal in the story.
5. Mickel (cited in Hieatt, 1977, p. 358) refers to an 'extraordinary act of charity . . . an act of sacrificial love'; Harris, on the other hand, (ibid, p. 352) speaks of 'a purely "conventional" ending, in which "the heroic wife acts with . . . inhuman generosity" '. Hieatt steers a shrewd middle course: 'The wife's attitude . . . is firm, never abject; she . . . [demands] her due "alimony" in the form of a dowry to found an abbey' (ibid, p. 355).
6. In Fowles's hands the Continental setting gives an intellectual as well as an emotional atmosphere: see e.g. the use made of Barthes in 'The Cloud'.
7. These are most numerous, as one might expect, in the title story, in which we are referred to *Eliduc* ('the Arthurian cycle', p. 19; the insistence that Breasley's *Moon-hunt* springs out of 'both a homage and a kind of thumbed nose to a very old tradition', p. 24; Breasley's actual re-telling of *Eliduc* which is referred to on pp. 58–9; and the way in which Diana is called 'the Mouse', reminding us of the weasel which is the agent of revival in *Eliduc*, but which in 'The Ebony Tower' David runs over and kills ('something orange-brown [Diana's colours], a mouse, but too big for a mouse', p. 107). We are referred also to 'The Enigma', the use of the word itself on pp. 24 and 83 being surely not accidental, and above all to 'The Cloud'. Here the

'curious trisyllabic call' which 'wasn't English' on p. 10 performs in part the same function as the 'un-English song' of the 'hidden warbler' on p. 247, though it will remain unidentified for non-birdwatchers until the call of the oriole, which plays an increasingly important part in 'The Cloud', is described as 'trisyllabic' on p. 286. Further points of contact include the unexpected thunderstorm remembered from Breasley's childhood (p. 31), matching the sudden appearance of the storm (p. 301); the reference to sodomy on p. 49 prefiguring its actual occurrence on p. 297; the 'angler' in 'peasant blue' on p. 76 matching the 'fisherman . . . in faded blues' on p. 258; and the use of a kiss on the top of the head as a form of sexual signing-off, first used in this way on p. 99, and recurring on p. 265. There is also the frequent use of 'one', which is so conspicuous a feature of the style in both 'The Ebony Tower' and 'The Cloud' as to suggest some kind of echoing. Nor should we ignore the references to other works by the same author. In 'The Ebony Tower' the Freak is reading *The Magus* (p. 65); we are reminded of *The Collector* when Breasley is said to have 'collected' at one point in his life (p. 23), and when his work is described as proceeding towards its 'final *imago*' (p. 31, emphasis in original). Diana 'Thinks she's Lizzie Siddal', on whom Fowles based his description of Sarah Woodruff (Huffaker, 1980, p. 145) which in turn makes Breasley 'that ghastly little Italian fudger' (pp. 24–5) – i.e. Rossetti; a further pointer in the direction of *The French Lieutenant's Woman* is the legitimate but meaningless kiss on the mouth exchanged between David and Beth (p. 114), recalling the equally arid osculation of Charles and Ernestina (*FLW*, p. 229). Paintings by the same mediaeval artist, Pisanello, feature prominently in both works (*ET*, p. 19, *FLW*, p. 208). Where *Daniel Martin* is concerned, the naked swim in the forest pool (p. 61) reminds us of a similar episode in Italy (*DM*, pp. 124–5), while the triangular relationship between Breasley, Mathilde, and Jean-Pierre matches in quite close details that between Daniel, Phoebe, and Ben in the later work. In a more general way, we note the tendency of the hero to try to hide behind a platitude ('He felt a traitor . . . but in a good cause', p. 96: cf. Charles's advice to Sarah, *FLW*, p. 157, or Nick's to Alison, *M*, p. 48), and Fowles's habit of reversing the normal literary sequence of pursuit followed by possession ('He watched her present metaphorical nakedness, and thought of the previous literal one', p. 94).

8. At the risk of anticipating my own argument, I might add that just as *Eliduc* dramatises the contradictions in the ethic of knighthood, so it could be said that 'The Ebony Tower' dramatises the contradictions inherent in the role of artist-hero. (Fowles's marginal note on the typescript endorses this reading.)

9. In Classical mythology, Diana was goddess of the moon: thus the success of Breasley's work is yet a further reproach to David for the failure of the quest for Diana which constitutes his own 'moon-hunt'.

10. I owe this point to Huffaker, 1980, pp. 124–5.

11. The implied allusion to Lewis Carroll (whose real name was C. L. Dodgson) picks up the mention of Alice in Wonderland in 'Poor Koko' (p. 161).

12. I owe this point to Huffaker, 1980, p. 130.

13. Nor are these the only parallels with other works in the collection. Like Diana, Catherine, imprisoned in her own grief, tries to free herself by making a pass at a second-rate artist; like David, Paul declines the offer. Like Marcus Fielding, both Catherine and her late husband seem – but are nowhere definitely stated – to have committed suicide (but see note 16 below). Like the narrator of 'Poor Koko', Catherine takes issue with 'visuals', in this case the noxious TV producer Peter. And

the insensitivity to landscape and atmosphere, the over-fed bickering insularity, of the characters in 'The Cloud' stand in silent but accusing contrast to the way in which Breasley has accepted and responded to the landscape in which he has chosen to live.

14. Fowles is fond of the *mise en abyme* or inset tale and uses the technique frequently: Breasley's remark in 'The Ebony Tower' (p. 61, final two lines) may indeed rate as the shortest known example of the method.

15. Personal interview: the particular reference was to p. 577 of *Daniel Martin*, but see also p. 560 of *The Magus*.

16. Fowles has commented here: 'Catherine's the implied author, throughout; she does not die, she writes'.

17. For more ambitious narratives leaving permanently unanswered questions see 'The Art of Gho'tography', in Jones, 1978, pp. 75–128, or 'The Cloak', in Dinesen, 1957, pp. 37–58.

18. The analogy is with Wells's 'The Time Machine', which depicts a future world in which humanity has split into distinct and opposed species: the gentle, frail, decadent Eloi, too feeble and disorganised to produce anything for themselves, who inhabit a daylight world, and the violent and sinister Morlocks, blinded by light, who live underground and emerge at night to capture and devour any Eloi they can find. The correspondence with 'Poor Koko' (as with *The Collector*) is striking: we note, moreover, that in the latter the Morlock figure, Clegg, lives partly underground, just as in 'Poor Koko' the burglar operates almost entirely nocturnally.

19. Fowles finds my comments in this paragraph 'priggish', but endorses the final sentence: 'that was at least partly the idea'.

20. 'The extramarital affaire becomes particularly siren-like after several years of marriage . . . But . . . it is a flight from reality; and if children are involved, a flight from responsibility . . . A child is a law against adultery' (*A*, pp. 163 and 166). We note even in *The Magus* Nick's 'innate sense that [he] ought to find all [he] needed in Alison' and his corresponding rejection of the 'clean surgical abscission [between] loins [and] heart' (*M*, p. 633).

6   DANIEL MARTIN

1. 'I also set out with a rather curious idea that I would throw away one asset I suppose I do have which is the ability to tell stories and to keep people reading . . . [*Daniel Martin*] is told much more in terms of fragments, with great jumps in time' (Plomley, 1981).

2. The second term in particular is a standard one in scenarios: see, for example, Pinter's screenplay of *The French Lieutenant's Woman* (1981).

3. Such a policy offers a number of attractions. Since its practitioner does not even try for what he wants, he is cushioned against the pain of competing and being found wanting. By placing him in situations he is bound to find uncongenial, it enables him to soak in a reassuring mixture of pity for himself and contempt for his surroundings. And by preventing him from sinking his full energies into what he is doing, it fossilises his personality, insulating it against suffering, change, and development.

4. My first efforts to explain this feature (Loveday, 1980) now seem to me to have been mistaken.

5. The phrase (which occurs also on p. 224 of *The French Lieutenant's Woman*)

suggests Arnold (who in the sonnet *To a Friend* writes that Sophocles 'saw life steadily, and saw it whole') and Ruskin ('Not only is there but one way of *doing* things rightly, but there is only one way of *seeing* them, and that is, seeing the whole of them', Lecture ii, *The Two Paths*, 1859, emphasis in original).

6. It is perhaps churlish to note that though the scene is written by a woman, its form – a sexual episode involving two women and a man – closely parallels the male fantasies recounted both in *Daniel Martin* and elsewhere in Fowles's fiction.

7. Part of her humanising influence is to give 'The Prick' a name, Steve (p. 480).

8. It is noteworthy, in connection with Fowles's expressed aim of writing a modern *Education sentimentale* (see above, p. 103), that for much of his writing career Lukacs himself held this to be the finest novel ever written.

9. I am thinking here of David Malevich the film producer, of the American couples Abe and Mildred and the Mitchells, of Ahmed Sabry the Egyptian comedian, even of Labib the Lebanese driver.

10. We should note here also that although Lukacs has to allow the paradox whereby realist authors may choose to oppose the progressive forces which they depict in their fiction, Dan does in fact bring his life into line with his art and ends by joining Jane in the Labour Party. This act of political commitment, however sheepishly undertaken – one is reminded of Ginsberg's splendid line 'America I'm putting my queer shoulder to the wheel' – emphasises the left-of-centre position which Jane maintains throughout the book, and further reinforces her solidarity with the Lukacs line.

11. The quotation that follows, though from an entirely different context, is strikingly appropriate: 'One can only stand back and admire this Oxford ruling class, so certain, so limited in its ideas, so conscious from youth of its rightful destiny, so uninterested in other forms of humanity, so perfectly preserving, after three generations, the entire mentality of late Victorian rationalism' (John Vincent, *The Sunday Times*, 6 June 1982).

12. In fact Andrew can be more easily explained in psychological than in political terms: that is, as the doer to counterbalance Anthony the thinker, the two of them providing flanking supports for the central male character.

13. The reference is on p. 628; see also 'Love might be a prison: but it was also a profound freedom', p. 641.

14. I owe the formulation of this point to McSweeney (1978, pp. 32–3).

15. They shared a house at Oxford; both are connected with visual media; both are unsuccessfully married and are having *affaires* with girls young enough to be their daughters; and both (in Barney's case see p. 504) are planning to get out of the rat-race and write their autobiographies!

16. The term, borrowed from Genette (1972, pp. 206ff), refers to the limited point of view of a narrator who is also a character in his own story.

7 THE ROMANCES OF JOHN FOWLES

1. I am aware that such a belief is not necessarily present in all socialist traditions, and that – to name but two – Fabianism and Marxist-Leninism lay great stress on the importance of small enlightened groups working like yeast within the doughy mass of society. My point is that democratic socialism, as defined above, is not a movement of this effectively elitist kind.

162 *Notes*

2. Fowles consistently prefers to explain human behaviour in biological rather than social terms. Thus (as we saw in Chapter 1) the Few are described as *biologically* superior to the Many (*A*, p. 9), while elsewhere Fowles speaks of his 'notion of art as vocation (that is, something to which one is *genetically* suited)' (*The Tree*, p. 66, emphasis added). In the light of this insistence on the biological and genetic origins of inequality it is hard to understand what he means when he writes that 'All the evils of history are attributable to a shortage of schools' (*A*, p. 136).

3. A few examples must suffice, chosen wherever possible from works in which Fowles is writing as himself rather than through a narrator:

    Journalese: 'Nothing defanged destiny more surely than these potent plants' (*Islands*, p. 48).

    Unintentional rhyme: 'the heart of this art' (*The Tree*, p. 100); note also (from Fowles's narrators) 'mock shock'/ (*MI*, p. 509: *M*, p. 591), and 'go pro' (*DM*, p. 489).

    Incorrect etymology: '[weaning and waning] are related etymologically' (*The Enigma of Stonehenge*, p. 73). The SOED gives entirely separate derivations for these two words.

    Solecism: 'Enormity' twice misused (pp. 39 and 42 of *The Enigma of Stonehenge*) to mean 'excess in magnitude', a usage which the SOED describes as incorrect; 'the future's attention', 'any tool's lasting worth', 'the tree's qualities' (*The Enigma of Stonehenge*, pp. 52, 83, 109) – on p. 13 of *A Practical English Grammar* (Oxford, 1980), Thomson and Martinet point out that 'of + noun' should be used for possession with inanimate possessors.

    We may add, from *The Magus*: 'Julie's fascination for Maurice' (p. 317; 'for' should be 'with'); 'Tony Hill put . . . June and *I* . . . in the main part' (p. 330, emphasis added).

    Cliché: See Lever (1979, p. 86) and Conradi (1982, pp. 97–8) for examples.

4. See also Chapter 3, note 7 above.

5. Though even here it is tempting to read the final scene on Hampstead Heath as a merciful decision to commute a death sentence to one of life-long exile! (For a different reading of 'The Cloud', see Chapter 5, note 16 above.)

6. In view of the suggestive parallels revealed between Shaw and Fowles in the area of evolutionary theory, it may be worth continuing the quotation from Frye: 'Thomas Hardy and Bernard Shaw both flourished around 1900 and both were interested in evolution. Hardy did better with tragedy, and saw evolution in terms of a stoical meliorism, a Schopenhauerian immanent will, and an activity of "chance" or "hap" in which any individual life may be expendable. Shaw, who wrote comedies, *saw evolution as creative, leading to revolutionary politics, the advent of a Superman, and to whatever metabiology is*. But it is obvious that Hardy and Shaw are not substantial philosophers, and they must stand or fall by their achievements in poetry, fiction, and drama' (Frye, 1957, p. 64, emphasis added).

7. Andrew provides an interesting test case. On the one hand he is an Oxford graduate and the heir to a sizeable estate which he works in an appropriately pastoral and feudal fashion, rescuing stray sheep with his shepherd's crook and resolutely stamping out trade unions (*DM*, pp. 343–5). On the other hand he seems only too happy to accept the decidedly second-rate Nell; he is very clearly neither a creative nor a penetrating thinker; and his role as a man of action in the discovery of the woman in the reeds ('[Dan] senses [in Andrew and Mark] a contempt for him . . . the

bohemian, the effete middle-class aesthete', *DM*, p. 31) seems to put him firmly on the wrong side of the tracks.

8. This covers freedom of thought ('a theory of relativity among theories of absolute truth', *A*, p. 116); freedom of conscience ('Existentialism is the revolt of the individual against all . . . systems . . . that attempt to rob him of his individuality', ibid, p. 115); freedom of will ('Freedom of will is the highest human good', ibid, p. 25); freedom of action ('There is an invitation in existentialism to reject traditional codes of morality or behaviour', ibid, p. 116); and freedom to be oneself ('[an existentialist] never belongs as every organisation wants its members to belong', ibid).

9. An assumption of this kind about the unique claim to respectability of the realist novel presumably underlies Fowles's 'shock' that *The Collector* could be taken to be 'a mere suspense story' (Newquist, 1964, p. 221).

10. In *Mantissa* there is a similar, but more rapid and more extreme, progression through the stages already noted. Stage one is got over extremely briskly with the departure of Miles Green's wife (*Mantissa*, p. 15); stage two is transcended when Erato storms in and tears up the pages of Miles's story, revealing that the little therapeutic community in whose hands he had believed himself to be was nothing more than a figment of his imagination. The rest of the book consists of an exploration of stage three, though whether we are intended to think of his intracranial tête-à-tête with Erato as involving two people (as was the case with Nicholas) or one (as at the conclusion of *The French Lieutenant's Woman*) is, like much else in *Mantissa*, left somewhat unclear.

11. It could be argued that Fowles implicitly acknowledges this: he has admitted that 'my novels don't read like socialist novels . . . I don't see how it is possible to write a socialist novel' (personal interview).

12. An alternative view might be that intelligence rather than class background is the criterion. The example of Sam, however, who is hardly lacking in native wit, seems to disprove this (see pp. 66–7 above).

13. See the discussion of this point in Chapter 3 (pp. 40–1) above.

14. See his interviews, *passim*; e.g. 'if there is one thing that all the books I like have it is narrative' (Amory, 1974, p. 34).

15. The defensive tone which he adopts in *The Tree* when describing his imaginative life is quite striking: '*Slinking* into trees was always slinking into heaven'; 'no fruit for those who hide in trees untouched by man; no fruit for *traitors to the human cause*'; 'the *wicked* green man'; 'I write fiction in a *disgracefully haphazard* sort of way'; '*addicting* myself, and *beyond curability*, to the pleasures of discovery'; 'powers of concentration, of *patience in acquiring true specialised knowledge*, that would *disgrace a child*' (*The Tree*, pp. 14, 36, 66, 78 twice, and 80, all emphasis added). We are reminded that Fowles has referred to fiction-writing, not only as narcissism ('Notes on an Unfinished Novel', p. 137), but even as onanism ('Hardy and the Hag', p. 28).

16. This is not entirely true of *The Magus*, nor in a sense of *Mantissa*; but these exceptions, which are in any case explicable, do not disprove the broad generalisation. I exempt *Eliduc* as being a translation rather than an original work.

17. Fowles has consistently affirmed his faith in Freudian and post-Freudian theories of literary creation. Where his own work is concerned, he has endorsed Gilbert Rose's psychoanalytic reading of *The French Lieutenant's Woman* (Rose, 1972; for

Fowles's own comments see 'Hardy and the Hag'), and has urged critics to pay closer attention to 'the benign psychosis of the writing experience' ('Hardy and the Hag', p. 29).

Bibliography

PART ONE: WORKS BY JOHN FOWLES

John Fowles: Fiction

In every case, the original publisher is Jonathan Cape (London), and a paperback edition is published by Panther (Frogmore, Herts). Unless otherwise stated, the American edition (published by Little, Brown of Boston) appeared in the same year as the English one.

Fowles, John, 1963   *The Collector*
—   1966   *The Magus* (The American edition appeared in 1965.)
—   1969   *The French Lieutenant's Woman*
—   1974   *The Ebony Tower*
—   1977a *The Magus: A Revised Version*, with Foreword (The American edition appeared in 1978.)
—   1977b *Daniel Martin*
—   1982   *Mantissa*

John Fowles: Non-Fiction, including Editions and Translations

Unless otherwise stated, the original English publisher is Jonathan Cape (London), and the American publisher is Little, Brown of Boston. For details of offprints, broadsides, and limited-edition publications, please see the bibliographies mentioned below (Olshen, 1980 and Roberts, 1980).

Fowles, John, 1964   *The Aristos: A Self-Portrait in Ideas* (Boston: Little, Brown. The English edition appeared in 1965).
—   1968   *The Aristos*, revised edition (London: Pan. The revised American edition, published in New York by New American Library/Signet, appeared in 1970).
—   1973   *Poems* (New York: Ecco Press).
—   1974a *Cinderella*, by Charles Perrault (1697), adapted and translated by Fowles, illustrated by Sheilah Beckett (the American edition appeared in 1976).
—   1974b *Shipwreck*, with photographs by the Gibsons of Scilly (the American edition appeared in 1975).
—   1977   *Ourika*, by Claire de Durfort (1824), translated with an Introduction and Epilogue by Fowles (Austin, Texas: W. Thomas Taylor).
—   1978   *Islands*, with photographs by Fay Godwin.

Fowles, John 1979   *The Tree*, with photographs by Frank Horvat (London: Aurum Press. The American edition, dated 1979, appeared in 1980).

—.   1980a *The Aristos: A Self-Portrait in Ideas*, second revised edition (not issued in America).

—.   1980b *The Enigma of Stonehenge*, with photographs by Barry Brukoff (no American edition).

—.   1980c *Monumenta Britannica, Parts One and Two*, by John Aubrey, edited by John Fowles, annotated by Rodney Legg (Sherborne: Dorset Publishing Company. No American edition).

—.   1982   *A Short History of Lyme Regis* (Wimborne: Dovecote Press).

—.   1983   *Lyme Regis, Three Town Walks* (Lyme Regis: The Friends of the Museum. No American edition).

In addition Fowles has translated a number of works for the National Theatre, including Molière's *Don Juan* and de Musset's *Lorenzaccio*. These translations have in some cases been used on stage, but have not as yet been published.

John Fowles: Afterwords, Introductions, Prefaces

Unless otherwise stated, the original publisher is Jonathan Cape (London).

Fowles, John, 1969 Introduction, Glossary, and Appendix to *Mehalah, a Story of the Salt Marshes*, by S. Baring-Gould (London: Chatto and Windus).

—   1971   Afterword to *The Wanderer, or The End of Youth [Le Grand Meaulnes]*, by Alain-Fournier, translated by Lowell Bair (New York: New American Library).

—   1974   Foreword and Afterword to *The Hound of the Baskervilles*, by Sir Arthur Conan Doyle (London: John Murray and Jonathan Cape).

—   1975   Foreword to *Hawker of Morwenstow: Portrait of a Victorian Eccentric*, by Piers Brendon.

—   1978a Introduction to *Mirmar*, by Naguib Mahfouz (Cairo: Heinemann, in association with the American University in Cairo).

—   1978b Foreword to *The Lais of Marie de France*, translated by Robert Hanning and Joan Ferrante (New York: E. P. Dutton).

—   1980a Introduction to *After London or Wild England* by Richard Jefferies (Oxford: Oxford University Press).

—   1980b Foreword to *The Sunday Times Book of the Countryside – Including One Thousand Days Out in Great Britain and Ireland*, eds Philip Clarke, Brian Jackman, and Derrick Mercer (London and Sydney: Macdonald General Books and Macdonald and Jane's).

—   1981a Introduction to *The Book of Ebenezer Le Page*, by G. B. Edwards (London: Hamish Hamilton).

—   1981b Introduction to *Agatha Christie – The Art of her Crimes: the paintings of Tom Adams*, commentary by Julian Symons (New York: Everest House). An English version is published as *Tom Adams' Agatha Christie Cover Story* (London: Paper Tiger).

Fowles, John 1981c Introduction to *The Royal Game*, by Stefan Zweig, translated by
Jill Sutcliffe.

— 1981d Foreword to *The Screenplay of The French Lieutenant's Woman*,
by Harold Pinter and Karel Reisz (London: Jonathan Cape in
association with Eyre Methuen).

John Fowles: Selected Articles

Fowles, John, 1964a 'I Write Therefore I Am', *Evergreen Review 8* (Aug-Sept), pp.
16–17, 89–90.

— 1964b 'On Being English But Not British', *Texas Quarterly 7* (Autumn),
pp. 154–162.

— 1968 'Notes on Writing A Novel', *Harper's Magazine 237* (July), pp.
88–97. Expanded version appears as 'Notes on an Unfinished
Novel' in Bradbury, 1977 (q.v.), pp. 136–150; references in the
text are to this later version.

— 1977 'Hardy and the Hag', in *Thomas Hardy after Fifty Years*, ed.
Lance St John Butler (London: Macmillan) pp. 28–42.

— 1978 'The Man and the Island', in *Steep Holm – A Case History in the
Study of Evolution*, compiled by the Kenneth Allsop Trust and
John Fowles (Sherborne: Dorset Publishing Co) pp. 14–22.

PART TWO: WORKS ABOUT JOHN FOWLES

This section includes bibliographies, criticism, and selected interviews.

Amory, Mark, 'Tales out of School', *Sunday Times Magazine* (22 Sept. 1974) pp. 33–4,
36.

Baker, John F., 'John Fowles', *Publisher's Weekly 206* (25 Nov. 1974) pp. 6–7.

Barnum, Carol, 'Archetypal Patterns in the Fiction of John Fowles: Journey towards
Wholeness', unpublished PhD dissertation, Georgia State University, 1978.

Benton, Sarah, 'Adam and Eve', *New Socialist* (May/June 1983) pp. 18–19.

Binns, Ronald, 'John Fowles: Radical Romancer', *Critical Quarterly 15:4* (Winter
1973) pp. 317–34.

—, 'A New Version of *The Magus*', *Critical Quarterly 19:4* (Winter 1977) pp. 79–84.

Boston, Richard, 'John Fowles, Alone But Not Lonely', *New York Times Book Review*
(9 Nov. 1969) pp. 2, 52, 54.

Bradbury, Malcolm, 'The French Lieutenant's Woman', *Observer Review*, 3 Aug. 1980,
p. 19.

Conradi, Peter, *John Fowles* (London: Methuen, 1982).

—, '*The French Lieutenant's Woman*: novel, screenplay, film', *Critical Quarterly 24:1*
(Spring, 1982) pp. 41–57.

Delaney, Frank, Unpublished interview with John Fowles on *Bookshelf* (BBC Radio 4,
10 Sept. 1981).

—, Unpublished interview with John Fowles (BBC 2, 13 Nov. 1982).

Docherty, Thomas, 'A Constant Reality: The Presentation of Character in the Work of
John Fowles', *Novel 14:2* (Winter, 1981) pp. 118–34.

Fleishman, Avrom, '*The Magus* of the Wizard of the West', *Journal of Modern Literature 5* (April 1976) pp. 297–314.

Freeman, David, Unpublished interview with John Fowles (Radio Oxford, 7 Oct. 1982).

Halpern, Daniel, 'A Sort of Exile in Lyme Regis', *London Magazine* (March, 1971) pp. 34–46.

Hieatt, Constance B., '*Eliduc* Revisited: John Fowles and Marie de France', *English Studies in Canada 3* (Fall, 1977) pp. 351–8.

Huffaker, Robert, 'John Fowles: A Critical Study', unpublished PhD dissertation, North Texas State University, 1974.

—, *John Fowles* (Boston: G. K. Hall, 1980).

Kaplan, Fred, 'Victorian Modernists: Fowles and Nabokov', *Journal of Narrative Technique 3:2* (May, 1973) pp. 108–20.

Lever, Karen M., 'The Education of John Fowles', *Critique 21:2* (1979) pp. 85–100.

Loveday, Simon, 'The Style of John Fowles: Tense and Person in the First Chapter of *Daniel Martin*', *Journal of Narrative Technique 10:3* (Fall, 1980) pp. 198–204.

McSweeney, Kerry, 'Withering into the Truth', Review of *Daniel Martin*, *Critical Quarterly 20* (Winter, 1978) pp. 31–8.

Mansfield, Elizabeth, 'A Sequence of Endings: the manuscripts of *The French Lieutenant's Woman*', *Journal of Modern Literature 8:2*, John Fowles Special Number (1980–81) pp. 275–86.

Mason, Michael, 'Good fiction and bad history', Review of *The French Lieutenant's Woman*, *Times Literary Supplement* (27 Nov. 1981) p. 1391.

Morse, Ruth, 'John Fowles, Marie de France, and the Man with Two Wives', *Philological Quarterly 63* (winter, 1984) pp. 17–30.

Newquist, Roy, 'John Fowles', (in) *Counterpoint* (Chicago: Rand McNally, 1964) pp. 218–25.

Olshen, Barry N., *John Fowles* (New York: Frederick Ungar, 1978).

Olshen, Barry N. and Toni A., *John Fowles: A Reference Guide* (Boston: G. K. Hall, 1980). Obtainable in UK through Holt Saunders).

Palmer, W. J., *The Fiction of John Fowles: Tradition, Art, and the Loneliness of Selfhood* (Columbia, Missouri: University of Missouri Press, 1974).

Plomley, Roy, Unpublished interview with John Fowles on 'Desert Island Discs' (BBC Radio 4, 16 Jan. 1981).

Rankin, Elizabeth, 'Cryptic Coloration in *The French Lieutenant's Woman*', *Journal of Narrative Technique 3* (Sept. 1973) pp. 193–207.

Roberts, Ray A., *John Fowles: A Bibliographical Checklist* (*American Book Collector 1:5*, New Series, Sept./Oct. 1980).

Rose, Gilbert J., '*The French Lieutenant's Woman*: The Unconscious Significance of a Novel to its Author', *American Imago 29* (Summer, 1972) pp. 165–76.

Rothschild, Judith Rice, 'John Fowles and *The Ebony Tower*: Marie de France in the Twentieth Century', (in) *The Twenty-Seventh Annual Mountain Interstate Foreign Language Conference*, Research Council of East Tennessee State University (1977) pp. 129–35.

Sage, Lorna, 'Profile 7 – John Fowles', *New Review 1:7* (Oct. 1974) pp. 31–7.

—, Unpublished interview with John Fowles, on videotape at the University of East Anglia, 1976.

Thorpe, Michael, *John Fowles* (London: Longman, 1982).

Wakerman, J., (ed.), *World Authors 1950–1970* (New York: H. W. Wilson, 1975).

Walker, David H., 'Subversion of Narrative in the Work of André Gide and John

Fowles', (in) *Comparative Criticism: A Yearbook*, vol. 2 (Cambridge: Cambridge University Press, 1980) pp. 187–212.

Watt, Ian, 'A Traditional Victorian Novel? Yes, and Yet . . .', Review of *The French Lieutenant's Woman*, *New York Times Book Review* (9 Nov. 1969) pp. 1,74–5.

Wolfe, Peter, *John Fowles, Magus and Moralist* (Lewisburg; Bucknell University Press, 1976; rev. ed. 1979).

PART THREE: WORKS CITED IN, OR RELEVANT TO, THE TEXT

Auerbach, Erich, *Mimesis* (New Jersey: Princeton University Press, 1953, originally 1946).

Beer, Gillian, *The Romance* (London: Methuen, 1970).

Bennett, Tony, *Formalism and Marxism* (London: Methuen, 1979).

Bradbury, Malcolm (ed.), *The Novel Today: Contemporary Writers on Modern Fiction* (London: Fontana/Collins, 1977). See Fowles, 1968, in Articles above.

Campbell, Joseph, *The Hero with a Thousand Faces* (London: Sphere Books, 1975, originally 1949).

Camus, Albert, *La Chute* (Paris: Gallimard, 1956).

—, *L'Etranger* (Paris: Gallimard, 1957, originally 1942).

Chrétien de Troyes, *Arthurian Romances*, translated with an Introduction by W. W. Comfort (London: Dent, 1914).

Culler, Jonathan, *Structuralist Poetics* (London: Routledge, 1975).

—, 'Fabula and Sjuzhet in the Analysis of Narrative', *Poetics Today I, iii* (1980) pp. 27–37.

Daellenbach, Lucien, *Le récit spéculaire: essai sur le mise en abyme* (Paris, Seuil, 1977).

Dinesen, Isak, *Last Tales* (London: George Allen & Unwin, 1957).

Forster, E. M., *Aspects of the Novel* (Harmondsworth: Penguin, 1962, originally 1927).

Frye, H. Northrop, *Anatomy of Criticism* (Princeton, New Jersey: Princeton University Press, 1957).

—, *The Secular Scripture* (Cambridge, Mass: Harvard University Press, 1976).

Genette, Gérard, *Figures III* (Paris: Seuil, 1972).

Harris, Julian, *Marie de France: The Lays Guigemar, Lanval, and a Fragment of Yonec; With a Study of the Life and Work of the Author* (New York: Institute of French Studies, 1930).

Jones, R. G. L., *Tricks of the Light* (London: Methuen, 1978).

Jung, C. G., *Modern Man in Search of a Soul*, translated by W. S. Dell and Cary F. Baynes (London: Routledge, 1961, originally 1933).

Kates, Bonnie R., 'Novels of Individuation: Jungian Readings in Fiction', unpublished PhD dissertation, University of Massachusetts, 1978.

Leach, Edmund R., *Genesis as Myth and Other Essays* (London: Cape, 1969).

—, *Lévi-Strauss* (London: Fontana, 1970).

Leavis, F. R., *The Great Tradition: George Eliot, Henry James, Joseph Conrad* (London: Chatto and Windus, 1948).

Loveday, Simon, 'Northrop Frye: Aspects of the Anatomy', unpublished MPhil. dissertation, Oxford University, 1978.

Mickel, E. J., *Marie de France* (Boston: Twayne, 1974).

Pinter, Harold, and Reisz, Karel, *The Screenplay of The French Lieutenant's Woman* (London: Jonathan Cape in association with Eyre Methuen, 1981). See Fowles, 1981d, in Introductions, above.

Scholes, Robert, *Elements of Fiction* (New York: Oxford University Press, 1968).

Todorov, Tzvetan (ed. and tr.), *Théorie de la Littérature* (Paris: Seuil, 1965).

Index

172 *Index*

Dickens, Charles, 113
Great Expectations, 156 n.4
Dinesen, Isak, 160 n.17
Docherty, Thomas, 156 n.1, 156–7
n.9
domaine, *see under* Fowles, John,
four themes
Don Juan, see under Fowles, John,
translations by
Durrell, Lawrence, 37

Ebony Tower, The, 2–3, 5, 26, 70,
82–102, 117, 133–8, 140, 144,
152–3, 158–60, 162 n.5
evolution, 4, 52, 58, 63, 65–7, 132,
162 n.6
existentialism, 18, 27, 45, 58–9, 65,
70, 77–8, 114, 143–5, 163 n.8
existential projection, 138–45, 149,
162 n.6
Eagleton, Terry, 158 n.3
Eleusinian mysteries, 41
*Eliduc, see under Ebony Tower,
The*; *see also* Fowles, John,
translations by
Eliot, George, 63
Eliot, T. S., 35, 125
Enigma of Stonehenge, The 2, 4,
133, 151, 162 n.3

Few and the Many, the, *see under*
Fowles, John, four themes
Flaubert, 113, 133
L'Education sentimentale, 103,
115, 119, 161 n.8
Fleishman, Avrom, 41
Forster, E. M., 8, 69
Howard's End, 44
Fowles, John
childhood influences, 1–2, 130–1,
155 nn.1 and 2; *see also*
Fowles, John, chronology
chronology, xi-xiii
class attitudes, 22–4, 130–1, 140,
149–50, 163 n.12; *see also*
Fowles, John, four themes:
the Few and the Many
as experimental novelist, 55–60,

109–11, 132–5, 144, 152–4;
see also Fowles, John,
interventions in own fiction;
see also Fowles, John,
relationship with own fiction
film adaptations, 1, 48, 69; *see
also* Fowles, John, film and
the novel
film and the novel, 103–4, 107,
109–10, 160 n.2; *see also*
Fowles, John, film
adaptations
four themes: domaine, 3–5, 7, 9–10
27, 32–3, 52, 68–9, 121, 129,
139, 142–4, 153–4, 155 n.3;
the Few and the Many, 3–4,
7, 22–3, 40–1, 62–4, 66–7,
80, 120–1, 129–32, 139–41,
149–50, 156 n.5, 161 n.1,
162 nn.2 and 7 (*see also*
Fowles, John, class
attitudes); freedom, 3–4, 7,
27, 41–5, 48, 51–2, 57–9,
63–5, 73–4, 78, 80, 101,
122–3, 129, 144–5, 146–8,
150, 151–4, 163 n.8;
masculine and feminine, 3,
5–7, 9, 24–6, 42–4, 60–2,
70–1, 73, 75, 98, 121–6, 129,
141–2, 157 n.10 (*see also*
Fowles, John, treatment of
female characters)
interventions in own fiction,
56–8, 69–70, 72, 132–5, 158
n.12; *see also* Fowles, John,
as experimental novelist; *see
also* Fowles, John,
relationship with own fiction
nature and its importance in
his work, 1, 4–5, 130–2, 142
relationship with own fiction,
75–7; *see also* Fowles, John,
as experimental novelist; *see
also* Fowles, John,
interventions in own fiction
translations by: *Cendrillon,
Don Juan, Lorenzaccio,
Ourika*, 1; *Eliduc*, 1, 82, 158
n.1, 163 n.16